M000223603

"Care to Dare sends a vital and urgent message to every leader: empathy and attunement are not a waste of time in today's business climate, but essentials for success. George Kohlrieser makes the business case for kindness as the platform that allows leaders to challenge their followers. And he does so with authority, depth, and verve. Every leader who wants results needs to read this book."
Daniel Goleman, bestselling author, *Emotional Intelligence*

"I wondered if George Kohlrieser could create a worthy sequel to his masterful *Hostage at the Table*. Well, he, Susan and Duncan have, and then some! Genius in its simplicity, this book shows us that the Secure Base Leader provides a combination of safety and risk that creates the only possible means to success at innovation. 'Innovate or die' is the seminal characteristic of today's environment; *Care to Dare* is the key."
Tom Peters, co-author, *In Search of Excellence*

"If you read only one book on leadership, it should be *Care to Dare* by George Kohlrieser, Susan Goldsworthy and Duncan Coombe. Filled with actionable advice, the book shows leaders how to discover their secure bases in order to sustain their effectiveness and energize their teammates to do so as well."
Bill George, Harvard Business School, author, *True North* and former chief executive officer, Medtronic

"This book will not only help you learn – it will help you act! A book for leaders across all cultures, its message is clear – Care enough to Dare and you will transform teams, organizations and business culture."
Marshall Goldsmith, author, *MOJO* and *What Got You Here Won't Get You There* and America's preeminent executive coach (*Fast Company* magazine).

"*Care to Dare* ties together the essential and very human elements of leadership into a program you can make work. Read this

powerful and very readable book. It will help you see your strengths and weaknesses as a leader and will help you grow as a person."
John A. Davis, Faculty Chair, Families in Business Program, Harvard Business School

"Kohlrieser, Goldsworthy and Coombe's captivating book makes a compelling case for the need to have, and to be, a Secure Base. Their clear prose and relevant examples bring the concept to life, empowering all of us to become better leaders."
Nick Shreiber, former President and CEO, The Tetra Pak Group

"I have found Secure Base Leadership to be a powerful concept that has practical applications for any business. When leaders Care to Dare, they can build higher levels of engagement and deliver more creativity and innovation for their organization."
Søren K. Vilby, President & CEO, Nielsen & Nielsen Holdings, Denmark

"Secure Base Leadership works at both a personal and professional level. George, Susan and Duncan have identified nine characteristics that can make a real difference to the performance and impact of any leader."
Andrew Milton, COO, Constance Hotels

"This is an exceptional book with a message that is critical to the challenge of developing better leaders. In short, being personal and connecting on a human level is the key to what really matters in life and business. George has done a great job of explaining how and why this matters so much if you want to lead others effectively."
David Rock, cofounder of The NeuroLeadership Institute, and author, *Your Brain at Work*

A WARREN BENNIS BOOK

This collection of books is devoted exclusively to new and exemplary contributions to management thought and practice. The books in this series are addressed to thoughtful leaders, executives, and managers of all organizations who are struggling with and committed to responsible change. My hope and goal is to spark new intellectual capital by sharing ideas positioned at an angle to conventional thought—in short, to publish books that disturb the present in the service of a better future.

BOOKS IN THE WARREN BENNIS SIGNATURE SERIES

CARE TO DARE

CARE TO DARE

Unleashing Astonishing Potential through Secure Base Leadership

By George Kohlrieser

Susan Goldsworthy and Duncan Coombe

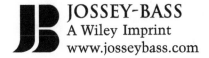

JOSSEY-BASS
A Wiley Imprint
www.josseybass.com

This edition first published 2012
© 2012 John Wiley & Sons

Under the Jossey-Bass imprint, Jossey-Bass, 989 Market Street, San Francisco CA 94103-1741, USA
www.jossey-bass.com

Registered office
John Wiley & Sons Ltd, The Atrium, Southern Gate, Chichester, West Sussex, PO19 8SQ, United
Kingdom

For details of our global editorial offices, for customer services and for information about how to apply
for permission to reuse the copyright material in this book please see our website at www.wiley.com.

The right of the authors to be identified as the authors of this work has been asserted in accordance
with the Copyright, Designs and Patents Act 1988.

All rights reserved. No part of this publication may be reproduced, stored in a retrieval system, or
transmitted, in any form or by any means, electronic, mechanical, photocopying, recording or
otherwise, except as permitted by the UK Copyright, Designs and Patents Act 1988, without the prior
permission of the publisher.

Wiley publishes in a variety of print and electronic formats and by print-on-demand. Some material
included with standard print versions of this book may not be included in e-books or in print-on-
demand. If this book refers to media such as a CD or DVD that is not included in the version you
purchased, you may download this material at http://booksupport.wiley.com. For more information
about Wiley products, visit www.wiley.com.

Designations used by companies to distinguish their products are often claimed as trademarks. All
brand names and product names used in this book are trade names, service marks, trademarks or
registered trademarks of their respective owners. The publisher is not associated with any product or
vendor mentioned in this book. This publication is designed to provide accurate and authoritative
information in regard to the subject matter covered. It is sold on the understanding that the publisher
is not engaged in rendering professional services. If professional advice or other expert assistance is
required, the services of a competent professional should be sought.

Library of Congress Cataloging-in-Publication Data

Kohlrieser, George, 1944-, Coombe, Duncan, 1972-, Goldsworthy, Susan, 1960–
   Care to dare : unleashing astonishing potential through secure base leadership / by
George Kohlrieser, Susan Goldsworthy, Duncan Coombe.
      p. cm.
   Includes bibliographical references and index.
   ISBN 978-1-119-96157-4
1. Leadership.   2. Attachment behavior.   I. Goldsworthy, Susan.   II. Coombe, Duncan.   III. Title.
   HD57.7.K645 2012
   303.3'4–dc23

                              2012012433

A catalogue record for this book is available from the British Library.

ISBN 978-1-119-96157-4 (hbk) ISBN 978-1-118-36127-6 (ebk)
ISBN 978-1-118-36126-9 (ebk) ISBN 978-1-118-36128-3 (ebk)

Set in 11/15pt Garamond by Toppan Best-set Premedia Limited

To the young people in my life—Paul, Andrew, Ben and Lily— who keep me inspired and represent the Secure Base Leaders of the future. Our world needs you.

-George

For Pamela, the epitome of a secure base mother, and for Nigel, in appreciation of our journey.

-Susan

To my original and enduring secure bases, my parents Patricia and Anthony.

-Duncan

TABLE OF CONTENTS

PREFACE

The iconic founder of numerous businesses under the brand name Virgin, Sir Richard Branson is not only one of the richest and most entrepreneurial men in the United Kingdom, he also appears to be one of the most balanced and playful. The eldest of four, Branson is dyslexic, and as a result he struggled academically. However, he refused to let that disability limit him. From a very young age, he focused instead on building his businesses. Leveraging his ability to connect with other people, his first venture took the form of a student magazine. He was just 16 years old.

Sir Richard is perhaps most famous for his airline. In his autobiography, he wrote about his decision to start that venture:

"My interest in life comes from setting myself huge, apparently unachievable challenges and trying to rise above them . . . from the perspective of wanting to live life to the fullest, I felt that I had to attempt it."

When his grandmother was 99, she wrote to Richard saying that the last decade of her life had been the best. She inspired him with the powerful message, "You've got one go in life, so make the most of it." Says Sir Richard, "I have done my best to live up to her wish." He also credits his mother with shaping his thinking: "My mother was determined to make us independent."

He writes in his book Losing My Virginity, *"When I was four, she stopped the car a few miles from our house and made me find my own way home across the fields."*[1]

Often seen as a transformational leader, Sir Richard chooses to hire motivated people, then he inspires energy around a goal and expects people to achieve it. He believes in helping people achieve things they didn't know they were capable of and enjoys being a catalyst to the success of others. He believes that you learn by testing theories and making mistakes. At the same time, he is known for treating employees as an extended family. His blog on the Virgin homepage exemplifies his very personal, warm and engaging style.

As well as running his business empire, Sir Richard commits energy to Virgin Unite, a not-for-profit foundation which focuses on entrepreneurial approaches to social and environmental issues. One funding recipient, Caroline Hart, left a comment on the Virgin website explaining what his help meant to her cause: "Sir Richard Branson is the real deal and I can say that from personal experience. Richard got behind a fundraising idea that I had and because of his help we were able to rebuild a tsunami-hit school in India. He and his business are what we need more of if the world is to get back on its feet."

Screw Business as Usual, *Sir Richard's latest book, enrolls others in his dream, which his website describes as turning "capitalism upside down—to shift our values, to switch from a just profit focus to caring for people, communities and the planet." He explains: "Over the last few decades as I've started up one exciting business after another, I thought that life and work could not get any better. In writing this book, I've realized that we've really been on a practice run, getting ready for the greatest challenge and opportunity of our lifetime. We've got a shot at really pulling together to turn upside down*

*the way we approach the challenges we are facing in the
world and look at them in a brand new entrepreneurial way.
Never has there been a more exciting time for all of us to
explore this great next frontier where the boundaries between
work and purpose are merging into one, where doing good
really is good for business."[2]*

Have you ever been led by someone like Sir Richard Branson
who cared for you like family and dared you to achieve more than
you ever thought possible for yourself, your organization and even
society?

We three authors have all been inspired by leaders who changed
the way we saw ourselves. We've also been on the other side,
influencing others to achieve more than they ever thought they
could. We have had the privilege of working with leaders from all
over the world, including CEOs, board members, teachers, doctors
and nurses who recognize themselves or their best bosses in Sir
Richard's approach.

While truly awe-inspiring in his achievements, Sir Richard is not
unique in his people-and-goals centered leadership philosophy.
George's book, the international bestseller *Hostage at the Table:
How Leaders Can Overcome Conflict, Influence Others, and Raise
Performance*, included one chapter on this very topic. He explained
how hostage negotiators, business leaders or anybody in a position of
influence succeed when they are "secure bases" for others. For the
purposes of leadership development, we define a secure base as:

**a person, place, goal or object that provides a sense
of protection, safety and caring *and* offers a source
of inspiration and energy for daring, exploration,
risk taking and seeking challenge.**

Many *Hostage at the Table* readers and others we work with
were eager to know more about how they could both be a secure
base and have secure bases. *Care to Dare* shows them and you

how to provide that magical combination of safety and stretch and how to become a "Secure Base Leader" no matter where you are working and regardless of your title or your profession.

George's use of the hostage metaphor created a new frame of reference for leadership: he showed leaders how not to be helpless or powerless in the face of an obstacle, whether it be a person, place, thing or even themselves. Secure bases provide a "hostage-free" psychological state. How? People who have secure bases are not held back by their fears: they dare to overcome even the greatest obstacles. Think of Nelson Mandela, who spent 27 years in prison and never felt like a hostage, or Gandhi, who transformed India without any formal political power.

Care to Dare shows you how to become a Secure Base Leader so that you release your followers from the fears that get in the way of their performance. This book is the result of our collective thoughts, experience and research on the subject. It teaches you how you can unleash astonishing potential by building the trust, delivering the change and inspiring the focus that underpin sustainable high performance. Secure Base Leadership works at the personal, team and organizational level. You care enough to dare people to reach for their dreams and, in the process, you return to your very own humanity.

Collaborating on this book makes sense for the three of us authors who have known each other and worked together in various capacities for more than a decade. The content reflects our different perspectives; our three sets of experience add up to a powerful combination of broad academic theory and profound practical knowledge. Our goal is to give you insight, understanding and coaching so that you can put these concepts into action today.

George first became acquainted with the concept of secure base when he was pursuing his doctorate in clinical psychology. Like all psychology students, he read the post-war research of John Bowlby and Mary Ainsworth concerning attachment theory. The basic premise of this theory is that humans are innately driven to seek closeness to, and comfort from, a person who gives them a sense of protection. Throughout his lifelong education, George has been privileged to meet and learn from many leading thinkers like Carl Rogers, Elizabeth Kübler-Ross, Jim Lynch, Eric Berne, Eva Reich, Warren Bennis and Daniel Goleman. Their work has informed George's understanding of leaders as human beings. His experience working with law enforcement agencies as a hostage negotiator and domestic violence mediator required him to be a secure base in many tense situations. These experiences, one of which he describes in Chapter 1, confirmed to him the dual need to be a secure base and have a secure base. His interest in the secure base concept deepened throughout his career as a clinical psychologist and his service in roles such as the director of the Shiloah Institute, a counseling center, and as President of the International Transactional Analysis Association.

Over time, George moved into the world of executive education. Through venues such as the landmark High Performance Leadership program at IMD business school, George has had the opportunity to share his work with thousands of leaders all over the world. He has seen too many examples of leaders who fail because they lack secure bases. He has also seen the power of Secure Base Leadership in action and the fundamental difference it can make in people's lives.

Susan and George met in 2001 while she was Vice President, Communications at Tetra Pak, the world's leading liquid food processing and packaging company. He invited her to be a leadership coach at IMD and she also had the pleasure of working with him in the writing of *Hostage at the Table*. A former Olympic finalist, Susan experienced the power of secure bases and the "Mind's Eye" at a young age during an international swimming career that led her to be ranked sixth in the world. She has combined qualifications in communications, organizational psychology, marketing, coaching and the neuroscience of leadership with a Masters in Consulting and Coaching for Change and more than 20 years of

senior management experience in global organizations. Mother-
hood has also been a powerful inspiration for her from both
perspectives: "having a secure base" and "being a secure base."
An experienced executive coach, lecturer and leadership consultant, Susan is passionate about working with people to turn knowledge into behavior and to create the conditions for healthy high
performance.

Duncan met George while studying for his MBA at IMD. George
invited him to be a leadership coach at IMD as well. Inspired by
the core psychological theory of secure base, Duncan sought to
further explore its value in organizational life. His exploration culminated in his 2010 doctoral thesis on the topic of Secure Base
Leadership. His role in the research, which distilled the nine characteristics of Secure Base Leadership, contributed greatly to this
book. As a faculty member at Ashridge Business School and as
a leadership consultant to numerous for-profit and not-for-profit
organizations, Duncan is driven by a desire to improve individual
and collective well-being. He has taught Secure Base Leadership
throughout the world and has seen its power and applicability
across cultures and industries.

The three of us are united in our belief that Secure Base Leadership can transform leaders, teams and organizations. As a Secure
Base Leader, you can *Care to Dare*. Notice that the title reflects
the two sides of Secure Base Leadership: caring and daring. You
cannot have one without the other. Secure Base Leaders unleash
astonishing potential by building the trust, delivering the change
and inspiring the focus that underpin high performance.

What do we mean by "high performance"? Our definition of
high performance is challenging yourself and others to see and
achieve what is beyond normal expectation. High performance
becomes "robust" or "sustainable" when people remain attached
to both people and goals in their pursuit of success. In our experience of working with high performance leaders, many have strong
attachments to goals and have achieved success from a materialistic

perspective. However, they may feel a sense of loneliness or lack of fulfillment because, in pursuit of their goals, they have lost or weakened their connection to people. When the drive to achieve financial goals is not balanced by the bonding to people, there is a danger of many physical, psychological and social consequences that include psychosomatic stress, addiction, burnout and depression—all of which obviously detract from overall success.

From extensive interviews with executives from all over the world as well as quantitative surveys with more than one thousand executives, we have identified the nine characteristics that Secure Base Leaders display on a daily basis. During the interviews, we were fascinated to watch executives realize the *who* behind the *what* of their success. People often forget the way their thinking has been influenced, and it can be an emotional and powerful moment when they recognize the people, goals and other entities that have shaped them.

A leader truly stands on the shoulders of others; the myth of a leader being a self-made person is only half true. Our research shows that a primary difference between a successful leader and a failed leader is the presence or absence of secure bases in his or her life. Having secure bases reduces anxiety and fear, and it increases trust and risk taking. In an organization, the secure base may be a boss, peers, colleagues, the corporation itself, the work or even the product.

Secure Base Leadership is more than a set of skills—the "doing." It is first and foremost a way of "being." Since leadership is a learned behavior, you can always learn new ways to be a Secure Base Leader. In this book, we give lots of actionable advice to help you learn the skills that will put you in the right state of mind to encourage the right actions. Because people gain insights from the experiences of others, we share stories, both long and short, including some of our own. In the cases where confidentiality was requested, we have changed the names of the characters.

This book will take you on a journey during which you will discover your own secure bases, past and present, and determine how you can be a secure base for other people in your life at work and at home. You cannot reap the full benefit of this book if you simply read the words. When we write, "Ask yourself . . . " we want you to pause, think and even capture your insights in a journal. In so doing, you will build your self-awareness and take a big step toward change. We encourage you to pick a few of the characteristics to work on. We hope that you will engage in the personal quest we propose in Chapter 7 in order to identify the secure bases who have influenced you.

Along this journey be prepared to delve into your past. You will find that the lines between work and home, professional and personal blur as you do this work. You are indeed one human with one brain, one set of fears and one very deep well of astonishing potential. Just as you need to draw upon your personal life in order to develop as a leader, you will learn to be a better secure base to people outside of work by becoming a Secure Base Leader. In fact, many people we work with find the concepts equally important in their roles as parents, spouses, siblings and friends. We encourage you to make those links. Let yourself be a complete person. Let yourself be fully human. Let yourself live all your dreams with full joy.

In fact, our greatest hope is that you can be fully human and also accept the full humanity of others. When enough people within an organization care to dare and practice Secure Base Leadership, they humanize the organization itself. Organizations become better places for people to be, where they can feel valued and supported and where they can feel encouraged and inspired.

Practice Secure Base Leadership on a daily basis and you can contribute to making any group, be it a family, a team or an organization, a healthier, more fertile and vibrant place to be. People who come to understand and apply the concepts of Secure Base Leadership have a life-changing experience.

If you allow it to be, this book itself can become a secure base for you, encouraging and inspiring you as you progress on your leadership and life journey.

Enjoy the read and embrace the adventure!

GEORGE, SUSAN & DUNCAN

&

"Deep within humans dwell those slumbering powers; powers that would astonish them, that they never dreamed of possessing; forces that would revolutionize their lives if aroused and put into action."

–Orison Swett Marden
1850–1924
American Writer

&

ACKNOWLEDGMENTS

This book exists thanks to the caring and daring exhibited by so many of the people in our lives. We are deeply touched by the support we received during the entire process of bringing this book to fruition. First and foremost, we are exceptionally grateful to the three members of our book project team: Marie O'Hara for her skillful managing of the project, her tireless support with all aspects of the book and for her amazing ability to build bonds and create collaborative relationships; Frederick Wieder for his excellent research skills, ideas and insights for content and structure, and detailed work around the notes; and Katherine Armstrong, editor extraordinaire, for her professional brilliance, insight, energy and commitment in shaping our work into the book you are reading. This book would not have happened without the combined dedication, knowledge and skills of these three collaborators.

Thank you to Francisco Szekely, co-director of IMD's High Performance Leadership (HPL) program, for your friendship, insights and profound understanding of Secure Base Leadership. You are a true Secure Base Leader.

Over the years, we have had the privilege to support hundreds of executives who have had the courage and commitment to undertake deep personal work at HPL and the advanced program (AHPL). They have provided us with a wealth of ideas, examples and insights that continue to inspire and teach us and which contributed greatly to the fabric of this book. In particular, we thank all of the leaders who shared their experiences and allowed us to use their stories to illustrate Secure Base Leadership in action.

We thank the HPL coaches, especially those who conducted interviews and supported us throughout the process. Olle Bovin, Sharon Busse, Joyce Crouch, Isobel Heaton, Jean-Pierre Heiniger, Andreas Neumann, Robyn Renaud, Leonie Schneider-Kuttig, Bente Thomassen and Ilaria Vikelis: We thank you for your essential contribution to the book and for your continuous encouragement. You are very special to all of us.

We appreciate the insights and encouragement from our HPL program collaborators whose expertise has enhanced our work. Thank you Jamie Andrew, Dan Klein, Peter Meyers and Terry Small.

We are grateful to IMD, one of the world's leading business schools, for creating such an outstanding environment where the real world meets real learning.

We would like to thank the publishing and editing team at Wiley, with special mention to Rosemary Nixon, editor, for her support and dedication to getting this book written. Thanks also to Nick Mannion and his marketing team and to the production and editing team led by Michaela Fay and Tessa Allen.

Special thanks to Marianne Wallace for her detailed work on the final manuscript, to Karen Sharpe for her support early in the process and to Mark Pritchard and his team at Pritchard's Creative Design for producing the graphics.

Special thanks from George:
I am especially grateful to IMD's president, Dominique Turpin, for his unwavering support. I appreciate the exceptional faculty at IMD who inspire me and with whom I work closely, in particular: Bill Fischer, Robert Hooijberg, Kamran Kashani, Ginka Toegel, Anand Narasimhan, Maury Peiperl, Ben Bryant, Preston Bottger, Winter Nie, Dan Denison, Joe DiStefano, Ulrich Steger, John Weeks, Don Marchand, Joachim Schwass, Shlomo Ben-Hur and Jack Wood.

Thank you to IMD's Corporate Development Group (Stein Jacobson, Hischam El-Agamy, Jim Pulcrano, Joanne Scott and Josephine Schoolkate) for your unwavering support. And to Marco Mancesti and Cedric Vaucher: Thank you for your ongoing collaboration around the research.

My deepest thanks to my wonderful, very patient and extremely competent IMD assistant Cristina Couto.

I have witnessed Secure Base Leadership in the countless senior executives in the organizations I have worked with. I very much appreciate the Malaysian influence that Tan Sri Azman, Roshan Thiran and Alvin Ung have had on my work and my life.

I also want to thank Dan Goleman, William Ury, Peter Senge, Bill George, David Rock, Tom Peters, Jim Collins and Marshall Goldsmith—the thought leaders whose work has inspired me.

The inspiration for this book is built firmly on the shoulders of my secure bases: Liz Pringle, Azim Khamisa, David Steindl-Rast (Brother David), Alberto Vollmer, Robyn Fryer, Marijke Wusten, the priests and teachers from my seminary days, and, of course, my parents and grandfather.

Lastly, my deep thanks to Warren Bennis. I am truly honored that, like *Hostage at the Table*, this book is part of the Warren Bennis series. In our relationship that has spanned many years, he always offers unquestionable support while also daring me to take the next risk.

Special thanks from Susan:
Grateful thanks to the following people who supported me with a *Care to Dare* spirit in the creation and development of this book as an extension of my life: my husband Nigel, son Jack, daughter Sydney, mother Pamela, brother Steve and sister-in-law Trish.

I am indebted to Nick Shreiber for our professional relationship at Tetra Pak, for being a secure base in relation to this book and my career and for his invaluable friendship.

For acting as a sounding board and being secure bases through-out the writing process, I am thankful to Annie Tobias, Joyce Crouch, Sharon Busse, Robyn Renaud, Jean-Pierre Heiniger and Michael Kenyon. For their ongoing inspiration and belief, I am grateful to Joy and Johannes Bronkhorst, Ethel and Jean Chalopin, Lorraine and David Murdoch, and Jack and Nina Queen. And for the stimulating approach and insights, I thank Jean-François Manzoni and Jack Wood.

I continue to be inspired by the Tetra Pak Market Operations Management Team (TPMO), a high performing group still bonded years after disbanding. Nils Bjorkman, Philippe Tafelmacher, Alastair Robertson, Steve Wyatt, Michael Zacka, Eric Baudier, Jorge Montero, Claes DuRietz and also Katarina Eriksson and Annie Busby: I thank you for the challenge, fun and learning that provided some of the practical experience for this book.

Finally, I thank the people I have had the honor to coach and to work alongside in the spirit of this book: I have learned from you all and I am deeply touched that you have shared parts of your minds, hearts and souls with me.

Special thanks from Duncan:
My conviction about the power of secure bases is a direct reflection of the profound experience of having Anthony and Patricia as my parents and Nicola and Robert as siblings. The foundation of love you provide supported me as I pursued my research and writing.

I have more gratitude than words can express for my awe-inspiring, graceful and strong wife, Linda, who supported me throughout the PhD and book writing processes. We have committed to being a secure base to each other and there is no greater blessing and privilege than to be partners with her in life.

Thank you to Darren Good who has been my research colleague, confidant, co-author and, most important, truly special friend.

Gratitude also to Eric Nielsen, Dave Kolb, Ron Fry and Peter Whitehouse for their critical support through my PhD process and for helping with the research that underpins this book. In particular, I thank Eric for his invaluable guidance as a leading secure base scholar and his attention to detail in ensuring the rigor of the research. In addition, I would like to express gratitude to George Kohlrieser and IMD for their enormous support throughout this research project. I would also like to thank David Cooperrider and Richard Boyatzis for being such significant role models of scholars making impact in the world.

I am deeply aware and appreciative of all of the friends, family members, teachers and authors who have shaped me personally and professionally. This book is an extension of all that I am, and therefore it's an extension of all that you have contributed to my growth and development. Thank you.

PART I

CHAPTER ONE

YOUR LEADERSHIP OPPORTUNITY

When working with leaders, George often tells the story of the first time he was physically taken hostage:

In the mid-sixties, I had just come out of graduate school and started working as a psychologist accompanying police on domestic violence cases. One night, I was riding with Dan, a lieutenant, when a call came through of a possible hostage situation at a nearby hospital. We rushed into the emergency room where we learned that a patient being treated for a stab wound had taken a nurse, Sheila, hostage. In a psychotic state, he was shouting and screaming.

Dan quickly assessed the situation and realized that since we were in the emergency room it was not possible to use tear gas or rush through the door. He decided that the best option was to have someone go calmly into the room and try to talk to the man.

With all the doctors, nurses and police officers standing around, I felt pretty safe that that "someone" would not be me, the "new guy." Dan looked around the room once, then twice, and then he turned to me and asked, "George, how would you like to do it?" I said, "Sure, why not."

I entered the room to find the patient, a man named Sam, holding a pair of scissors to Sheila's throat. I began by asking questions: "What do you need, Sam?" "What do you want?" "How can we help you right now?" After a few minutes of screaming and yelling, he cut the skin on Sheila's throat. Sam then started across the room. As he charged forward pointing the scissors at my throat, he kept screaming, "I'm going to kill you and everybody I can!" I kept calm, put my hands onto his arms and, looking into his eyes, asked more questions. I knew from the briefing that his ex-wife had stabbed him, injuring him severely, during an argument over the custody of their children. Focusing his mind onto what was important to him, I asked, "What about your children, Sam?"

"Don't talk about my children. Bring them here and I will kill them too," he answered.

Now, while not the response I wanted, his answer was a concession—a positive step because it was the first time Sam had responded to one of my questions.

"Do you want them to remember you as a murderer?"

Then there was a pause during which Sam's energy changed. I had found a way to connect with him.

"We have to talk about your kids. How do you want them to remember you?"

We carried on talking and he calmed down enough for me to negotiate for Sheila's release. A few minutes later, I asked him, "Do you still need the scissors? Would you throw them on the floor or hand them to me?" Given this choice, he hesitated and then gave me the scissors—a sign that he trusted me enough to give up his weapon.

I pointed out that we needed to continue his medical treatment. Since it was necessary to handcuff him, I asked, "Would you like me to handcuff you, or shall I ask the police to do it?" "Would you like to be handcuffed in the front or back?" He answered, "George, I would like you to do it and I want to be handcuffed in the front." So I did, and we slowly walked out of the room.

As he was being led away, Sam said, "George, you're all right. I am glad I didn't kill you." I replied, "Me too, Sam." He then thanked me sincerely. I asked him what he was thanking me for and he said, "For reminding me how important my children are to me."

After he was taken away, I held it together long enough to ask Dan to step away from the group of people. I then experienced a wave of powerful, overwhelming emotions. I shouted at Dan, "How dare you send me into that room! I could have been killed!"

"But George, you were the right person. I've been watching you and I knew you were ready to deal with a situation like this. I knew you could do it."

I've since been physically taken hostage three additional times, and I've diffused hundreds of potentially violent situations. Now, more than 40 years later, when I'm in a challenging situation, I can still hear Dan's voice saying, "I knew you could do it," and I am once again inspired.

Dan saw a potential in George that George could not see in himself. Recalls George, "He didn't treat me as a junior or a trainee; he treated me like all other members of the team. In a high-stakes situation, Dan decided that I was capable and I was the right person. He offered me the opportunity to stretch myself."

In a tense moment, Dan remained calm in his general behavior, exhibiting confidence in his team. Instead of panicking or raising his voice, he simply and calmly asked, "George, how would you like to do it?"

After the hostage situation was resolved, he responded to George's outburst with a single statement: "But George, you were the right person" which brought George back to the fact that he had been successful.

Let's look also at the keys to George's success in this harrowing situation. He, too, remained calm. He developed an empathetic understanding of Sam's motivation; by the end, Sam even felt bonded to George. George tapped into Sam's potential and possibility by bringing up the subject of his children instead of focusing on the negative aspects of the future (including certain prison). He asked questions and gave options, thereby granting human dignity and choice to the very man who held scissors to his neck.

In this anecdote, the real interest lies in the fact that Dan "led" George in essentially the same way George "led" Sam. They were both, to be precise, a "secure base"—Dan for George and George for Sam. They each provided a sense of protection and comfort from which another person received energy and inspiration to explore, take risks and seek challenge.

Dan and George are not unique. Great leaders all over the world unleash astonishing potential within themselves, their people and their organizations by building the trust, delivering the change and inspiring the focus that together underpin engagement and create the conditions for innovation. They achieve sustainable high performance simply by tapping into their own secure bases and becoming a secure base for other people. We define high performance as:

challenging yourself and others to see and achieve what is beyond normal expectation.

In this place, you push beyond your comfort zone and do what you thought was impossible. You move to the very edge of risk and possibility.

You, too, can become a Secure Base Leader in your work and your life. No matter where you work and with whom you work, how little support you feel, how small your budget, or how busy you are, you can learn specific skills and develop a way of being and doing that delivers sustainable results through inspired relationships. You can learn to care to dare.

If you are like many executives we meet, you may have been "taken hostage" by a boss, a team, an employee, a customer, a situation or by the pressure to achieve results in the form of numbers, targets or key performance indicators. In other words, you may feel powerless and unable to escape these constraints. In the pursuit of financial success, you may even have lost sight of the importance of relationships and how they impact real and sustainable success. Secure Base Leadership, based on trust, confidence and challenge, is the best way to liberate yourself, your team and your organization from being held hostage.

Although extremely deep and powerful, Secure Base Leadership does not take years to learn. In fact, the keys to developing as a Secure Base Leader are already within you: within your life story, within your experience and within the way you have internalized successes and failures. Through our research, we identified the nine characteristics of a Secure Base Leader, and over the course of this book, you'll learn how to develop these characteristics in yourself. We'll answer these questions:

- Why should you be a Secure Base Leader?
- How do you provide care, safety and comfort?[1]
- How do you provide daring, challenge and risk?
- How do you put these ideas into action right away? In other words, what do you do next Monday morning at work?

WHAT IS A SECURE BASE?

Let's start by going back to the beginning. Your beginning.

Your first secure base was likely your mother, your father, a grandparent or another significant caregiver. Your relationships with these people are fundamental to understanding yourself as an adult and as a leader.

The term secure base arose from the post-war attachment theory research of John Bowlby and Mary Ainsworth.[2] Attachment theory revolves around the basic premise that all humans have an innate desire to seek closeness to and comfort from a person who gives them a sense of protection. In the post-World War II period, the United Nations hired Bowlby to find out why babies in "sterile" hospitals died of infection while those surrounded by disease often lived. He determined that mother-excluding protocols and severe nursing styles in the sterile hospitals often deprived babies of attention and loving care. On the other hand, babies who had access to their mothers or sensitive caregivers tended to survive the diseases around them. He concluded that a bond gave the babies resilience and strength.

Following Bowlby's work, researcher J.W. Anderson noticed how children would explore but always keep their mothers as a base—a *secure* base. Toddlers would play around the area but from time to time return to the mother for some form of comfort. It was intriguing that different children appeared to behave differently. Some would stay very close to their mothers, afraid to take a risk, while others would explore the outer edges of the play area while paying very little attention to their mothers. What was common, however, was that when frightened or upset all children turned to their mothers, who demonstrated two sets of behaviors. On the one hand, their behaviors of acceptance and being accessible indicated a provision of safety, while on the other hand, their behaviors of providing opportunities for risk empowered the children to discover their own solutions and to pursue their autonomy.[3]

Building on this concept, for the purposes of our work in modern organizations, we define a secure base as:

a person, place, goal or object that provides a sense of protection, safety and caring *and* offers a source of inspiration and energy for daring, exploration, risk taking and seeking challenge.

Note that to our way of thinking a secure base is someone or something that inspires or brings forth energy within an individual. With this inspiration and energy, individuals step out of their comfort zones and strive to fulfill their untapped potential.

To understand why we all need secure bases, consider how the human brain works. When an actual or perceived threat to survival emerges, the primal brain will prompt the individual to resist change or avoid risk to protect the self. However, when a person has a secure base, he can turn the focus from pain, danger, fear and loss to focus on reward, opportunity and benefit.

While the strongest secure bases often take the form of people, secure bases can also be anything that shuts down the early warning system in the brain and provides the energy and inspiration to seek challenge. In our view, places, goals and objects can be secure bases, as can a country, a religion or God, an event, a group, or even a pet. Any entity that through a relationship enhances the person's inner sense of safety and inspires exploration can be a secure base. The stronger the secure base, the more resilient the person becomes in the face of adverse or stressful circumstances. Because the need for a secure base is rooted deep within the brain, the secure base concept applies universally across all cultures and generations.

Multifaceted, the concept of a secure base presents paradox after paradox and layer after layer. A secure base provides protection and encourages risk taking. A secure base both waits and intervenes. People need both people and goals as secure bases. You can only be a secure base for others when you have multiple secure bases yourself. Let's explore these dynamics in more detail.

THE SAFETY/RISK PARADOX

Figure 1.1 shows the interplay between the two primary dimensions of being a secure base: safety and risk. The safety is reflected in caring, while the risk is reflected in daring. A secure base provides the safety, security and comfort that enable exploration and risk taking. A secure base simultaneously shuts down the brain's

FIGURE 1.1   THE SAFETY/RISK PARADOX

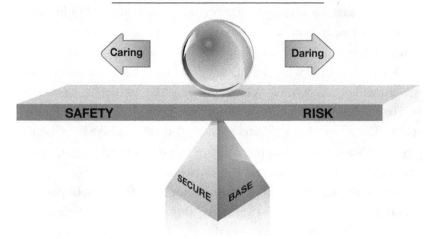

focus on fear, threat and even survival *and* encourages curiosity and risk taking while inspiring exploration. In this way, a secure base brings out the inherent potential in the individual.

If you only provided safety, you would be a source of great comfort for the other person; however, without inspiring him to explore, take risks or seek challenge, you would actually overprotect him and limit his potential. On the other hand, if you encouraged risk without providing safety and security, you would be demanding exploration without giving the support necessary for the person to gain confidence in that risk taking. In that situation, he is likely to feel overexposed and vulnerable and then resort to defensiveness as an instinctive reaction to feeling unsafe. Providing only one side of the equation reduces the ultimate performance of the people you want to lead—either because they are too comfortable or because they are too anxious.

As we conducted our research on high performance leaders, we heard these two stories that demonstrate how childhood secure bases who balance safety and risk have an enormous and lasting impact:

Andrea's German and biology teacher had high expectations and was very results-oriented; at the same time, the personal development of his pupils was close to his heart. She recalls, "He encouraged us to go beyond thinking in 'black and white' or 'right and wrong' categories; he very much encouraged us to look out for 'grey zones' and to consider them as well. He triggered critical as well as creative thinking and clearly pointed us to personal responsibility and accountability. My teacher was an authentic, respectful person and was very passionate about what he did. His way of acting and approach to life highly motivated me and enabled me to achieve more than I would have ever believed to be possible."

Gudrun recalled a time when she was only four or five and her family went skiing in Switzerland. It was snowing and cloudy but her father took her up to the Stockhorn, a rather difficult skiing area, and skied down with her. On their return, her mother was upset and said, "This is madness. She is just a small child and it is very dangerous." Her father replied, "Yes, and she did very well. There was no problem." Gudrun recalled that she had felt absolutely secure when skiing through the snowfall and remembered the pride she felt about how she had skied that day and about how her father had believed in her.

Andrea's teacher clearly cared for her and dared her to achieve high performance. Likewise, Gudrun's father provided an extraordinary example of how the power of presence, the depth of relationship and the impact of words can influence a person's thinking. Today, Gudrun still remembers her father's voice saying, "She did very well." Who did she choose to listen to? In this case, she paid attention to the words of her father rather than the anxiety of her mother.

Gudrun seemed quite happy with her father that day. Sometimes you may not actually appreciate your secure base at the time he or she pushes you. Think of those times you "hated" your parents for "making" you challenge yourself. Think of that teacher who gave you extra work because she knew you could do better. Secure bases push you out of your comfort zone. On the other hand, a friend you love may not be a secure base at all if she doesn't challenge you to explore and take appropriate risks.

A WAITING GAME

Bowlby made it clear that a secure base should intervene only when required or requested, not proactively. As he said, "It is largely a waiting game."[4] In our frame of reference, it is about being available and on standby. That's why even a very "busy" person can act as a secure base to many people. A secure base is a good listener who picks up on signals (whether verbal or non-verbal) and pays close attention to the needs of the other person, rather than imposing solutions too quickly. Also, instead of advocating a position, a secure base applies the judicious use of questions to challenge thinking.

Secure bases do not think for other people. They don't "rescue" them. They don't do what the person can clearly do herself. A secure base lets the person do something herself and then helps her to make meaning of the experience.

PEOPLE AND GOALS

Figure 1.2 captures another dimension of secure bases: the combination of attaching to both people and goals. Bonding to people is pretty obvious. People need interpersonal attachments to feel worthwhile, to deserve to exist and to feel loved.

"Bonding to goals" is less obvious. To do so, set a target or goal for yourself and then commit to the steps needed to achieve that goal. Here are some examples that show bonding to goals:

- Jacob aimed for the goal of becoming an excellent presenter. He achieved it at his company annual event after 18 months of practice.

FIGURE 1.2 THE STRENGTH OF A SECURE BASE

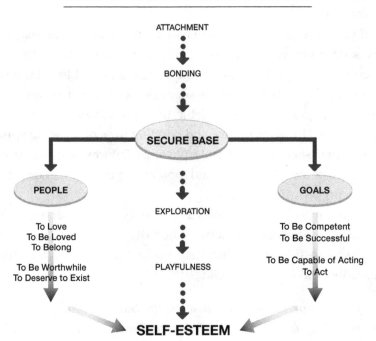

- Andreas set himself the goal of becoming a better leader, as measured by a pre- and post-360° feedback survey. By creating a plan and putting in place clear actions, he was able to improve his leadership skills over a 12-month period.
- Kathleen set herself a goal of becoming a Chief Technology Officer by age 45. She achieved this goal at age 43 by changing companies.
- As a team of co-authors, George, Susan and Duncan have been bonded to the shared goal of completing this book.

People simply must be bonded to goals in order to feel capable of acting, to achieve and to have success. Bonding to goals provides the determination and resilience to overcome obstacles and achieve results. The very act of bonding to a goal brings energy to the pursuit.

If you have people as secure bases but not goals, you may feel very secure but you may play it too safe and not take the risks necessary to maximize your potential. You may feel loved but not successful. If you have goals as secure bases but not people, you often will experience considerable material success but be quite impoverished in terms of love and bonding to people. Some apparent external successes are truly personal failures because of the hidden costs of high stress and potential burnout. Secure Base Leaders prevent these failures.

People who have only goals as secure bases can become what are called "independent loners." When they lack bonds to people like Pascal in this story, they may suffer from illness, addiction, depression and chronic loneliness:

Pascal, a senior leader with a scientific background, grew up with a lack of bonding to both his mother and his father, who was physically and emotionally abusive. He managed to be very successful in his career but at a great cost. He always focused on numbers at the exclusion of people. Shortly after marrying a woman he loved deeply, Pascal had a major emotional reaction provoked by feelings of rejection and jealousy, and he physically attacked his wife. Shocked by his own behavior, he sought medical help and was put on medication for a decade. He felt that there was something fundamentally wrong with him and he could not trust himself. This affected his leadership style as he did not trust anyone else, either. Employees liked his sense of humor but were unable to bond with him as a leader.

Once Pascal was able to grieve for what he had missed with his own parents, he was able to understand that he was a highly independent loner filled with pain. He could then forgive himself and fully re-bond with his wife. As with all

*resolved grief, Pascal's process ended with a feeling of
gratitude. His inner peace dramatically improved his
leadership. For the first time he was able to create authentic
relationships with his colleagues, peers and boss—and thereby
move into outstanding high performance.*

This story highlights the difference between high performance and *sustained* high performance. Many leaders carry wounds with them from their past that affect their leadership without their conscious knowledge. To move on effectively, Pascal needed to stop being a hostage to his past, get over the event that occurred with his wife, and forgive his parents for not being secure bases for him.

Keeping the balance between bonding to people and bonding to goals is fundamental for healthy functioning, high self-esteem, and high performance at work. When you lack attachment to people or to goals, you may develop a fear of rejection, a fear of success, or a fear of failure that stops you from reaching your full potential. Extremely powerful, fear stops people from reaching for stretch goals because they feel inadequate. Secure bases help them focus on potential success, protect them from their insecurity and inspire the courage to act.

Ask yourself:

• How bonded am I to both people and goals? Do I have the right balance?

TO BE A SECURE BASE, YOU NEED SECURE BASES

It is important both to *have* secure bases and to *be* a secure base for others. We learn through imitation and modeling. If you have experienced the power of a secure base in your life, you are then able to use it as a "model" of how to be a secure base for others.

Ideally, you will have multiple secure bases that change depending on your stage in life and your need. It is never too late to find secure bases for yourself. Likewise, it is never too late to learn how to be a secure base for others. You learn from the caretaking roles in your life: looking after a pet, being in love, becoming a parent or becoming a leader who cares.

SECURE BASES AND MINDSET

Secure bases play a very active role not only in how people learn skills but also in how they make meaning of the world. The secure bases in our lives, from childhood to present day, influence what we believe.[5] The secure bases we choose shape the mind, which in turn shapes focus, which in turn shapes result. In this book, we focus on the forces that have influenced your thinking and mindset. We undertook research that involved extensive interviews with global leaders and quantitative surveys with more than 1,000 executives (see "About the Research" section in the Appendix). By asking leaders about their own motivation, we discovered the factors that shaped the beliefs they hold about themselves. Their answers related to their own self-beliefs. However, when asked about who or what influenced the way these beliefs were formed, executives often experienced a kind of "a-ha moment" as they realized their thinking had been unconsciously influenced by significant people, events or experiences in their past or current lives.

Everyone holds both empowering and limiting beliefs. Some people focus more on the empowering beliefs while others focus more on the limiting beliefs that stop them from acting and succeeding. We all have a story of a teacher who encouraged us to achieve great things as well as a story of a teacher who poisoned our minds into believing that we had no talent in a particular field or area. This story describes Jack's choice of focus:

When Jack was 17 and working hard for his final IB exams, he received a history paper back from his teacher with the words, "I don't know why I bother" scrawled across the end. With his family as a secure base, rather than be distracted by the negative words, Jack decided to prove the teacher wrong and achieved much higher grades than predicted in his final exams.

The important point to remember is that you have a choice about whether you accept or reject someone else's views or opinions. You do not have to be held hostage by others' words or deeds. You choose whether someone is going to influence you positively or negatively. We now understand that the way we react to influences is so individual that it is impossible for any two people to have the same behavior, even if they grew up in the same family and the same environment. What means something to one person may mean something altogether different to another.

Ask yourself:

- Who are the people who have influenced the beliefs I hold about my own abilities and those of others?

SECURE BASE LEADERSHIP

In choosing to be a Secure Base Leader, you step into a deeply influential position that contributes to the "making" of a man or woman. Although deeply ingrained, other people's self-beliefs can be influenced and, more precisely, they can be influenced by you. You choose whether your influence is going to be positive or negative.

In the words of leadership guru Warren Bennis, "The basis of leadership is the capacity of the leader to change the mindset, the framework of another person."[6]

This is a delicate point to understand: the interplay between inherited characteristics, outside influences and choice. You do not become a great leader by yourself. You become a great leader in part through the influence of your secure bases. In short, you stand on the shoulders of those people who have influenced you. You act as a great leader when you use *your* influence to unleash the positive potential of the people who follow you, in other words when you choose to be a Secure Base Leader and you let others stand on *your* shoulders.

We define Secure Base Leadership as:

the way a leader builds trust and influences others by providing a sense of protection, safety and caring *and* by providing a source of inspiration that together produce energy for daring, exploration, risk taking and seeking challenge.

Figure 1.3 demonstrates how Secure Base Leadership unleashes potential and results in achievement.

Leadership is all about inspiring and harnessing energy. You harness your energy to mobilize individuals, teams and organizations to use their energy in the service of a goal or mission you articulate. In the process, you and your followers achieve more than you ever thought possible.

Managers have direct reports. Leaders have followers. Through their followers, leaders are able to achieve outstanding results.

FIGURE 1.3 SECURE BASE LEADERSHIP

DARING
Risk, Challenge, Exploration

Energy, Inspiration

CARING
Security, Protection, Comfort

Unleashed Potential

Achievement

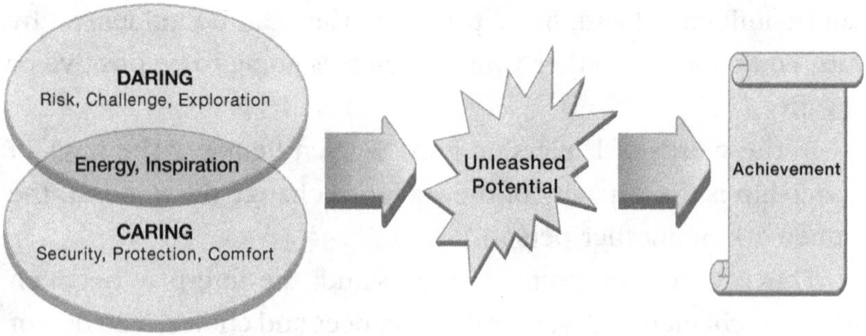

Secure Base Leadership emphasizes both the relational nature of leadership (people) and the operational aspect of getting work done in a positive manner. It certainly involves how you deal with decision-making, issues, situations and problems. However, it is more than just driving numbers. It is about how you inspire people. By articulating inspiring goals that can themselves become secure bases for your people, you will realize success in terms of results. We know you have to deliver results, and through Secure Base Leadership, you will. By focusing on people, you can inspire and engage others to achieve more than they ever thought possible.

MYTH: Your personal life has nothing to do with your leadership effectiveness.

Not true. Your personal journey defines who you are as a leader. You bring both inspiration and limitations from your personal life into work. You manifest your very humanity in your leadership.

The combination of people and goals as secure bases allows a person to trust, be creative, take risks, explore and be playful. When we ask people about how they describe being on a high performing team, they often say it was intense but also a lot of fun. In other words, they experienced a tight connection to both goals and people.

What we hear on the ground mirrors the findings of leadership and organizational researchers Micha Popper and Ofra Mayseless. They suggest that "the leader's provision of a sense of security makes possible the activation of other behavioral systems such as exploration. This might be manifested in the capacity of followers to take risks and be creative, leading to learning and personal growth."[7] They further suggest that the opposite would also be true. If the followers feel insecure as a result of the leader's behavior, then risk taking, exploration and learning will diminish.

Continuing this line of thought, they propose that the leader who is a secure base will help followers develop new mental models as well as achieve greater "self-confidence, autonomy, competence, self-efficacy and self-esteem."[8]

When Leaders Fail

Leaders fail when they:

- Do not inspire others
- Lack awareness of the impact they are having on other people
- Neglect relationships in the relentless pursuit of goals
- Do not manage themselves and their emotions

Even icons like Steve Jobs failed at some point in their careers. Walter Issacson, author of the tech giant's authorized biography, told the story of Jobs' firing at Apple. Book reviewer Lev Grossman provides this summary:

Nine years after Jobs founded Apple, he was driven out of the company, and Isaacson makes it clear that he gave his colleagues no choice: his obsession with control, his tirades and crying jags, his inflexibility in the face of a changing market and his reluctance to bathe all made him a toxic presence.[9]

At that point in his career, Jobs definitely did not lead as a secure base. However, Grossman continues with:

But he returned in triumph in 1996 a changed man, with enough control over his demons to save Apple and build it into the world's most valuable company.

Jobs' story stands as an example of why leaders fail as well as an inspiration for those who need courage to become self-aware and change in pursuit of leadership greatness.

Through the executives attending our workshops around the world we see firsthand how secure bases are an important foundation of leadership. Your personal journey defines who you are as a leader. For that reason, much of your work to become a Secure Base Leader will involve becoming aware of the people, events and experiences that have influenced you. That is why we will take you back to your personal life throughout this book and provide specific guidance and exercises to help you reflect upon the people, events and experiences that have shaped your thinking and impacted your leadership.

Your Leadership Successes and Failures

One way to reflect upon your leadership performance patterns is to write up three success stories and three failure stories from your life. They can be personal or professional, from your childhood, adolescence or adulthood. Write with as much or as little detail as you would like.

Read through the stories and notice what aspects appeared in each of the success stories and what was absent from the failure stories. For example, did your success stories all involve working with others while your failures reflected times you worked alone? Or did your successes have a supportive authority figure in common? Was such a figure lacking in your failure stories?

By examining the factors behind your successes and seeing the absence of those factors in your failures, you can identify the patterns or themes that are most important for success, not only at work but also in your personal life.

BELAY YOUR PEOPLE: THE COMPONENTS OF SECURE BASE LEADERSHIP

You demonstrate Secure Base Leadership when you combine comfort and risk, support and stretch, protection and challenge—when you bond with your people and focus them, the team or the organization on stretch targets. It is a dynamic balancing act between providing safety through bonding and encouraging risk through a focus on possibility.

In many ways, being a Secure Base Leader is like "belaying" a rock climber. Although different manifestations of this safety system exist on different rock faces or indoor climbing walls, the basic concept remains the same. As illustrated in Figure 1.4, a rope

FIGURE 1.4 BELAYING AS METAPHOR FOR SECURE BASE LEADERSHIP

Climber
(Taking Risks Safely)

Belayer

SECURE BASE

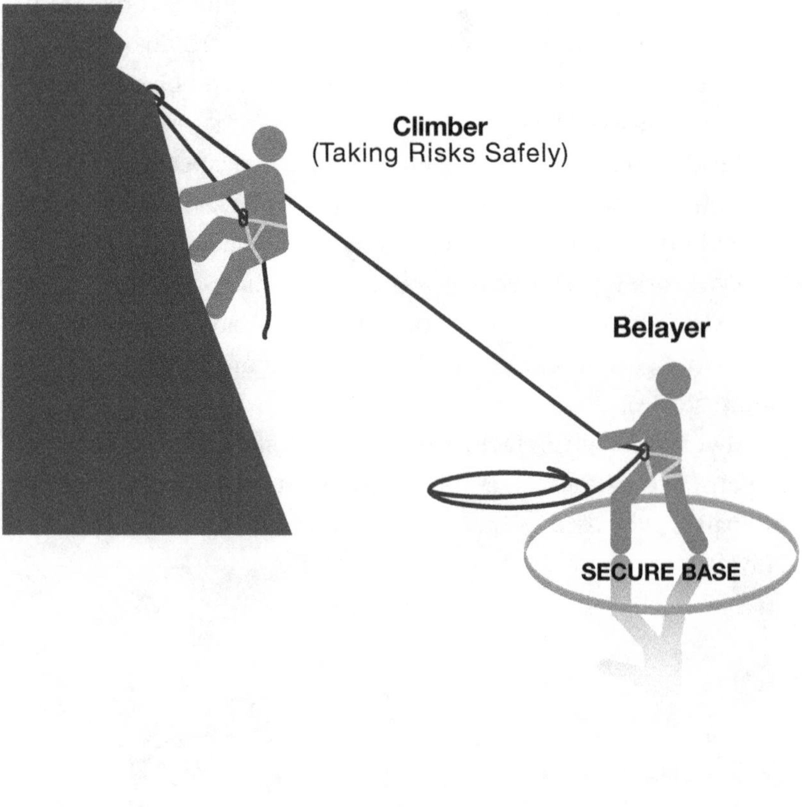

is looped through an anchor above the immediate climbing area. The climber is attached to one end of the rope. The belayer, using a special device clipped to his harness, holds the other side of the rope so that the climber has enough slack to move, but not enough to fall any great distance. As the climber advances up the mountain or wall, the belayer watches the climber intently and takes up slack as needed.

Essentially, the climber can take the risks inherent in the climb precisely *because* the belayer is providing the sense of safety. As we delve into the details of Secure Base Leadership, you'll see that we explore this metaphor in more detail because both the process and the presence of belaying reflect the nuances of Secure Base Leadership.

Clearly, encouraging someone to climb before you secure the belay would be irresponsible. Likewise, stretching someone through professional challenges before you have established a strong platform of safety can result in frustration and stress. Therefore, the first "step" of Secure Base Leadership is to develop that sense of safety and protection by "bonding." When you encourage stretch and challenge, you actually reinforce the bond of trust because you are saying "I believe that you can succeed. I trust you." The power of Secure Base Leadership is in this self-reinforcing dynamic.

Ask yourself:

- Would my people say I do a good job "belaying" them?

BONDING THAT DEVELOPS TRUST

Critical to Secure Base Leadership, bonding is:

forming an attachment that creates more physical, emotional, intellectual and/or spiritual energy than the person or people involved could generate independently.

Bonding is an emotional connection that is different from friendship. As you'll see in Chapter 3, Secure Base Leaders bond with their followers. Ultimately, that bonding results in trust—trust that the leader is acting with the best interest of the followers in mind, trust that the leader will support the followers should they falter or fail and trust that the leader knows the level of challenge that is appropriate. It is, quite simply, like having someone on belay.

All bonds start as "attachments" that are basic connections. An attachment progresses to a bond when there is an exchange of emotion and a depth of contact—a "chemistry," if you will. However, bonds are not permanent, nor should they be. "Separation" from a bond at the right time is natural, just as it is natural for a child to leave a parent. When leaders do not allow bonds to evolve, they inhibit the separation that comes with growth. In this case they hold their followers hostage. A Secure Base Leader encourages his people to move on and up, taking on bigger and greater challenges, and he watches with pride and with caring. In today's highly competitive world, bonding to people is the biggest challenge and a true test of a Secure Base Leader.

EMBRACING LOSS TO DELIVER CHANGE

"Grief" is a word one rarely hears within work settings, yet it is a natural part of life that is as relevant in the workplace as it is in personal life. Any time a person suffers a loss—the loss of a person through death, the loss of a bond with a colleague who was laid off, the loss of a team because of a reorganization—she can become resistant to "reattaching" and forming new bonds to people, goals or work. The only way to move on from the loss is through grief. Through the process of grieving, people come back to the joy of work, to the joy of parenting or even to the joy of life. They get over whatever was lost. They regain energy. At work, therefore, they return to full productivity.

People experience loss on a daily basis and in all transitions. In addition to the big losses in life, people can also grieve the loss of an office, the loss of a project, the loss of a client, the loss of a reserved parking spot or even the loss of a favorite pen. When you learn to embrace grief as a natural emotion rather than something to be avoided, you begin to be able to deal more effectively and more compassionately with any loss or change.

Organizations are constantly dealing with change, and even the best-handled changes create loss that necessitates grieving. As you will read in Chapter 4, Secure Base Leaders understand grief as a natural process. They manage change in a way that focuses on the benefit instead of the pain. Because they have created a bond of trust, they authentically create space for people to express their fears and vent their feelings of disappointment. At the end of the process, people reach a stage of forgiveness and gratitude, and they are ready to move on to new attachments and challenges.

DIRECTING THE MIND'S EYE TO PROVIDE FOCUS

From the foundation of a bond so strong that it allows for grieving and reattachment, Secure Base Leaders, like the belayer, encourage followers to explore, take risks and stretch. They do so by directing the focus of their followers toward possibilities. Just as your mindset was influenced by your secure bases, you, as a Secure Base Leader, can influence the mindset of others so that they focus on the positive, thereby creating empowering beliefs that help them achieve goals.

As you will discover in Chapter 5, the "Mind's Eye" is the part of the brain that manages our focus. The Mind's Eye directs the focus of a "flashlight" to shine on either the positive or the negative. You can choose to look at the negative, the pain, the danger and what is going wrong and thereby create limiting beliefs that can stop you from taking risks to achieve the results you want. Or you can choose to look at the benefit, the gain and what is going right. Secure Base Leaders influence the way others make that choice. They ensure that the Mind's Eye of the individual or team is focused on the goal, the benefit, the desired results, the learning, the opportunity and the possibility.

ACHIEVING RESULTS BY "PLAYING TO WIN"

"Playing to Win," the subject of Chapter 6, is a leadership approach that combines a high level of caring and a high level of daring. When you "Play to Win", you value both relationships and challenge. You push toward benefits instead of being taken hostage by fear. Many people "Play Not to Lose" because they are controlled by fear and anxiety; they avoid taking risks in order to pursue benefits. Other people "Play to Dominate" by focusing too much on the result and disconnecting from the people around them or by being too much of what *Emotional Intelligence* author Dan Goleman calls "pacesetters." People cannot keep up with a leader like this.

A pacesetter can be positive in the short term with a highly motivated team. When a pacesetter learns to stay bonded to people while focusing on stretch goals, he can move toward the "Playing to Win" approach and become a Secure Base Leader. Together, leader and followers achieve the highest level of performance: the climber, knowing he is safe with the Secure Base Leader belaying him, takes risks and reaches farther to arrive at the top of the climb. "Playing to Win" is the leadership approach in which you lead at your best in a sustainable way and have your deepest impact on others and your organization.

SUSTAINABLE HIGH PERFORMANCE

If you are like most leaders, you are surrounded by volatility, uncertainty, complexity and ambiguity. You know the world is becoming increasingly more volatile, more uncertain, more complex and more ambiguous. How do you achieve results across cultures in such a world? How do you sustain your organization's performance amid these challenges? Just as importantly, how do you sustain *your own* performance amid these challenges?

If you keep driving for results by squeezing every ounce of energy out of yourself and your people, you will burn out and also lose their best effort. Instead, you have to inspire energy in a way that does not deplete you. Your followers have the potential to go the distance with and for you. You simply have to unleash their astonishing potential.

As a Secure Base Leader, you drive bonding that builds relationships and trust. Trust-based relationships drive engagement.[10] Engagement promotes retention and loyalty, and it reduces cost and stress. Even more importantly, with your full belief in their potential, your followers will be inspired not only to achieve ambitious personal goals but also to fulfill the very mission of your organization. With your influence on their Mind's Eye, they will believe that anything is possible. When the going gets tough or when inevitable change brings about loss, this high level of engagement will buoy them up so that together you can deal with the complexity, uncertainty, volatility and ambiguity of today's world.

As a Secure Base Leader, you deliver sustainable results by inspiring others to perform at their very best, even in changing environments. You create conditions that bolster loyalty and engagement as well as creativity and discovery. You promote excellence, inspiration and high self-esteem. In the end, when you care to dare and embrace Secure Base Leadership, your organization is more likely to deliver sustainable high performance with outstanding results.

This performance can be achieved without a big price tag: Secure Base Leadership does not cost money. It also does not have to take a lot of your time. It is simply a way of using your time with people differently and, most importantly, tapping into a deeper part of yourself to connect with your followers at a deeper level.

Ask yourself:

- Am I a Secure Base Leader?
- Do I balance a focus on results with a focus on people?
- Do I provide a safe enough environment to allow people to take risks?
- Do I intervene too quickly or wait too long?

WHAT'S NEXT? WHAT WILL YOU DO ON MONDAY MORNING?

Part I of this book gives you an overview of Secure Base Leadership. After the introduction in this chapter, you will learn about the nine characteristics of Secure Base Leaders that we discovered in our research (Chapter 2). In Part II, you will explore the components of Secure Base Leadership—bonding (Chapter 3), grief (Chapter 4), Mind's Eye (Chapter 5) and Playing to Win (Chapter 6)—as well as gain tips to develop the characteristics most applicable to each of those components.

Just as tennis players become experts through deliberate practice and good coaching, you can become an expert Secure Base Leader. It will take practice and you will need to build awareness of the secure bases in your life. The process, as you'll discover in Part III, involves delving into your past and embracing your present. You will discover the "roots of your leadership," recognize the secure bases you have in your life and even learn about becoming your own secure base (Chapter 7). From there, you will read about becoming a secure base for others (Chapter 8) and transforming your own organization into a secure base (Chapter 9).

Although developing as a Secure Base Leader is a highly personal process, it is tangible and attainable. Understanding and then incorporating the nine characteristics into your daily leadership behavior will help you to create an environment where people feel safe and protected enough to step out of their comfort zones, take risks and seek challenge. By picking a few of these characteristics to work on, you can improve your own performance as a Secure Base Leader and thereby improve the performance of your employees, your team and your organization.

As you will read in Chapter 10, Secure Base Leadership is fundamentally about humanizing your leadership and, by extension, your organization. It is all too easy in this world to forget about people, including yourself, and the universal needs we all have to be connected, to be inspired and to grow. When we go too fast in an effort to keep up with change, we can dehumanize challenge. It is our hope that this book gives you permission to return to your humanity and to keep the human dimension flourishing and thriving in your teams, organizations, families and, by extension, society.

Key Learnings

- A secure base provides safety, protection and comfort as well as the inspiration for exploration, risk taking and challenge.
- Your secure bases have influenced not only your leadership but also who you are and what you choose to focus on.
- Secure Base Leaders build the trust, deliver the change and provide the focus that together underpin engagement and lead to high performance.
- Secure Base Leaders form bonds, embrace loss through grief, focus the Mind's Eye on the positive and "Play to Win."
- Secure Base Leaders manage their own Mind's Eye to focus on the positive and the benefits, and they influence others to focus theirs in that direction too.
- A Secure Base Leader is like a belayer who provides security to a rock climber so that he can take risks and climb to the top of the mountain.
- Secure Base Leadership does not cost money. The only investment you make is the choice to use your time differently.
- Leadership is a set of learned behaviors. You can develop any of the nine characteristics and become a Secure Base Leader who unleashes personal and organizational potential.

&

"Dream more than others think practical. Expect more than others think possible. Care more than others think wise."

–Howard Schultz

1953–

Chairman and CEO of Starbucks

&

FREQUENTLY ASKED QUESTIONS

Q: This sounds like a lot to take in . . . is it really possible to learn all of this?

A: Take it one step at a time. This chapter gave an overview of the whole book. You now have the big picture. From here you will learn more about these concepts in each chapter, and you will get the chance to learn how to fully integrate the material.

Q: How is *Care to Dare* different from other leadership books I have read or from leadership theories I have heard about?

A: Caring and Daring together is what makes Secure Base Leadership different. It is "soft" and "hard" at the same time. Furthermore, the personal exploration you will do in this book will lead you to understand the reasons why you lead the way you do. Your leadership role is the tip of the iceberg of who you are as a person. This book aims to get deep beneath the surface level of your leadership behaviors to develop a new way of leadership "being" and "doing."

CHAPTER TWO

SECURE BASE
LEADERSHIP IN ACTION

When she was eight years old, Susan watched the Mexico City Olympics on television and thought to herself, "I want to be part of that." Although she enjoyed swimming, she was not particularly tall, strong or broad-shouldered. Many people would say to her parents and to her coach, "It's a shame Susan isn't bigger—she'll never make it to the top being so small." However, Susan's grandfather, Jack Brown, who had been a flyweight boxer in his youth, would always tell her, "The bigger they are, the harder they fall." In her mind, Susan swam with the belief that it was actually an advantage to be smaller—she was more swift in the water, faster at turns and better able to maneuver quickly. It never even crossed her mind that it was a disadvantage to be short.

Fast forward eight years. Just before the Olympic trials, Susan was walking up the steps outside the competition venue with Jack Queen, the coach of Great Britain's 1976 Women's Olympic swimming team. "But what if I don't make it?" asked Susan. "You've already done the qualifying time," said Jack. "If you are walking along the road and you come to a one-foot gap in the pavement, you step over it and carry on walking. Now, imagine you are on top of a twenty-story building and there is a one-foot gap between that building and the next one.

Even though the height is different, it's the same one-foot gap."
"But what if I don't do the qualifying time in the trials?" said
Susan. "Go down two steps," said Jack. "What?" said Susan.
"Go down two steps," replied Jack. Confused, Susan moved
down two steps. "Your goal is at the top of these stairs. You
were standing next to me a moment ago. By what you've just
said, you've moved yourself two steps further away from your
goal," said Jack.

These two Jacks framed a self-belief within Susan that
inspired her to compete in the finals of the Olympic
Games in Montreal and earn a host of other international
swimming honors. At the European Championships, as she
lined up for the final of the 200m butterfly, she turned
around and looked at her 6' 2" rival from Russia and
thought to herself, "You're too big to beat me." She ended
up winning a bronze medal, coming in behind two East
German swimmers.

Susan and Jack Queen have remained in touch. Many years
later, he sent her a card that said: "Just think of us as sharing
the same shadow. If you feel downhearted or exhilarated by a
job well done, then go stand in the sunlight and look at your
shadow—that's my hand on your shoulder."

Jack Brown and Jack Queen certainly fit the bill as secure
bases. Susan trusted both Jacks enough to incorporate into her
belief system their words and faith in her. They focused Susan's
Mind's Eye away from the negative and potential pain onto the
positive and potential gain. Along with her mother and her
outstanding club coach, Al Richards, they gave Susan a sense
of protection and feeling of comfort while also inspiring, challenging and motivating her to reach to the very top of her field;
they cared about her and then dared her to reach for her
dreams.

Your leadership opportunity is to translate this concept to the business setting so that you, your team and your organization can reach Olympic levels of performance.

Bowlby coined the term "secure base" while researching the dynamics in parent-child relationships. Through our research, we have confirmed the dynamic in actual work settings. More importantly, in exploring the secure base concept more thoroughly in relation to high performance leadership, we have discovered what a Secure Base Leader *actually says and does*. We have distilled our findings into the nine characteristics that we will introduce in this chapter and explore in more detail in Part II. Our goal is to create a practical guide for you and other leaders who wish to improve their own Secure Base Leadership skills.

CHARACTERISTICS OF SECURE BASE LEADERS

The behaviors of Secure Base Leaders are clear, practical and learnable. In fact, you may already be exhibiting some of the nine characteristics described in Table 2.1 and, through reading this book,

TABLE 2.1 SECURE BASE LEADERSHIP CHARACTERISTICS

1. Stays Calm
2. Accepts the Individual
3. Sees the Potential
4. Uses Listening and Inquiry
5. Delivers a Powerful Message
6. Focuses on the Positive
7. Encourages Risk Taking
8. Inspires through Intrinsic Motivation
9. Signals Accessibility

begin to understand the impact of those tangible behaviors on your own leadership. Any leader is capable of learning, practicing and delivering on Secure Base Leadership. Linked to the bonding cycle and the Mind's Eye, these nine characteristics work at the individual, team and organizational levels.

MYTH: Leadership is not personal.

Not true. Great leaders form significant bonds with people inside and outside the company; they accept and value people as individuals. Leadership is innately personal.

Secure Base Leaders engage in a high level of caring and also encourage a high level of daring. In this way, both the leader and their followers can reach the highest levels of performance and have the most positive impact on others. We call that place the "sweet spot" of leadership. This sweet spot is of particular relevance to organizations focused on learning, innovation and change.

Unfortunately, we can't give you a precise recipe for the sweet spot. Secure Base Leaders mix together the nine characteristics in just the right way, at just the right time, to provide just the right amount of safety and encourage just the right amount of risk. Some people require more of one than the other. Some days require more of one than another. It comes down to knowing people and being able to pick up signals about their moods and motivations. This artful, dynamic balance is the wisdom of the leader or, as some say, their intuitive side. As Colin Powell, former U.S. Secretary of State, says: "Leadership is the art of accomplishing more than the science of management says is possible."[1]

Secure Base Leadership is indeed an art, and it does indeed mobilize people to achievement.

A Great Boss

Think of the best boss you've ever had.

• What words describe him or her?
• What did he or she do that was so effective?

When we ask senior leaders these questions, we hear words such as:

Even-tempered	Courageous
Supportive	Willing to fail
Focuses on others	Gives constructive feedback
Fair	Inspirational
Consistent	Visionary

Notice that the column on the left describes caring and the one on the right describes daring.

As you learn about the characteristics of Secure Base Leaders, you are likely to recognize the best bosses you've ever had. In fact, it is very likely that they were great bosses precisely *because* they provided that magic combination of comfort and challenge, safety and stretch.

Let's explore each of the characteristics in detail.

1. STAYS CALM

One of the words used most frequently by the people we interviewed about Secure Base Leaders was "calm." A Secure Base Leader remains composed and dependable, especially when under pressure—times at which other leaders may have an "amygdala hijack" (see box on next page). In fact, this characteristic is so fundamental that a leader needs to master it before he is able to portray other characteristics. That's why we shine the development spotlight in this chapter on "Stays Calm."

Amygdala Hijack

Normally, a sensation—such as a visual cue—is routed to a part of the human brain called the thalamus. The thalamus acts as an "air traffic controller" to keep the signals moving. In a typical situation, the thalamus would direct the impulse to the cortex—in this case the visual cortex—for processing. The cortex "thinks" about the impulse and makes sense of it. "A-ha," it says, "This is an exclamation mark! It means I should get excited." That signal is then sent to the amygdala, the part of our brain that controls emotions. The amygdala then releases a flood of peptides and stress hormones into the body, thereby creating emotion and action commensurate with exclamation-point level excitement. The amygdala functions for both positive and negative stimulation.

In what Daniel Goleman labelled "The Hijacking of the Amygdala,"[2] the thalamus has a different reaction. Like any skilled air traffic controller, the thalamus can quickly react to potential threat. In that case, it bypasses the cortex—the thinking brain—and sends the signal straight to the amygdala, essentially "hijacking" it with an unreasoned response. Now, what makes this more interesting is that the amygdala can only react based on previously stored patterns such as the instinctive fight-or-flight mechanism. Sometimes this kind of express-lane reaction can save our lives ("run from the woolly mammoth!"). More frequently, it leads us to say something harmful or to escalate a situation. In some cases, it can even lead to violence.

To minimize the damage from an amygdala hijack, it is important to practice behavior that leads to de-escalation. Even though your brain may be flooded with electrochemicals, you still have options. You do not need to stay hijacked: you can choose to take a deep breath and regain control of your actions.

2. ACCEPTS THE INDIVIDUAL

Our research shows that a key component of being a Secure Base Leader is an acceptance and acknowledgment of the basic worth of the person as a human being—beyond being an employee or being viewed as just a job description. In the words of Carl Rogers, it is about "unconditional positive regard."[3] Secure Base Leaders show caring for the human being before focusing on the issue or problem. They separate the person from the problem. As far as possible, they avoid judging and criticizing people. This approach makes the other person feel legitimized and affirmed. This response occurred in our interviews even when the person was remembering a dialogue involving some difficult feedback or conflict. Essentially, secure bases maintain respect for the person at all times. This characteristic is about making leadership personal and about keeping people as the primary focus.

It is important to note that this characteristic reflects the notion of valuing, honoring and appreciating every person as worthwhile and deserving to exist. See Chapter 3 for tips to develop this characteristic.

3. SEES THE POTENTIAL

Secure Base Leaders see the employee's potential talent versus his current functioning or "state." This characteristic goes beyond acceptance of the person's inherent value and possibly even goes beyond what the person expects from himself. Importantly, this characteristic is not about short-term potential. Instead, it is about a deeper vision or even a dream for the person's deepest potential— not in one year, but in 10 or 20 years. If Jim Collins says success is about BHAGs (Big Hairy Audacious Goals),[4] this is about BHAP (Big Hairy Audacious Potential). Given that the Secure Base Leader often has more experience, more wisdom and a broader perspective on opportunities than the employee, he is well-positioned to look for and inspire this sense of potentiality. The individual may not yet see or believe what is possible within. See Chapter 3 for tips to develop this characteristic.

Not Just a Big Teddy Bear

Don't get the impression that Secure Base Leaders are all fluff and no action. Far from it. Rather than shying away from some of the tougher aspects of management and leadership, Secure Base Leaders embrace these challenges with humanity.

Feedback: Secure Base Leaders can deliver tough, even painful feedback and still be able to inspire others. Because they shine their Mind's Eye on the positive and see the potential in every individual, they deliver painful feedback and followers say "thank you" because they feel the positive intention from the Secure Base Leader.

Push: Secure Base Leaders push "the edge of the envelope" and really challenge their people. They do so by inspiring courage, not by invoking fear, threats and control. In guiding followers' thinking, Secure Base Leaders train them to look for the gain over the pain, to focus on the goal rather than any immediate discomfort and to stretch themselves beyond what they thought reasonable or possible.

Accountability: Secure Base Leaders don't let people off the hook. Because they believe in the capability of their people, they hold them expressly accountable for achieving goals. Sometimes wrongly accused of being "unreasonable," they don't accept excuses and will disagree with followers who want to take the easy way out. They are, in many ways, the epitome of "tough love."

4. Uses Listening and Inquiry

Our research reflected a stylistic preference of Secure Base Leaders toward listening and inquiry rather than "telling" and advocacy. The people we interviewed described how secure bases listened to them and asked questions rather than providing solutions or telling them what to do in difficult situations. The Secure Base Leaders did not follow the all-too-common pattern of launching into monologues to convince others of their point of view. Instead, they mastered the arts of asking open-ended questions and engaging in a dialogue to seek a greater truth. Because deep dialogue is one of the most powerful tools available to a Secure Base Leader, we give development tips related to this characteristic in both Chapter 4 (within the context of embracing loss) and Chapter 8 (as a key component of becoming a secure base for others).

5. DELIVERS A POWERFUL MESSAGE

Secure Base Leaders have the ability to impact people deeply with single sentences or gestures. They are masters at coming up with pithy sentences, or what we call "bull's eye transactions," that carry tremendous power and impact and that seem to be remembered for many years and in some cases a lifetime. (A "transaction" in this case is a verbal or non-verbal exchange between two people; a full conversation is composed of many distinct transactions.)

We also noticed that bull's eye transactions often happened in the heat of the moment—or "live." In other words, Secure Base Leaders are good at introducing these bull's eye transactions when it really matters, not hours or weeks later when the moment has passed. Rather than launch into a long, rambling speech, Secure Base Leaders appear to have the ability to cut to the chase and say the right thing at just the right time. See Chapter 4 for tips to develop this characteristic.

6. FOCUSES ON THE POSITIVE

Secure Base Leaders are good at directing the Mind's Eye of other people to focus on the positive rather than the negative. In so doing, they help others to see their potential and the opportunity for learning, even in a crisis or time of difficulty. The people we interviewed particularly appreciated and remembered their Secure Base Leaders for their ability in this regard. See Chapter 5 for tips to develop this characteristic.

7. ENCOURAGES RISK TAKING

In very concrete ways, Secure Base Leaders give their people opportunities to reach their potential, many times with some personal risk
attached. This characteristic goes beyond acceptance and beyond
seeing the potential: it takes those concepts into direct action.
Secure Base Leaders actively dare people to unleash their potential
by providing tangible opportunities for risk taking. They support the
autonomy of their followers, and their followers do not feel over-
controlled. See Chapter 5 for tips to develop this characteristic.

8. INSPIRES THROUGH INTRINSIC MOTIVATION

There was not a single reference to money in any of the interviews
we undertook. In other words, when leaders are invited to talk about
the people and events that have influenced them, they do not reference money or financial reward at all. On the other hand, our interviews were full of references to potential, learning, development,
passion, contribution (i.e., making the world a better place) and
meaning. Therefore, we conclude that Secure Base Leaders understand the importance of "intrinsic motivation" to get the best out
of people rather than relying on extrinsic motivation.

What is "intrinsic motivation"? Intrinsic motivation refers to
doing something because it is inherently interesting or enjoyable.
Compare that to extrinsic motivation in which a person does something because it leads to an outcome that is separable from the pure
task. When intrinsically motivated, a person is moved to act for the
fun or challenge involved rather than because of external pressures
or rewards.[5] See Chapter 6 for tips to develop this characteristic.

9. SIGNALS ACCESSIBILITY

People believe that their Secure Base Leaders are always accessible
and available rather than detached and unavailable or "too busy."
Don't panic that you are about to lose your weekends and evenings
to your colleagues! It turns out that physical proximity and fre-

quency of interaction are less important. In fact, many Secure Base Leaders are neither in regular contact nor physically present to the people they influence. Many of the most powerful conversations were, in fact, very brief. Rather, what was important was the *perception* that the secure base would be available if needed. The idea of being supportive and accessible has more to do with a sense of the person and of the relationship rather than the actual amount of time spent together. One could almost think of this characteristic as the psychological presence of a secure base who plays a role even when not physically there. See Chapter 6 for tips to develop this characteristic.

In this and each of the next four chapters, we provide development tips for one or two of the characteristics. We begin here with Characteristic #1: "Stays Calm" because it is one of the most important and challenging characteristics. Yet it is essential for both bonding and handling stressful situations.

We begin each Characteristic Spotlight with quotes from our research that exemplify the main concepts within the characteristic.

CHARACTERISTIC #1: "STAYS CALM"

In our research, leaders repeatedly used expressions such as these to describe how Secure Base Leaders stay calm and help others to stay calm:

> *"And he reacted very calmly. He said, 'Okay, yeah, I am hearing you.'"*

> *"He asked in a very nice way, without shouting and without making a big whatever."*

> *"They would always think properly and treat people properly."*

> *". . . calm and support. I could be upset, but he would support me."*

> *"When everyone else was panicking, she remained calm."*

Before people bond with you, they will want to know you are dependable and predictable; calmness contributes to those perceptions, and agitation and stress send the opposite message. Staying calm is also critically important in providing opportunities for risk taking. Your calmness helps the other person stay calm in the face of challenge. If you bring further emotion and fear to a situation that is already full of emotion and fear, you only make things worse. Imagine how the rock climber would feel if the person holding the belay expressed nervousness or distraction: she'd be very unlikely to want to jump to that next handhold.

The dependable and predictable aspect does not imply a dull or uncreative secure base; it implies a person who can be relied upon in terms of support and behavior even when under stress. A secure base is not described as agitated and erratic. This story demonstrates the critical importance of a leader staying calm:

In sharing how he had handled the crisis on September 11, 2001, New York City Mayor Rudy Giuliani told George that the most important thing he did on that day was to remain calm amid the chaos. The city he ran was unprepared for such a devastating attack. As he endeavored to lead in the hours after the planes struck the towers, the mayor realized he was beginning to unravel. He chose to take a walk in a garden close to the Twin Towers to compose himself. He looked for the trees and the sky but could see nothing but a grey-brown cloud. He could, however, see the grass. He grounded himself with that gaze. He explained, "I needed to calm myself in order to be calm for others. I had lost people, they had lost people. My father, who had been a New York City policeman, had told me: 'Never make a decision in high emotions. Always calm yourself first, because otherwise, you are likely to make a mistake.' His words rang in my head that day." This memory helped guide him during the hours and days after the tragedy.

This characteristic is particularly evident in stories related to failure or risk. Consider this story from an executive we worked with:

We had a major product crisis that could potentially cost the company millions. Vice Presidents began to panic and searched for who was to blame. But our CEO remained calm, referred to our values and implemented a step-by-step program to deal with the issue while constantly communicating with the necessary stakeholders. His calm kept us calm.

Is remaining calm easy? No. However, it is a learnable skill. It is about managing your emotions under pressure and keeping your amygdala in check (see box earlier in this chapter). It is also a matter of keeping a larger perspective on the world and not taking things too personally.

Ask yourself:

• Have I ever said or done something when I was not able to remain calm and later regretted it?

HUMAN EMOTIONS, "STATE" AND RESULTS

Clearly, we cannot completely separate the emotional and rational aspects of ourselves. Basically, the human brain is designed to serve us as social creatures. The way we see and how we feel about ourselves and the world around us are inextricably linked to the views and emotions of others. Given the fact that many people spend more of their waking time with colleagues than they do with their families, it is important that leaders understand how they can positively or negatively influence the mindsets, emotions and moods of those around them.

Perhaps one of the best-known recent stories about a leader positively influencing the emotions of others involves an event that took place just after a takeoff from New York's LaGuardia Airport:

On January 15, 2009, as Flight 1549, carrying 150 passengers, started to lose height following the failure of both engines, 57-year old pilot Chesley B. "Sully" Sullenberger III prepared to land the plane on the Hudson River. Passenger Mark Hood of

Charlotte, North Carolina describes that moment and what Sullenberger said as follows: "I can tell you verbatim: 'Brace for impact.' He said it in a calm, cool, controlled voice. It was a testament to his leadership. Had he let any tension leak into his voice, it would have been magnified in the passengers." Sully has since explained that he simply did what the training manual had taught him to do in such a situation. With his training as a secure base, he even remained calm enough to call his wife shortly after the emergency landing and say "You may see something about a plane on the news, but don't get excited. It wasn't that significant."

Others pick up on your state of mind, just as the passengers picked up on Captain Sully's state. What is a "state"? According to Eric Berne, the founder of Transactional Analysis, a state is "a coherent set of feelings, thinking and behavior."[6] We have broadened that concept to include the idea that state reflects how we are at any one moment in time—our physiology, attitude, emotions, mood, behavior and beliefs as they all come together.

Your state determines the result you achieve. States can be positive or negative. Moods and emotions can affect our state. Paul Ekman defines a mood as an ongoing emotion.[7] Once you are aware of an emotion, you can trace its cause and change it. Left unchanged, an extended period of emotion becomes your "mood." A very extended mood can also develop into a character trait. Some people remain trapped in a chronically negative mood which then affects their state and subsequently influences others.

The ability to manage your own state is fundamental to managing yourself and to influencing the state of another person. Given the high probability of disappointment, failed expectations and loss in the world, you are vulnerable to being pushed into a negative state unless you have learned to self-manage. It is highly likely that you have learned self-management from one or more of your secure bases.

Assess Your Secure Base Leadership Behaviors

On a scale of 1 to 5 (1 = never, 5 = always), rate how frequently you:

- Remain calm when under pressure
- Are dependable and predictable in terms of moods and emotions
- Remain approachable for support, even in stressful situations

If you rated yourself less than a "3" for a particular behavior, make note of this characteristic as a development priority (see Chapter 8, Become a Secure Base for Others).

S-t-r-e-s-s

While a little bit of stress is positive and even necessary to help you perform at your best, too much prolonged stress can cause physiological and neurological wear and tear known as "allostatic load." Research shows a 45% increase in people's stress levels over the last 30 years and also indicates that depression will overtake heart disease as the number one disease by 2030.[8]

Stress is our reaction to a dangerous or frustrating situation from which we feel we cannot escape or our reaction to a situation in which we cannot respond to external stimuli. In other words, being stressed is like being held hostage. Some of the greatest causes of stress are loss, uncertainty, exclusion, negative relationships, and chronic loneliness from social isolation.

Inescapable or uncontrollable stress can be very destructive and can even be a cause of death in rodents.[9] People in most modern societies are, unfortunately, very aware of the physical symptoms of stress such as headaches, back pain, weight gain or loss and heart disease. Stress also has other less well-known costs:

(Continued)

- Stress is the strongest inhibitor of both brain plasticity (the ability of the brain to create new pathways based on new experience) and neurogenesis (the creation of new brain cells). Without these functions, you cannot learn.[10]
- Prolonged stress can lead to depression, which decreases cognitive functioning.
- Stress contributes to disease through a mind-body connection often known as "psychosomatic illness." These diseases, according to Rossi and other researchers, actually "turn on" genes that activate certain symptoms.[11]

What can you do to avoid chronic stress? Along with exercising regularly, eating well and getting enough rest (the obvious basics), you can practice mindfulness techniques, which have been proven to make a significant difference. Learning to be less automatically and habitually reactive to unhelpful thoughts, emotions and impulses is possibly a prime way in which mindfulness helps to remodel the brain and thereby protect the body from the damaging effects of chronic stress and depression.[12] Since loss is a major cause of stress, developing the ability to get over loss through grieving (see Chapter 4) also reduces chronic stress.

Tips to Develop Characteristic #1: "Stays Calm"

1. **Change your mood.** While it is tough to change your state when you are in a bad mood, it is possible. Raise your self-awareness and acknowledge that you are "in a mood." That process, by itself, helps you be more mindful of your state and how it is impacting you and others.
2. **Watch what you say and how you say it.** Tone and manner of communication matter to others. Clearly, under stress even the best leaders will be feeling the pressure. At these times, still aim to present yourself in a calm and predictable manner, rather than reacting emotionally. By remaining outwardly calm, you will be able to instill

confidence in those around you and alleviate a greater sense of panic. A good trick is to take a deep breath before you say anything. That small moment of space may be enough for you to check yourself and escape from an amygdala hijack.

Practice checking yourself when you are challenged or verbally attacked by someone else. In those situations, you're likely to attack back instinctively. In so doing, you are letting yourself become a hostage to the situation. Instead, take a deep breath and ask a question instead of making any kind of statement.

3. **Practice a mindfulness exercise.** Learn to stay calm by practicing a simple mindfulness exercise. Make yourself comfortable by sitting in a chair, feet flat on the ground, arms in your lap. Take about 20 seconds to draw four deep breaths. Focus on your toes first and imagine the muscles relaxing. Then slowly work through your feet, up to your calf muscles, your thigh muscles, your buttocks—each time relaxing the muscles. Then move to the tips of your fingers, through your wrists, your forearms, up to your shoulders—each time concentrating on relaxing your muscles. Then move to your shoulders, your neck muscles and your face muscles. This whole process only takes a few minutes and yet, when practiced daily, can make a significant difference in the levels of stress you experience.

BECOMING AN EXPERT

Each of the nine characteristics of Secure Base Leadership, including "Stays Calm," is a learnable behavior that you can practice on a regular basis. Let's take a step back and consider the relationship between learning, practice and becoming a true expert. This information will not only help you excel as a Secure Base Leader, it will also help you to develop others as well.

Many people believe that those who excel at something are just innately talented or skilled. However, according to Swedish researcher Anders Ericsson, as much as 95% of talent is learned and only 5% is truly genetically based. Recent research shows that out-standing performance is, in fact, the product of years of deliberate practice and coaching. Ericsson concludes that it takes three things to become an expert:

1. Practice—for 10,000 hours
2. Deliberate Practice—practicing over and over and correcting mistakes
3. Having a Coach or Mentor—who gives you feedback[13]

In *Developing Talent in Young People*, Benjamin Bloom shared similar findings and also specified the role that families play. He examined the critical factors that contribute to talent by investigating the childhoods of 120 elite performers who had won international competitions or awards in fields ranging from music and the arts to mathematics. He also discovered that all the performers he investigated had three things in common. In addition to intensive practice schedules and devoted teachers or coaches, all of the elite performers he studied also had enthusiastic support from their families in their early years.[14] Clearly, these young talents had secure bases around them.

You can develop any of the nine characteristics of Secure Base Leadership. Improving on any of these areas takes daily practice and self-correction. Pick one characteristic to work on and focus on daily practice; you will start to notice the difference.

Ask yourself:

- What are some practical things I could do to develop one of the nine characteristics within the next 24 hours?
- Who can help me?

Bear in mind that having a coach, a mentor or a third party to support you will help tremendously. That person may become one of your own secure bases. We are back to the idea that to be a Secure Base Leader, you need to have secure bases in your life.

Identify people who will care about you and dare you to perform at your best.

It is important to note that a Secure Base Leader is not perfect. None of the people we interviewed displayed all nine of the characteristics all of the time. However, if you focus on and improve in more areas, you will create more of a secure base environment and more powerfully propel forward those willing to work toward greatness.

Key Learnings

- There are nine characteristics of Secure Base Leadership.
- The characteristics link to Mind's Eye and bonding.
- The characteristics work at individual, group and organizational levels.
- These characteristics are learnable behaviors.
- Leaders can practice any one of the skills on a regular basis to improve it.
- You do not have to be excellent at all nine characteristics. However, the more areas you focus on and improve, the more of a Secure Base Leader you become.
- Improving on any of these areas takes daily practice. Pick one and focus on it for at least 28 days in a row; you will start to notice the difference.

&

"Becoming a leader is synonymous with becoming yourself.
It is precisely that simple, and it is also that difficult."

-Warren G. Bennis
1925-
American Scholar, Organizational Consultant
and Leadership Author

&

FREQUENTLY ASKED QUESTIONS

Q: Nine characteristics sound like a lot to learn. How I can be good at all of them?

A: Take it one step at a time. In our experience executives are indeed able to incorporate the nine characteristics into their daily life. Doing so takes deliberate practice and you won't do everything on the first day. Our advice is to relax, choose the ones most important to you now, and start experimenting. You can always come back to the book in the future to add to your repertoire.

Q: I get stressed sometimes. And there are other people in my organization who seem to be successful when not being calm. Is staying calm really related to performance?

A: While those other people might be successful in the short term, they will not achieve sustainable high performance. The cost of stress to themselves and the negative impact of their erratic behavior on their relationships will erode their impact over time.

PART II

Chapter Three

Build Trust through the Bonding Cycle

On January 12, 2010, Christa Brelsford, a PhD student with a Master's Degree in Engineering, was in Darbonne, Haiti. Her brother, Julian, a volunteer with Haiti Partners, had asked her to conduct a feasibility study on a wall that would protect a rural area from floodwaters.

At 4:53 p.m., the first shockwave of the infamous earthquake hit the small town. Christa, Julian and her hosts clambered down the stairs of the two-story house they were visiting. Christa tripped and fell head first. The building collapsed around her.

Even while pinned under three slabs of concrete, Christa, an accomplished rock climber with a national reputation, thought of Hugh Herr, a mountaineer who had lost both legs below the knee after being stranded on a mountain in 1982. "I figured if he climbed again after that, I would, too."

Within about an hour, a local teenager, Wenson Georges, arrived with a pickaxe and soon freed the young American he knew only as someone who had helped him with his English. Christa's right leg was crushed below the knee. Wenson scooped her up in his arms and climbed on the back of a motorcycle. As they sped their way to a U.N. camp, Christa saw houses in rubble and bodies in the street.

Wenson stayed with her all night. He stood to block the floodlights from her eyes. He gave her the shirt off his back. At some point during the night, a four-year old held her hand.

Christa knew if she closed her eyes, she would die. So she stared at the stars and, in excruciating pain, "watched Orion march across the sky." "I'm from Alaska: I know my constellations," she explained. Over the course of the night, she made her list: Walk again. Give something back to Haiti. Help Wenson.

She did make it out of Haiti and into a hospital in Miami, Florida, where doctors had to amputate her lower leg.

Four surgeries and a prosthetic later, Christa not only walked, but also climbed again. She credits Ethan, her boyfriend then and husband now, for helping her through the process of re-learning how to live. "He knew what I could do before I did. I'd ask him to do something, and he'd tell me to do it myself."

She used the national spotlight shined on her to raise $150,000 to rebuild the school where her brother Julian worked just ten months after the earthquake. Her organization, Christa's Angels (www.christasangels.org), continues to contribute to the area.

Christa's strong sense of purpose had been instilled by her parents who raised their children in the Quaker tradition. "It always seemed obvious to me that I should use my life to make the world better. If I could bargain with God, I'd happily trade both legs—the one I still have and the one I don't—for the ability to reshape the world such that a minor earthquake in Haiti wasn't turned into a humanitarian catastrophe."

"My dad also showed us that the act of trying counted for a lot. Even if you didn't succeed, you needed to 'try all the way.' That's what he did with Wenson: he 'tried all the way' and, against all odds, obtained a visa for him to study in the U.S."

With that, she checked off the last item on her horrific night's list.

Christa credits her mother with planting the seed of her can-do attitude: "When I was about five, I asked my mom if we could go cross-country skiing. She said yes, and so I got on all my stuff. I clipped into my skis and waited for her outside. When she opened the door, she looked surprise and said, 'Gosh, you are independent!' I asked, 'What does independent mean?' and she replied, 'It means you can do whatever you want.'"

"I still believe that with enough work, I CAN accomplish anything."

Survivors like Christa Brelsford often have more than luck in common. They are often deeply bonded to multiple people, ideals and goals, and they are able to draw energy from those to fight against the odds. Certainly, Christa was deeply bonded to her parents and Ethan. However, she was also able to bond profoundly and instantly with Wenson, who pulled her from the rubble, and even with a young child who held her hand. She drew great strength from her bond with her homeland, the sky and her goals. She even set new goals and bonded to them as she lay bleeding through that terrible night.

It takes a certain kind of openness and vulnerability to bond like Christa. That is why we call bonding the "heart" of leadership. Central to our mission to humanize organizations, it is the guts and emotion of leadership. It is the "caring" part of *Care to Dare* that we find is often neglected in businesses. A leader can be extremely disciplined, focused and goal-oriented, but without interpersonal bonding, she will probably fail.

Bonding is the aspect of leadership that takes you from being a manager to being a leader. It is the part of leadership that makes people want to follow you, not just for your intellect and your ideas, but for the benefit that comes from trusting you as an individual, as a human being.

Think about the most impressive and inspiring leaders you ever worked with. Were they cold, distant, detached and aloof? Not likely. Were they warm, connected, attached and engaged—tough, yet inspiring? Very likely.

It is quite clear to us that the best leaders not only connect to others but also form an engaged emotional bond. They believe that other people are interesting and worthwhile. Going even further, the very best of those leaders think people are fundamentally good and trustworthy. They seek the best in people. They are able to look past the job description or the behavior of an employee and see the human being who sits behind the position, job competency or key performance indicator. These leaders are the ones with great bonding skills.

Professor Bill Fischer, co-author of *The Idea Hunter* says, "Be interested rather than be interesting."[1] When you demonstrate interest in others, you begin the very process of bonding.

WHAT IS BONDING?

Bonding happens through the warmth of a handshake, a smile, eye contact and normal daily dialogue. It happens by working together, playing together or through interacting around a common goal.

A form of synergy, we define bonding as:

forming an attachment that creates more physical, emotional, intellectual and/or spiritual energy than the person or people involved could generate independently.

This definition applies to all kinds of bonding. People like Christa bond to people, goals, objects, animals and ideals in this way. They receive energy from these entities and then either give the energy back (for example, to the goal of walking again) or transform it into positive action (for example, taking energy from the stars and using it to get through the night).

In this chapter, the kind of bonding we concentrate on is bonding between people. Bonding is a way of being in a relationship that may deliver a profound physical and psychological impact on both you and the other person. Bonding is an emotional connection that invites the other person to feel a sense of protection and safety as well as energy and inspiration. It goes beyond a simple attachment.

Bonding is not just nice to do. It is basic and fundamental to human nature. Karen Horney believed that we are motivated by the need for security and love. (Interestingly, another driver she noted is the need to achieve).[2] Joseph Chilton Pearce, author of the *Magical Child*, understood bonding as a psychobiological form of communication that goes beyond ordinary consciousness. As he put it:

> *"Bonding is a vital physical link that coordinates and unifies the entire biological system. Bonding seals a primary knowing that is the basis for rational thought."*[3]

Social in nature, humans cannot thrive without bonding. We need bonding to a family, to a tribe, to a clan, to a leader, to a team or to an organization.

If you do not bond, you will spend your life in search of what bonding was designed to give. Sometimes considered unimportant in the work environment, bonds are now understood to be critical to leaders' success. Yet, there are people, often top leaders in organizations, who have either stopped bonding or who never learned it in the first place. For some this missing skill is not only their most difficult leadership challenge, it also negatively impacts their personal lives. They block the bonding process for fear of being rejected, being used or being seen as "too soft." Unfortunately, what they do not realize is that by not bonding they neglect one of the foundations of sustainable high performance for themselves and their teams. The risk in today's high-pressured environment is that too much emphasis is placed on doing and acting rather than on being and belonging.

How do you know when you are bonded? When you feel compassion and empathy, share a common goal and are willing to take a risk on the other person, you are bonded. When you are not bonded or bonded only to material things, you will feel isolated and detached.

MYTH: It's Lonely at the Top

Not true. When you are performing at your best as a Secure Base Leader, you will be bonded to other people. You may have to make decisions on your own, but you don't have to feel lonely. Feeling lonely is always a choice. You can be in a crowded room and feel lonely, or you can be alone on a hilltop and feel bonded.

ABILITY TO FEEL EMPATHY AND COMPASSION

Ideally, bonding is a two-way process that gives sustenance to the people involved. It is more than a connection. It is more than rapport. It is an emotional give and take. One manifestation of bonding, therefore, is the ability to feel empathy and compassion for the other person. Empathy and compassion are the main ingredients of caring. We know from our research and work that leadership is inherently personal. Business is both rational and emotional; people bring their whole-selves to work.

Ask yourself:

- Am I able to put myself in someone else's shoes?
- Am I able to relate to other people's pain and frustration?
- Do I care about people?
- How do I demonstrate that caring?

SHARING A COMMON GOAL

Your goal as a leader is not to make friends with everyone, but rather to have bonds, to care and to inspire. In fact, a common misperception is that bonding equals friendship. You do not have to like someone to bond with her. You only need a common goal. Hostage negotiators are trained to create bonds with hostage takers, and encourage them to focus their Mind's Eye on a common goal (to resolve the situation, for example) even with the certain knowledge that the hostage taker will go to prison. Hostage negotiators succeed in 95% of cases precisely *because* they are able to bond around a common goal. People who have experienced pain in past relationships may be more comfortable bonding to goals instead of other people. For these people, bonding to a goal they can share with other people opens up opportunities for them to start to build relationships again.

WILLINGNESS TO TAKE A RISK ON THE OTHER PERSON

When you are bonded, you dare to take a chance on the other person as this story, shared by a business executive named Ralf, shows:

One of our employees, a 50-year old, had been treated for depression three times in the past 12 years. He had worked with the company for more than 20 years and, at one time, had been a successful sales executive. Since his last relapse, he had been given "paper pusher" jobs (e.g., statistics and business data analysis). No one wanted to give him operational responsibility. When I took over the department, it was suggested that I just simply fire him.

Instead, I asked him straight out about the reason for his depression, and then I listened to him tell his story. Through this dialogue, I learned that a certain event in his business life led to the first depression and then he quickly fell into a downward spiral. I told him that I was willing to give him a chance under the condition that we start with a clean slate. There would be no special work conditions and no references to his "health history" made by those around him.

Today, this employee is a motivated performer. He is reliable and always eager to help. Why did my approach work? The employee told me that I was the first one to ask him openly about his depression and be willing to listen. I gained his trust, so he was willing to give it a try. When I treated him like everyone else on the team, others realized I meant what I said.

This story exemplifies what a Secure Base Leader does. He communicates acceptance and takes a risk toward activating the potential in a person. Ralf looked for the reason why the employee was stuck, sought to understand his motivation and saw his potential. Ralf was willing to stand behind this man without taking on the responsibility for his actual performance. He provided comfort, protection, belief and energy to give him a chance to succeed. In Ralf's heart, even though he was taking a risk, he believed that the approach would work, and it did.

Ask yourself:

- When have I taken a special risk with an employee because of my bond with him or her?

STAGES OF THE BONDING CYCLE

Attachment, bonding, separation and grief are the four stages of the bonding cycle which is illustrated in Figure 3.1. You cannot understand bonding without understanding grief. You cannot understand attachment without understanding separation. And you cannot begin to understand the complexity of human relationships until you understand that we are each bonding to many things—

FIGURE 3.1 THE BONDING CYCLE

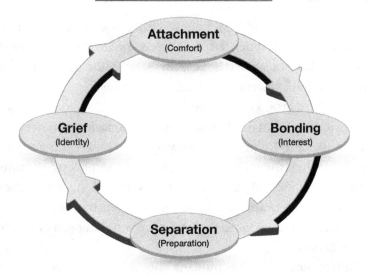

people, goals, objects, values, pets and ideals—at the same time. Some of those bonds are strong, some are weak. Bonds are created, separation occurs, and after going through the grief, you expand your identity, find a new attachment, and the process begins again. Of all the bonds in our lives, some are just moving into true bonding, and some are in the phase of separation.

The cycle of making, maintaining, ending and renewing emotional connections is a fundamental part of Secure Base Leadership.

ATTACHMENT

The first stage in the bonding cycle is attachment. Whether to a partner, a new job or a new project, people first become attached to someone or something. Everyone needs attachments; they provide a sense of **comfort**. When we are attached, we feel safe enough to let our natural guard down.

The Brain, Mirror Neurons and Bonding

Several years ago, it was believed that sociability, including bonding, was an inherited trait. New neuroscience research indicates that sociability is actually a behavior that is learned through a brain system called mirror neurons.

In 2004, a group of brain researchers working with monkeys in the Italian town of Parma made an amazing discovery. A neuron that fired when a monkey actually picked up a peanut also fired when the monkey saw someone else pick up a peanut. Originally called "Monkey See, Monkey Do" neurons, these special brain cells are now called mirror neurons because they fire whether one is doing the action or watching someone else do the action.[4]

Mirror neurons give humans the ability to learn through imitation. Dr. Vilayanur S. Ramachandran believes that the major leaps in human evolution came about because of our strong mirror neuron systems.[5] You watch someone do something and you imitate it. The more you copy an activity from someone else, the easier it becomes, and eventually you can do it almost without thinking.

Research indicates that the basic need for relatedness, empathy and bonding is actually a biological wiring that is activated through such a learning process. Bonding can be learned by watching others and experiencing how they bond. If mirror neurons are the biological system that makes bonding and empathy possible, it is a secure base, or at work, the Secure Base Leader, who turns the possibility into reality. Think of the worst boss you have ever had and think about the impact he had on others:

- Did he intimidate people and build a culture based on negative behaviors such as aggression or passivity, or through instilling fear?

- Have you seen a team that followed a team leader or member into a downward spiral based on her negative behavior?

  You may also have witnessed the reverse:

- Have you seen one team member turn around a negative culture through his positive behavior and mindset?

The mirror neuron system provides scientific validation of the need for empathy and authenticity in order to engage and inspire followers. It is central to "emotional intelligence"—a concept that calls for leaders to be self-aware and socially aware[6]—that is to have the ability to bond and empathize with those around them by managing their own emotions and influencing the emotions of others.

Attachment may or may not include significant emotion or interdependence. Attachment is a drive to be in proximity to, to be next to or to be connected. You know the difference between attachment and bonding in terms of the impact that the other person has on you and the way you feel when you part from them.

Leaders have a problem when they attach but do not bond. We often meet executives who can connect and attach to people but cannot bond with them.

BONDING

Bonding is the second stage in the cycle. Not every attachment leads to an emotional bond. However, all attachments have the *potential* to lead to bonding, be it short or long term, as in the case of many secure bases. Bonding flows from *what you do* with the connection initiated through attachment.

When the attachment leads to an exchange or source of energy, an emotion and depth of contact, a chemistry between people and a synergy around a common goal, it transforms into a bond.

Essentially, the depth and strength of the bond will depend on how much **interest** each person has and shows in the relationship—how much they each care about the attachment and the common goal. Bond a little, and you'll get a little flow of energy. Bond deeply and you will unleash enormous potential. Think of the belayer. If she is not truly committed or if there is only minimal trust between her and the climber, the climber will not have the full sense of safety and will not feel the energy needed to "go for it."

Bonding comes in many different forms: you can bond to people who are alive, to people who have passed on or to people you have never met but who nevertheless provide a source of inspiration.

There is parental bonding, family bonding, male bonding, female bonding, political bonding, team bonding, intellectual bonding, psychological bonding and societal bonding, to name the most obvious ones. Bonding is so pervasive that the psychological term "bonding" has slipped into common use. Within interpersonal bonds, the emotional exchange occurs on many levels that allow for mutual influencing: "I am open to you, you are open to me." And in a group or team: "We are open to each other." Bonding contributes to motivation, inspiration and resilience—all key aspects of engagement and all key conditions for innovation and change.

Not surprisingly, the deepest bonds in your life will be those you have with your secure bases.

SEPARATION

Separation is the third stage in the cycle. All bonds eventually lead to a transition or to an end—an uncoupling, a disconnection or a de-bonding. Separation occurs when people change jobs, when projects get completed, when people go through transitions, when relationships end or change, when a dream is reached or lost and when people retire or move homes. Death is also a form of separation. Everything comes to an end at some stage.

Change, if only through the natural passage of time, brings about separation. Separation includes any loss, conflict, jealousy, revenge or experience that disrupts the bond. Separation can also result from something positive such as getting a promotion (and leaving colleagues behind), getting married (and leaving the single life behind) or gaining a degree (and leaving student life behind). Separation is all about letting go of somebody or something, and is a **preparation** for something in the future beyond grief.

GRIEF

A person has the opportunity to progress to the fourth and final stage in the cycle: grief, which is an extension of the separation stage. Grief is the experience of saying goodbye in order to say hello. It ideally leads to a new attachment or to a renewal of an attachment. Grief involves the emotional experience resulting from the ending or transition of the bond. Completing the cycle means experiencing and expressing the depth of the grief. Grief allows you to expand your **identity**, embrace your future self and become ready to form new attachments that can lead to new bonds. The goals of grief are:

- Forgiveness
- Renewal
- Rediscovery of the joy in life, work or marriage

Central to change at the individual and organizational levels, grief is such an important concept in Secure Base Leadership that it is the subject of Chapter 4.

BEGINNING AGAIN

It is essential to understand that if you cannot grieve, you will never be able to bond effectively. In fact, for some people, their life strategy is to avoid pain or grief by never bonding; they are not willing to take that risk. These people can be defensive and become "independent loners" who put up barriers and walls to avoid pain and hurt and to protect themselves. For these people, the focus stays on the negative side of bonding—the fact that at some stage it has to end.

Your history with secure bases generally tells the story of how you handle the cycle of bonding—the cycle of making, maintaining, ending and renewing relationships.

Ask yourself:

- How effective am I at bonding—both in my professional life and in my personal life?
- What is my history of making, maintaining, ending and renewing bonds?
- Do I walk toward people or move away from them?
- Who were my role models for bonding as I grew up?
- How bonded is my team?

BUILDING TRUST THROUGH EFFECTIVE BONDING

The Reina Trust Building Institute cites research showing that trust is sorely lacking yet highly valued in today's business environment. Four out of five people surveyed had "only some" or "hardly any" confidence in the people running major corporations. Roughly half of all managers don't trust their leaders. Yet, at the same time, employees considered even a small increase in their ability to trust management to be as valuable as a 36% pay increase.[7]

In order to be able to dare people to achieve things beyond their own imaginations, Secure Base Leaders gain the trust of their people. Trust is built when leaders create a strong bond with their followers thereby providing a sense of safety and protection. Trust grows when leaders create empathy toward the followers and the followers feel cared for in return. When people trust a leader, they are far more open to constructive feedback and direction because then they believe that the leader has their best interests at heart. Trust embraces the whole person and allows you and your followers to be open and vulnerable—to be human.

Research conducted by Gallup covering 13 million people in the workplace showed that the highest levels of engagement occur when people feel that their immediate supervisors care about them as individuals.[8] Caring in this case is the outcome of bonding. Furthermore, the research showed that most people leave out of frustration with their bosses not their companies. The survey discovered that having a really strong relationship at work is indeed essential to one's level of engagement. Gallup further concluded that the level of emotional attachment to the job has a direct relationship to productivity, customer satisfaction, lost work days and turnover—key economic factors that matter to leaders.[9]

Given the impact on performance, creating trust through building bonds should be high on your list. By becoming a secure base to your employees, you can unleash their astonishing potential and thereby improve productivity, morale and results.

It takes a deliberate investment of time and energy, whether short or long term, to create a bond filled with trust. Bonding can occur in an instant or it can fail to occur after 25 years of working together. It is based on experiences such as the one below shared with us by an executive, Anders:

My most important success factor in life is the building of trusting relationships with people. Trust implies honesty, openness and respect. My team deepened its bonds through various events that led to building relationships and understanding each other.

The more successes we had as a team, the more energy we created in the team. We supported each other and I became a very proud leader of a very powerful team.

A personal incident showed me the success of what we "created" in this team. I broke my ankle and was totally dependent on others for any transport, movement—everything.

On the first day, a team member was at my door at 7:00 a.m. to take me to the office. The team worked out a schedule and I was supported every day for six weeks without asking for it.

I led this group of people through the process of becoming a deeply bonded, high performing team: its establishment, its formation, its understanding of purpose and eventually its successful output. We celebrated our successes by sharing and giving direction to the rest of the company.

A few of the team members asked me to be their personal mentor and some of those relationships are still going strong after many years, even though I am now in a new role and position.

As Anders' story demonstrates, people will go the extra mile for you, support you, and follow you if they feel bonded to you and a common goal. It is impossible to inspire others without bonding. Basic respect is an essential part of creating bonds. An understanding of the bonding cycle also helps you, as a leader, to better understand people's emotions and motivations.

Bonding is fundamental to Secure Base Leadership. It is also a fundamental part of being human.

TWO SECURE BASE LEADERSHIP CHARACTERISTICS THAT HELP YOU BOND

Two of the nine Secure Base Leadership characteristics are of special importance to bonding because they set the stage for a powerfully different relationship. Therefore, in this chapter, we shine the development spotlight on "Accepts the Individual" and "Sees the Potential."

CHARACTERISTIC #2: ACCEPTS THE INDIVIDUAL

In our research, leaders repeatedly used expressions such as these to describe how Secure Base Leaders accept the individual:

"He was not recognizing me for my performance, but rather he was recognizing me as a person . . . a human being."

"You want to treat people the way you want to be treated . . . love is maybe too big a word, but respect and kindness."

"It's about accepting the person for who they are and where they're at."

"He said, 'Just be yourself. Don't try and be anyone else.'"

"Her personal development, her personal growth was far more important than the specific business situation."

"My dad supports me in my dreams, even when I fail."

"My spouse is always there for me, even when my job causes family disruption."

Secure Base Leaders accept and acknowledge the basic worth of the individual as a human being. Accepting and valuing the person is the opposite of treating employees like numbers or cogs in a machine.

The idea of acceptance is very closely linked to one of our favorite phrases: "unconditional positive regard," a term coined by the famous psychologist, Carl Rogers.[10] He said that one should aim to approach others without negative judgment of their basic worth. This means you aim to accept another person unconditionally and non-judgmentally.

The benefit of this approach is that it shuts down the defensive reaction in the brain and allows the other person to explore all possibilities and suggest new paths without danger of rejection or condemnation. Imagine the person you feel the safest with in the world and how you feel and behave because of that sense of protection. Think of a person with whom you let your guard down and with whom you are able to think and act freely, creatively, energetically and spontaneously. People typically describe a relationship where there is no fear or judgment as a place where they can "be themselves."

Reflecting on his childhood learning, here is what President Bill Clinton said about acceptance:

> *"I learned a lot from the stories my uncle, aunts and grandparents told me: no one is perfect but most people are good; that people can't be judged by their worst or weakest moments; that harsh judgments can make hypocrites of us all; that a lot of life is just showing up and hanging on; that laughter is often the best, and sometimes the only, response to pain."*[11]

Will you have unconditional positive regard for 100% of the people 100% of the time? Not likely, as you are human. As a leader, you will sometimes need to judge or evaluate the other person's behavior—in a performance review, for example. However, Rogers was clear that we need unconditional positive regard as a foundation upon which all other transactions (verbal or non-verbal exchanges) or evaluative activities are built. Remember that the characteristic of acceptance goes to a deeper notion of valuing, honoring and appreciating the very heart of the person. It is quite simply about seeing each person as a legitimate and valuable human being.

This story shared with *Fortune* magazine by Indra Nooyi, PepsiCo Chairman and CEO, presents an example of acceptance:

> *"My father was an absolutely wonderful human being. From him I learned to always assume positive intent. Whatever anybody says or does, assume positive intent. You will be amazed at how your whole approach to a person or problem becomes very different. When you assume negative intent, you're angry. If you take away that anger and assume positive intent, you will be amazed. Your emotional quotient goes up because you are no longer almost random in your response. You don't get defensive. You don't scream. You are trying to understand and listen because at your basic core you are saying, 'Maybe they are saying something to me that I'm not hearing.'*

*In business, sometimes in the heat of the moment,
people say things. You can either misconstrue what
they're saying and assume they are trying to put you
down, or you can say, 'Wait a minute. Let me really get
behind what they are saying to understand whether
they're reacting because they're hurt, upset, confused,
or they don't understand what it is I've asked them to
do.' If you react from a negative perspective—because
you didn't like the way they reacted—then it just
becomes two negatives fighting each other. But when
you assume positive intent, I think often what happens
is the other person says, 'Hey, wait a minute, maybe
I'm wrong in reacting the way I do because this person
is really making an effort.'"[12]*

Assess Your Secure Base Leadership Behaviors

On a scale of 1 to 5 (1 = never, 5 = always), rate how
frequently you:

- Value your team members as human beings, not just as
  employees performing a role
- Accept people's limitations and weaknesses in a supportive
  way
- See the core goodness in people before judging or
  criticizing them

If you rated yourself less than a "3" for a particular behavior,
make note of this characteristic as a development priority (see
Chapter 8, Become a Secure Base for Others).

Tips to Develop Characteristic #2: "Accepts the Individual"

1. **Discipline yourself.** Develop a clear mindset and work to
   keep the value of acceptance in mind. It's one thing to read
   about this concept. It's another thing to live it and apply it on
   a daily basis.

2. **Get to know the person and the personality behind the organizational role.** Ask questions to learn about people's aspirations, fears and backgrounds as well as their deepest strengths and weaknesses. Recognize that every person on your team and in your organization is more than a "job description" or a "key performance indicator." They are all human beings with hopes and fears, dreams and vulnerabilities.

3. **Turn failure into learning.** When people make a mistake or fail, validate their worth as human beings and then deal with the failure by giving the necessary critical feedback. Ask them, "What did you learn from this mistake?" or "What would you do differently if it happened again?" Complexity and uncertainty mean that failure and mistakes are part and parcel of daily life; indeed, there is extensive evidence that failure is a necessary ingredient for innovation and exceptional performance. People will be more likely to take the necessary risks that may result in failure if they know that they will still be supported and validated for their effort and be accepted for their underlying worth as a person. This acceptance creates the foundation for curiosity, creativity and change.

   Andrew, a keen soccer player, learned from his coach: "A failure is not a failure if you learn something from it."

4. **Separate the person from the problem.** As soon as the person becomes the problem, you are likely to become a hostage to the problem. That position will prevent you from finding a resolution. Always remember you are dealing with a human being. Bear in mind that acceptance does not mean that you approve of all behaviors unconditionally.

   In his work as a hostage negotiator, George applied this concept as follows:

Even though I in no way approved of the hostage taker's behavior, I always found it essential to adopt an approach of acceptance and unconditional positive regard toward the person. It meant separating the person from the problem.

*When I did this, it became easier for me to see the human
being who was inevitably full of sadness, anger, regret, rage or
fear or was in some other high emotional state of distress.
When I could do that, I was more likely to create a connection,
a bond, which allowed me to resolve the dispute.*

CHARACTERISTIC #3: SEES THE POTENTIAL

In our research, leaders repeatedly used expressions such as these
to describe how Secure Base Leaders see the potential:

*"There were people around me who had more confidence in
me than I did."*

*"She could see me in another way than perhaps other people
in the organization."*

*"You are here because you are good. You are talented. You
are bright, and I am very happy that you are here and I will
support you and give you challenging roles."*

"I am absolutely sure that you can do it. Give it a try."

*"I always felt that my parents thought I could do anything and
there was no limitation on my ability to achieve and do."*

*"I had a dream when I was a child to win a Nobel Prize. And I
always thought that my father had a feeling that I could
achieve it. He never told me 'That's nonsense.' No, no, no.
He always told me 'Yeah, sure you will win.'"*

Secure Base Leaders see an individual's potential talent instead
of her current functioning. This characteristic goes a step beyond
accepting her as an individual: it says "I not only accept you, I also
believe in you" even though the individual may not yet see or
believe in herself, as this story shows:

*Ethel, a model in Singapore, was told frequently she did not
have the right "look" to make it big. One day, a representative
of the House of Ungaro was visiting from Europe and asked
her if she had ever thought about going to Paris. This question*

*planted a seed of hope in Ethel's mind. She moved first to
Europe where she became a runway model. She then moved to
the U.S. and she met Paul, a photographer, in San Francisco.
He saw something special in Ethel, and through working
together, she found her "look." Ethel went on to have a highly
successful career as a high fashion model, fronting campaigns
for houses like Armani and even appearing live on stage at
the Academy Awards show.*

Ask yourself:

- Was there a person at some point in my life who saw
  potential in me that I had not seen?

The opposite of a Secure Base Leader is the manager who dis-
courages growth and future possibilities. A boss who acts in this
way may be insecure, jealous, competitive or feeling under threat
from his own boss. Just as good parents always want their child to
be better than them, a good Secure Base Leader always wants to
leave a legacy that is bigger than what she can contribute as an
individual.

Confident and future-focused, secure bases communicate the
potential they see in others, as this anecdote shows:

*When a Danish executive was a young girl, she lived in a
small village and idolized her teacher. She told her she also
wanted to be a teacher in that school when she grew up. The
teacher said to her, "Oh no, you shouldn't be a high school
teacher here, it's too boring for you . . . you should do
something else. You have huge possibilities." She encouraged
the little girl to aim high and, many years later, she became
Deputy Permanent Secretary of the Danish Ministry of
Finance. Essentially, the teacher saw her potential way beyond
the village in which she lived and helped focus her mind to
dream of bigger things.*

Assess Your Secure Base Leadership Behaviors

On a scale of 1 to 5 (1 = never, 5 = always), rate how frequently you:

- Establish and hold a concrete vision of each direct report's unrealized potential
- Encourage each of your direct reports to realize his or her full potential
- Ask your direct reports about their hopes and dreams for their careers

If you rated yourself less than a "3" for a particular behavior, make note of this characteristic as a development priority (see Chapter 8, Become a Secure Base for Others).

Coachable Moments

How long does it take to coach someone? It can take as little as 30 seconds. When you have a secure base relationship, one transaction, one statement or one question can deliver a powerful message about the potential you see in the person.

When you have a moment of time, use it to give affirmation and ask questions using phrases like:

- "I am confident that under your management, this project will succeed. What kind of support do you need from me to achieve success?"
- "Whenever you try something new, things can go wrong. What did you learn from this experience? What could you do differently next time?"
- "What's an alternative approach? Can you share another option with me?"
- "You're good. I believe you could be great. Do you want to know how you can improve?"
- "May I share an observation about how you can contribute more?"

Tips to Develop Characteristic #3: "Sees the Potential"

1. **Develop a vision of the potential of every person in your team or organization.** This vision really considers what each person could achieve if given the opportunity. Proactively consider the real potential of each person and make sure that you are not limiting your thinking based on a partial view of past or current performance.

2. **Hold high expectations.** Do not be satisfied with a follower playing small or limiting himself in his self-vision and actions. In the words of Marianne Williamson, as quoted by Nelson Mandela:

   > "Our deepest fear is not that we are inadequate. Our deepest fear is that we are powerful beyond measure. It is our light, not our darkness that most frightens us. We ask ourselves, who am I to be brilliant, gorgeous, talented, fabulous? Actually, who are you not to be? Your playing small does not serve the world. There is nothing enlightened about shrinking so that other people won't feel insecure around you . . . And as we let our own light shine, we unconsciously give other people permission to do the same. As we are liberated from our own fear, our presence automatically liberates others."[13]

   If you see potential and set expectations accordingly, your followers are more likely to perform better. If you don't see their potential, they will likely not achieve it. Or, they may have to leave you as a boss to spread their wings.

3. **Hire people who have the potential to surpass you** and then invest in their development so that they do. Do not be afraid that you will "lose" because of the high performance of those who work for you. Instead, embrace your job as a leader who unleashes the potential in others. This philosophy is manifested in the manager who asks this question of a young recruit:

"Have you ever thought about becoming a top leader or even the CEO of an organization? You need to be thinking about what is possible for you in your career rather than thinking about your next assignment. You could become a top leader or CEO . . . always remember that."

Also consider this story that is rooted in the culture of advertising agency Ogilvy & Mather:

Whenever David Ogilvy hired a senior executive in any part of the world, he arranged for her to find a Matryoshka, a Russian doll, on the desk when she arrived at the office on her first day of work. When she opened up the doll, the nested dolls would become smaller and smaller until the new executive found a slip of paper wrapped around the last doll. Written on that paper were the following words: "Always hire people bigger than yourself. If you hire people bigger than yourself, we will become a company of giants. If you hire people smaller than yourself, we will become a company of dwarves."[14]

Key Learnings

- Bonding is the heart of Secure Base Leadership.
- Bonding is a natural human process: we are hardwired to connect with each other.
- You do not have to like someone to bond with them; you just need a common goal.
- If you do not allow yourself to bond, you stay in a state of detachment.
- Bonding creates the kind of trust that is essential for Secure Base Leadership.
- Accepting the individual is about unconditional positive regard.
- When you see great potential in your followers, they are more likely to achieve great things.
- To experience full joy, it is important to stay bonded to life.

&

"A person is a person through other persons; you can't be human in isolation; you are human only in relationships."

-Desmond Tutu

1931-

South African Activist and Retired Anglican Bishop

&

FREQUENTLY ASKED QUESTIONS

You will notice there are a few more questions and answers in this chapter than in others. That is because when we teach people about bonding we get lots of questions from those people who operate using the traditional model of "results are all that matter."

Q: What does bonding look like in the real world of work?
A: Bonding can be expressed in a number of small, simple ways:
  • A genuinely warm handshake and smile when you meet a customer
  • A question to a team member about something unrelated to work (asking about a holiday, family event or weekend)
  • Saying something thoughtful that demonstrates your awareness of the other person's interests
  • Picking up the phone to speak to someone in another office rather than sending an email
  • Making an effort to maintain a relationship during and after a difficult conversation
  • A reassuring comment or hand on a shoulder when a person is struggling to cope with a situation

Q: Do I need to be an extrovert to be good at bonding?
A: No, not at all. In fact, introverts can be excellent at bonding because they tend to listen and observe well, and they are

therefore tuned into the needs of others. Introverts are very good in the one-on-one situations in which bonding is most important and obvious. If you are an introvert, focus on the quality of your bonding rather than the quantity of people with whom you bond.

Q: Do I need to be a friend of everyone at work?

A: Will you be friends with everyone at work? No. Should you aim to be *friendly* to everyone? Yes. You do not need to interact socially with every person on your team or share special private moments with all of your colleagues. You should, however, aim to have a friendly relationship with as many people as possible.

Q: Isn't this a bit too touchy-feely? My work is competitive and demanding. My competitors would walk all over me if I attempted this caring stuff!

A: Remember, the bonding cycle is just the first half of the story. Next comes the risk taking. You have to get the caring in before you overload on daring. Performance won't be sustainable without the foundation of caring. Remember it's care to dare— not just "care" by itself.

Q: Some people have truly performed poorly. How can I accept that?

A: Aim to accept the person behind the performance not the performance itself. In fact, when you truly seek to accept the underlying humanity in a person, it is easier to be very frank and honest about poor performance. Direct and challenging feedback in the context of a caring relationship is extremely powerful.

CHAPTER FOUR

DELIVER CHANGE: EMBRACING LOSS THROUGH GRIEF

Formerly an investment banker, Azim Khamisa became a social activist after his 20-year old son Tariq was senselessly murdered by Tony Hicks, a 14-year old gang member, while Tariq was delivering pizzas in January 1995. Out of unspeakable grief and despair, Azim was inspired to transform his loss through the miraculous power of forgiveness. He was advised by a spiritual mentor to do a good deed to honor the memory of Tariq. In addition, Azim was inspired by his faith and the Koran, which states that after passing from this world, the soul remains in close proximity to the family and loved ones during the 40 days of grieving. After 40 days, the soul moves to a new level of consciousness. Grieving past this time impedes the loved one's soul's journey.

Believing that there were "victims at both ends of the gun," Azim forgave Tony and founded the Tariq Khamisa Foundation (www.tkf.org). Its mission is to transform violence-prone, at-risk youth into nonviolent achieving individuals and create safe and productive schools. A month after establishing the foundation, Azim invited Ples Felix, Tony's grandfather and guardian, to join him. "This was not the Dalai Lama meeting Mother Teresa," explains Azim. "Ples was a Southern Baptist who worked for the city of San Diego. I was a Sufi Muslim and an investment banker. If the two of us could come together in the spirit of reconciliation and forgiveness, couldn't anyone?"

Ples was delighted to join Azim, calling the request "an answer to my prayers." "I was racked with guilt," said Ples. "There is nothing I wouldn't do for Azim Khamisa and his family." Since November 1995, the two men have brought their story and message to the world through the Tariq Khamisa Foundation's Violence Impact Forums. The duo have reached more than half a million elementary and middle school children in person and over 20 million via video programs. In each interaction, they guide the youth to choose a peacemaker's life of non-violence and forgiveness.

Azim has also created a bond with Tony, not only campaigning on his behalf for his early release, but also offering him a job in the Tariq Khamisa Foundation should he be let out of prison.

Azim's story demonstrates the potential that leaders can unleash when they move through grief, become able to forgive and then move on. He tapped into his own energy and brought forth Ples's energy, too. Together, they have influenced millions. They may even have saved lives. We have had the privilege of meeting Azim and witnessing how powerfully he shares the message that forgiveness is actually for yourself: until you forgive, you carry the burden and the weight of the grief. This life lesson is also a fundamental lesson for all leaders.

Clearly, Azim has been "Playing to Win" in terms of his choices since Tariq's death. He has focused his Mind's Eye on the positive and created powerful bonds in order to honor the life of his only son. He has had the courage to move through the full process of grief and re-bond to a goal: the goal of reducing needless killings motivated by revenge.

In Chapter 3, we presented the bonding cycle and grief as necessary and completely human aspects of change and growth. Yet, many people, many executives and many organizations are so uncomfortable with loss, separation and grief that they fail to address these critical topics. In fact, each time we hold a leadership development program and include a session on grief, we get push-back from some participants who find it "too personal" or "irrelevant." Over time, however, they come to accept its power. Take Terry's story for example:

Terry, a senior manager, was sent to an executive education program because his bosses felt he wasn't as effective a leader as he needed to be. In early sessions, he became quite agitated when discussing loss. Finally, in a small group, it emerged that he had lost a young child several years earlier and had made the decision that he could never go through that pain again. With the support of his coaching group, he was able to begin grieving that terrible personal loss. By the end of the week, he decided to have a discussion with his wife who had wanted to have a second child.

Two months after the course, Terry's wife became pregnant and they are now the proud parents of another child. Not only did his grief process affect his personal destiny, it also impacted his leadership. He says, "I now feel courage to face risks I avoided before, to face pain I could not before and to live my dreams with joy. I am now more present with my team and energized about what we are achieving. Understanding grief changed my life."

We submit that there is no significant personal loss that will not permeate your leadership performance. Your work as a Secure Base Leader requires you to identify your losses and grieve them. If you do not "unload your heavy baggage" or burden of loss, you will not be able to access the energy you need to bond with and inspire others. The reason grief is so powerful is that it reflects in the mind, heart, body and soul the depth of the lost bond. The outcome of resolved grief is the ability to feel joy and gratitude again.

We believe that grieving is a normal, natural human process that does not require, in and of itself, a psychologist. Your work as a Secure Base Leader requires you to help others grieve their losses, whether personal or work-related. You do so within the boundaries of your relationship. When you embrace these concepts and allow your followers to move though the stages of grief with someone who cares, you will release their potential from the shackles of past pain. Resolving grief is essential to achieving results faster, with higher levels of motivation and engagement, and to delivering the change inherent in innovation, growth and even corporate survival.

One of the most ubiquitous companies of our time, Starbucks, chose to embrace grief, support employees and find a way to move on from tragedy at one of its locations:

When three Starbucks employees were shot and killed in 1997 at the Georgetown store in Washington, D.C., Howard Behar, then President of Starbucks North America and International, telephoned Starbucks CEO Howard Schultz who was in New York City. Schultz travelled to Washington D.C., spoke with the police and then went to the homes of each of the murdered Starbucks employees to express his sorrow and share in their tears. By having the courage to express his grief, Schultz demonstrated enormous compassion and respect toward the victims' families, and he supported friends and colleagues in dealing with the loss.

Immediately after the memorial service, Schultz hosted a press conference during which he announced that the Georgetown store would be remodeled with a memorial inside to honor the victims. He also announced that a portion of profits from that Starbucks location would provide support to the victims' families and would be donated to anti-violence and victims' rights charities.[1]

GRIEF, LOSS AND THE IMPACT OF BROKEN BONDING

For the purposes of Secure Base Leadership, grief has to do with the loss associated with change:

> *"Grief is the normal and natural emotional reaction to the change or end in any familiar pattern of behavior. Within those normal reactions exists the possibility of the entire range of human emotions."*

This description comes from the Grief Index published by the Grief Recovery Institute. The index highlights more than 40 types of losses that can dramatically affect our work and social lives as well as our physical and emotional well-being.[2] Grief is a universal experience that knows no boundaries of age, status or culture.

LOSS

All change involves loss: the loss of what was.

Loss, including the avoidance of anticipated loss, is one of the strongest motivators of human behavior according to a theory called "behavioral economics." Proposed by several notable economists, including two Nobel Prize winners,[3] behavioral economics indicates that people are disproportionately influenced by a fear of feeling regret and will often forgo benefits to avoid even a small risk of feeling they have failed. Therefore, people are likely to be more motivated by avoidance of loss than by potential benefits. Yet, people can learn to overcome this natural tendency; usually, they do so by modeling a secure base's behavior. They are then able to "Play to Win" by becoming more willing to take risks in order to seek a benefit.

Anticipating a loss can generate feelings as strong or stronger than an actual loss. In "anticipatory grief," many people live in constant pain because they are anticipating a loss before it actually happens. Anticipatory grief is quite common in organizations.

Ungrieved losses accumulate over time, one building upon another. All losses need to be grieved, whether automatically as in the case of a favorite ball-point pen gone missing or consciously for an extended period as in the case of a death. Grief is the experience of getting over something and saying goodbye. It involves the emotional experience that results from changing, ending or transitioning the bond. You cannot truly and fully say hello until you have said goodbye to that which you have lost.

BROKEN BONDING

The extent of the grief reaction will be commensurate with the degree of the perceived loss. Weaker bonds evoke less grief. The strongest bonds evoke the strongest grief. Losses of secure bases are the most difficult and important kinds of grief to face, both personally and professionally. As this story shows, the loss of a very deep bond can provoke a powerful response:

On June 3, 2011, inseparable twin friars, Julian and Adrian Riester, aged 92, died within hours of each other. Both men died of heart failure. The twins, who never revealed which one was born first, joined the Franciscan Order in their 20s. Their cousin, Michael Riester, told the Buffalo News, *"They had this intimate bond in which neither was selfish at all." Tom Missel, spokesman for St. Bonaventure University in New York where the friars spent most of their lives commented, "It really is almost a poetic ending to the remarkable story of their lives. Stunning when you hear it, but hardly surprising given that they did almost everything together."*[4]

Manifestations of broken bonding include psychosomatic illness, violence and aggression, addiction, depression, burnout, stress and conflict. Broken bonds can also lead to a broken heart.[5]

That's not to say that because they cause pain broken bonds should be avoided. On the contrary: separation is a natural and necessary part of the bonding cycle. A child needs to separate from parents into order to grow. A good boss encourages a high performer to take advantage of better opportunities. In fact, a parent or boss who refuses to let someone leave is holding that person hostage. Without separation, there can be no transition to something new.

Brain Science and Change

Our brains have a friend or foe "early warning system," a flashlight that changes focus based on very quick judgments about whether someone is a friend, and therefore treated "fairly," or whether they are a foe, and therefore treated with "suspicion."[6] This friend or foe mechanism in the brain has major implications for leaders. When the foe system is alerted by a perceived sense of threat, people will shut down, become distant and focus on problems as they attempt to reduce the perceived danger.

In order to engage and motivate large groups of people, Secure Base Leaders train themselves to block their own foe mentality and approach people with a sense of openness and acceptance. They also help followers to switch their flashlights from a foe focus to a friend focus where they are in a more open, available and accessible state.[7]

Brain science also demonstrates that people are fundamentally motivated by a sense of belonging. We all "need" social relationships in order to thrive and develop in a healthy way, both mentally and physically. What happens when one is socially excluded? Eisenberger and other researchers have discovered that social exclusion lights up the same parts of the brain as physical pain. Being left out, rejected or excluded causes very real sensations of pain. When people say "I feel hurt," they really do feel the pain.[8]

This finding has implications for implementing a change. It reminds you to approach people who are experiencing a change-driven loss with empathy and compassion.

Ask yourself:

- What losses have I had in my personal life? Have I grieved those losses and moved on?
- What losses have I had at work? Have I grieved those losses and moved on?
- How are ungrieved losses affecting my leadership?
- What do I need to "let go of" in order to fully experience joy in my life?

In the face of enormous loss, you, like Azim in the opening story, can move beyond your own pain to connect your energy to a greater purpose. Doing so is a positive expression of grief. Irina Lucidi's story provides another example of how unbearable loss can drive a person toward a positive expression of that grief:

On January 30, 2011, six-year old twins Alessia and Livia were reported missing by their mother, Irina Lucidi. The parents were separated and in the midst of a divorce. Their father, Matthias, had taken them for the weekend, and instead of returning them, he took them out of their home country of Switzerland and traveled around other parts of Europe for a week.

Matthias sent many messages by mail to Irina, and in his last one he claimed to have killed the girls. He wrote, "My dear, I wanted to die with my daughters but it didn't go that way . . . I will be the last to die. You will not see them again; they did not suffer and now rest in peace in a tranquil place."

On February 3, 2011, Matthias's body was found on a railway line in Italy. He had committed suicide by stepping in front of a train.

The pain of this tragedy surpasses words. How could Irina survive such a horrific event? George had the opportunity to support her and was impressed by her courage amidst despair. Irina was determined to do something to honor her children and to help ensure that no one else had to experience what she went through. This dramatic experience revealed to Irina that certain procedures and operations regarding the search for missing children could be improved. She came up with the idea to create a foundation.

Irina founded Missing Children Switzerland (www.missingchildren.ch). Officially launched on the twins' seventh birthday, October 7, 2011, the Foundation's activities revolve around two core areas: an emergency telephone hotline which is widely accessible and available and a support network for the families of missing children. The Foundation also works on the legal issues regarding missing children.

UNDERSTANDING THE STAGES OF GRIEF

Before you can support yourself and others in grieving, you need to understand the process of grief. The late Dr. Elisabeth Kübler-Ross was one of the first people to identify the stages of grief. Although initially proposed in the context of dealing with the death of a loved one, the stages are equally relevant for any type of loss. She said,

> *"One of the problems in our society is that we are taught to sedate all of our natural emotions, with the result that these emotions are repressed, leading to unnatural emotions. Repressed fear can turn into panic. Repressed anger can turn into rage."*

The work of Kübler-Ross encourages us to understand the benefits of expressing and labeling our emotions when dealing with loss.[9]

Building on her stages of grief and loss, the adapted curve in Figure 4.1 explains the stages of loss and grief in organizations and in life. Energy, self-esteem and ability to cope decrease for the first half of the process and then steadily increase in the second half. These stages can be seen in any loss. However, they rarely progress in a linear manner. It is quite possible, especially in dealing with

FIGURE 4.1 STAGES OF GRIEF

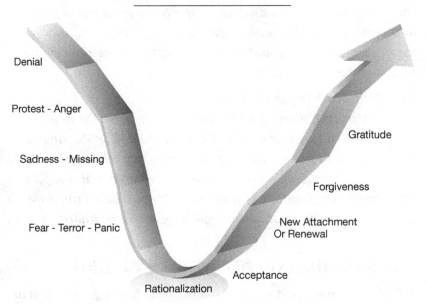

significant losses, to cycle through parts of the grief curve more than once before reaching completion. In such situations, the depth of emotion should reduce each time and the cycle should be faster.

Forgiveness and gratitude are the final stages of the grieving process. You know you have completed the grief curve when you can forgive yourself and others and come back to the joy of life.

How to Help Someone Grieve a Loss

Secure bases are vital in guiding people through difficult and sometimes tragic events. The old adage "A problem shared is a problem halved" has wisdom. Worries, fears and losses kept inside tend to grow and become larger and more worrisome. When you talk with someone about his losses or broken bonds, you reduce his level of anxiety and worry. You therefore help him move through the grief process. Like the belayer who catches a climber after a fall and then encourages him to get back on the rock face and climb on, the Secure Base Leader helps others to focus their Mind's Eye on the positive rather than the negative. They thereby help lift people out of despair and into hope through the process of grief.

In order to help a grieving person, first you want to be confident that you are indeed a secure base who is bonded to that person. Otherwise, your efforts to help may be construed as intrusive. Make sure you are in a good place for the conversation, both mentally and physically. Find private spaces and times.

Within your conversations, keep these tips in mind:

- Respect the person's grief and encourage the expression of emotions.
- Learn to be comfortable with crying. Tears are the body's natural process for eliminating toxins. Crying is a healthy part of grieving.
- Listen intently. Sometimes, all people need is someone to hear them.
- Empathize and recognize his right to his feelings.
- Do not try to provide solutions or rush him through the curve. Remember to ask questions.

Because grieving for a significant loss can take time, you are unlikely to finish the process in one sitting. Remain available and accessible. Remember also that no one is asking you to be a trained grief counselor or psychologist. If you sense the person needs more support than you can give, help him find an appropriate professional coach or counselor.

EMBRACING GRIEF TO DELIVER CHANGE IN ORGANIZATIONS

A new CEO enters an organization with energy and vision. Within a few months, he rolls out a new strategy, changes the management structure, implements an open plan office environment, closes down an underperforming business unit and introduces a new Business Intelligence system that worked well at his previous company. He is satisfied with progress.

A few months later, however, he faces a host of organizational problems. The new strategy is being ignored in some markets, engagement is at an all-time low, people are resigning or threatening to resign and he is in conflict with key members of the organization. What happened?

The answer is grief. Yes, grief based on loss. And if you are facing resistance to change within your organization, the source of that resistance is likely to be some form of grief or anticipated grief over a loss. Grief is seldom spoken about in organizational life; it is in fact one of the most common and least understood workplace phenomena. Familiar terms for grief in organizations include "loss" (as we've already discussed), "frustration" and "disappointment." Grief in organizations may appear in situations like:

- A new CEO struggles to win over an organization after the departure of the much-loved former CEO
- After not gaining a promotion, a high potential employee disengages and then subsequently resigns
- Ten years after a hostile acquisition people still talk about "us" and "them"
- An exit interview reveals resentment at the loss of a private office more than three years earlier
- An expatriate manager is relocated away from a country that he and his family have grown to love
- A previously successful salesperson loses his drive after the loss of a key contract
- A star performer becomes demotivated following a divorce

The change from the familiar state, whether for positive reasons such as a promotion or negative reasons such as a demotion, can often be the cause of great distress and can affect productivity and performance at significant levels.[10] Many people are surprised to learn that major gains also include losses that need to be grieved, even if only momentarily, for example:

- The loss of familiar colleagues after a promotion
- The loss of entrepreneurial spirit after a company progresses out of the start-up phase
- The loss of urgency after a huge project is completed
- The loss of complacency that may have developed after a sustained period of success
- The loss of familiar routines when a new computer system is introduced to increase productivity
- The loss of comfortable traditional chairs when the company moves to modern ergonomic models

As a leader, when you introduce anything new into an organization, you are requiring real people with real emotions about loss to let go of a previous bond and attach to something new. Through this process, you are creating a separation and a resultant grief reaction will naturally occur. The problem is that organizations tend to skip over the stages of grief and expect employees to bond to the new people or project or strategy or office layout immediately. Skipping stages by "forcing" the change can result in people getting stuck in their perceived loss and being unable to fully engage in a new bonding cycle—one in which they can say hello to new goals and new people.

In organizations, the stages of grief will have a distinct flavor:

- People may express denial through behaviors like ignoring requests, avoiding the implementation of new policies, or simply continuing with previous systems and strategies.
- Employees may vent anger through increased resistance to change. Conflict may rise to the surface more readily.

- Individuals may show fear by trying to negotiate the terms of the change and perhaps by threatening to resign. You may notice their hopelessness, despair, bitterness, cynicism, apathy and detachment coming out in low levels of commitment, engagement, motivation and energy.

In simple terms, if you as a leader are encountering shock, denial, anger, sadness or fear and panic, it is worth considering whether the source of these emotions and resistance might well be loss and grief.

Thierry, a former Swissair pilot, shared with us this story about Swissair's last days:

I can still remember where I was on the day of the 9/11 terrorist attack. I was on a flight to Brazil. There was a crew change in Sao Paulo as the flight was continuing to Buenos Aires. The captain of the new crew said to me: "Swissair will not survive the consequences of the terrorist attack in New York." And this proved to be true. Swissair had financial problems for quite some months even before this tragic event.

Still, the end of Swissair was a big shock not only for me and all other employees but also for our passengers. Swissair was like a big family and suddenly our secure base vanished. The first reaction was denial. It took many days before we were able to start the grief process.

We had tremendous support from our passengers and especially those who were not Swiss. To them, Swissair was an icon, a brand that represented Swiss-made quality.

The bankruptcy of Swissair became a major financial and political issue for the Swiss. After many high-level meetings between financial and political experts, a decision was made to provide money to guarantee continuing flight operations.

At this stage, we employees received no support from management. Moreover, as the size of the "new" company was much smaller, people had to be fired. The firing process took some time and there were strange situations in which pilots continued to fly already knowing the date when they would have to leave. I was lucky to be allowed to continue my job as a pilot. Still, I felt that something was definitively broken.

The handling of this dramatic event left deep wounds for each employee. It was like an endless nightmare. Looking back, I still feel sadness and anger that a few highly educated managers played a big poker game with the company and lost. To be more precise, it was the employees and the nation who lost, and the managers moved on to their next jobs.

MYTH: People naturally resist change.

Not true. Human brains are hardwired to seek expansion through curiosity, exploration, learning and change. In fact, our brains can create new neurons all the time. What people resist is the pain of change and the fear of the unknown.

Here are some specific ways to use your knowledge of the bonding cycle and grief curve to deliver change as a Secure Base Leader.

EMBRACE GRIEF

Remember that grief during change is natural. Expect and embrace it rather than fight it. When people exhibit behaviors associated with loss, remind yourself that they are behaving normally, even though they may not be the behaviors you want to see. By using this approach, you can avoid being taken hostage by people's reactions and behaviors. Moreover, by understanding the process of loss and grief as well as the bonding cycle, you can lead the change, instead of allowing resistance to the change to lead you.

ACCEPT EMOTIONS

Grief is not talked about much in the workplace because it is a personal emotional reaction to loss, not an intellectual one. Many leaders neglect the human side of their followers. Without full acceptance of the humanity of individuals, there is little or no room for emotion. A person cannot move to acceptance until they have felt and expressed their anger. However, traditional change programs rely solely on rational approaches that underestimate the natural grief reaction. You can encourage the change process and reduce resistance by creating safe environments for people to express emotions. Ask people about their feelings and then talk about your feelings and how the change is impacting you. Do not penalize people for momentary outbursts. Remember to see the potential in each individual instead of only his current state.

RECOGNIZE THE PAIN AND SELL ITS BENEFIT

Recognize the pain of others by putting words to it: "I know you miss the old team leader" or "I can imagine it's hard to get used to the new systems." Then, go on to "sell the benefit" of that pain: "The new team leader has contacts throughout the company that will pull in extra resources" or "The new system does analysis for you, so there's no more downloading data into a spreadsheet." Clearly, you will have more empathy with their pain and know what benefit to sell if you are connected; if you are truly bonded, you will have even more. Allow people to see your humanity. Through mirror neurons you become a model for how to deal with the loss.

SLOW DOWN

Paradoxically, the best way to accelerate the grieving process is to slow down. You can't book a one-hour meeting, say "this is the time we're going to express our emotions," and expect everything to come flooding out. It takes time for people to express the feelings associated with loss, and you can't schedule that time in Outlook. Suppression of feelings only short-circuits the cycle. Attempting to accelerate through the cycle, or skipping a stage, may produce short-term results, but you will find that people will actually remain stuck and the same issues will surface again in the future.

USE RITUAL

As part of the European Management Team at Digital Equipment Company (DEC), Susan experienced a powerful use of ritual to accelerate grieving. When the company was acquired by Compaq, DEC management at the European headquarters, led by HR, created a "celebration" event for the employees to say goodbye to the company they had known and loved for many years. Many rooms were set up with different activities: one room showed videos from the past years, another room was turned into a café-type area where people could sit and reminisce about "the old times" and another room had a company band playing rock music so people could dance. Employees could wander from room to room sharing feelings, laughing and crying, talking and dancing—all part of a ritual to mark the end of a very special company.

Most world cultures and religions have elaborate rituals around death and grieving. These developed because they help people "step into" the loss rather than try to avoid it. They encourage people to move through the natural grief curve. Within your organization, use ritual to acknowledge the separation and loss. Some ideas include:

- A farewell speech by a departing team member
- Going-away gatherings to reflect on what was

When Is It Time to Move on?

Delivering change as a Secure Base Leader is more art than science. Leaders often ask us about the balance between allowing the expression of grief and loss and communicating the benefit of the change. They wonder about timing. Here are some specific questions and answers that may help you:

When do I start focusing on the benefits of change instead of simply letting emotions come out?

People are more able to move through grief if they have a goal or benefit that draws them forward. In other words, you need to explain the "why" of a proposed change. The risk of focusing too much on the loss and grief is that the organization forgets about the positive reasons for the change or becomes paralyzed by loss and grief. So bring up a new goal early in the process, but don't expect people to attach to it for a while.

How long does a grief process take?

Major losses take can take years to grieve fully. More minor losses may take a matter of moments or months. There is a point in the change process when you have to make the decision to move forward. You may say, "Okay, we have had this conversation a few times now and it is time for us to move forward as a team and an organization." It is your job to define reality—to draw boundaries on behavior and encourage people to move forward.

How do I know when we are ready to move on?

You are ready to move on when (a) you can truly say to yourself that you have heard and understood the resistance and (b) others know that you have heard and understood their concerns. You will feel a shift in mindset and emotions.

The point is there's a time to grieve and there's a time to move on. If you are truly "Playing to Win," you will sense the right moment to move on.

- Working together to dismantle a project room after the deliverable is achieved
- Asking people to express their disappointment at changing the company name after a merger

Any event in which you take the time to allow the expression of the emotion resulting from the separation can be viewed as a ritual. Attempting to avoid "awkward farewells" or insisting on "being positive" does not help in a situation of loss or grief. Research shows that allowing people to put words to emotion actually reduces the level of the emotion in the amygdala (see Chapter 2), thereby giving a calming effect.[11]

MOVE ON TOGETHER

At the same time, it is important that people do not wallow in grief and become victims or complainers. They must be able to vent and then be encouraged to move on. A major mistake that business leaders make is failing to recognize that the management team often is a few steps ahead of others on the grief curve. They progress through the curve, come to a solution, and then announce the change to the others in the organization who are only just finding out about the loss. This change lag can cause frustration and anger at all levels.

Different people and different parts of the organization will go through the stages of grief at different speeds. Typically, the originators of the change and senior management will be ahead of the rest of the company. Do not get frustrated or surprised when issues you thought had been resolved months earlier are raised again. Some people may be encountering the reality of the loss for the first time.

By recognizing and handling grief effectively, you can actually increase the engagement and loyalty of those who work with you, as this story shows:

James had a direct report who came to him one day and explained that she needed to miss an important meeting because her mother was in the hospital. Immediately, James told her to take as much time off as she needed so she could be with her mother. When she returned to work a few days later, she told James that her mother explicitly asked her to thank James for his concern and his humanity. The employee is now even more engaged at work than she was before. James learned that the time given to her and her mother was worth far more to the organization than the potential time lost in on-the-job worry and unproductivity. He also learned that by giving to others he also gained himself.

TWO SECURE BASE LEADERSHIP CHARACTERISTICS THAT HELP YOU DELIVER CHANGE BY EMBRACING LOSS

In times of change and loss people clearly need a Secure Base Leader. They need leaders who care enough to dare them to move forward through grief. They need you to maintain the bond and encourage their growth even in the face of resistance. Make that *especially* in the face of resistance. In practical terms, this means *listening* to their concerns and points of view. At the same time, you need to *deliver a powerful message* that cuts through their resistance so that they keep their minds open to possibilities. Because these two fundamental Secure Base Leader skills are so critical to delivering change, we shine the development spotlight on "Uses Listening and Inquiry" and "Delivers a Powerful Message" in this chapter.

CHARACTERISTIC #4: USES LISTENING AND INQUIRY

In our research, leaders repeatedly used expressions such as these to describe how Secure Base Leaders use listening and inquiry:

> *"It's not about telling the other person what to do . . .
> it's more about inspiring and asking the right questions
> so that the other person can come to conclusions
> themselves."*

> *"She was listening, understanding, available and
> understanding of the feeling. She actually didn't say anything."*

> *"He set standards and discipline by asking tough questions
> and then following up."*

> *"She never told me what to think or feel. She only asked
> questions about my ideas, feelings and thoughts."*

> *"Actually listen most of the time and refrain from commenting
> or providing judgmental evaluation."*

Secure Base Leadership is about seeking a greater truth by listening and asking questions rather than speaking a lot and advocating a point of view. In this way, leaders can engage in a deep dialogue, a topic covered more fully in Chapter 8.

Remember that people have a basic human need to be heard. Listening does not mean that you need to agree with other people. You simply need to hear them and let them know that you have heard them. Often listening is simply the act of being actively silent, as this story shows:

Annie was angry with a colleague for the way he had treated her during a meeting. She called a friend who was a secure base and spilled her feelings. He listened in silence on the other end of the line. When she asked him if he was still there, he replied, "Do you really want to hear what I think?"

Shocked, she said, "Yes." He replied, "Well, I've been listening. Now, when you're ready to listen, I'll be happy to give you my perspective." This response stopped her from going on and on complaining and allowed her to let go of the emotion she was holding. In fact, she had been expecting him to agree with her complaints. Instead, what he did was listen and ask powerful questions to help her see the event in a different light.

Significant research supports the notion of asking questions.[12] It's not an accident that many of the approaches to leadership that have become popular over the past few decades include an underlying idea that the role of the leader is not to tell other people what to do. Instead, many researchers have determined that it is best for leaders to use powerful questions to guide their followers and encourage them to discover their own ideas and solutions.

This approach can actually liberate you. Instead of carrying the responsibility to have all the answers and be an all-around expert, you use your inquiry skill to draw the answers out of other people. In essence, it is only through questions that you unleash their answers and thereby their potential.

Adriana had a colleague who asked a number of open-ended questions to help her navigate a case in which a supplier wanted to be paid a bribe. He empowered her to find the solution and work it out rather than offer her an opinion or solution. Questions he asked included:

> *"Well, do you want to tell me about it?"*

> *"How do you want to handle it?"*

> *"What do you think is the best way to deal with the supplier knowing that bribes are against the company policy?"*

> *"What is the outcome you want to achieve?"*

Adriana's colleague did a good job balancing support and risk. He made himself available to help her and even accompanied her to the meeting, but in the end he allowed her to choose the course of action. He achieved this success not by advocating his point of view or giving solutions but by asking questions. Adriana still remembers what she learned and how he empowered her.

Assess Your Secure Base Leadership Behaviors

On a scale of 1 to 5 (1 = never, 5 = always), rate how frequently you:

- Listen actively
- Ask open-ended questions
- Ask questions before telling people what to do

If you rated yourself less than a "3" for a particular behavior, make note of this characteristic as a development priority (see Chapter 8, Become a Secure Base for Others).

Tips to Develop Characteristic #4: "Uses Listening and Inquiry"

1. **Practice active listening.** Be aware of the signals of body language and tone as well as the words someone says. Exercises around active listening, reflective listening, paraphrasing and empathic listening would all be relevant.[13]
2. **Ask open-ended questions.** Questions that seek opinions and ideas cannot be answered with a simple "yes" or "no." Instead of asking "Did the client upgrade his maintenance contract?" ask "What kinds of discussions did you have with the client about our value-added services?" Instead of asking "Are you frustrated by the change of policy?" ask "How do you see the change in policy impacting you?"

   When you are under pressure and the stakes are high, you may find it easier and more necessary to become directive by giving instructions and telling people what to do. In our experience, we have found that questions are more powerful than orders. Our research backs up this finding.

3. **Learn to use the power of pause and silence.** Once you have asked a question, allow the person the space and time to reflect and then respond. This technique is especially important during change when people may not know exactly what they think about something new.

4. **Be aware of the physical environment.** When discussing any potentially sensitive subject, think about where you want to be and how you want to position seating. Avoid having a "block" or "obstacle" like a table or lectern between you and the other party.

CHARACTERISTIC #5: DELIVERS A POWERFUL MESSAGE

In our research, leaders repeatedly used expressions such as these to describe how Secure Base Leaders deliver a powerful message:

"I am confident that you are doing the right thing."

> *"He wrote me a note that read 'I am confident that you are doing the right thing.' And this is huge to have a couple of words from him on a piece of paper. It's absolutely huge. I still have that piece of paper."*

"You always have a choice."

> *"She told me, 'You always have a choice.' Her words gave me a sense of freedom and empowered me in a critical moment when I was beginning to feel helpless and trapped."*

"Always leave with dignity."

> *"My HR colleague told me 'Always leave with dignity' when I was frustrated by a situation with my boss and had decided to leave the company. His words stayed with me and I managed the transition process with warmth and professionalism."*

"Stick with it."

> *"I was frustrated with continued delays in a project and was tempted to give up but my secure base told me clearly 'Stick with it.' I did and the results have been very positive for both me and the company."*

As you have read the quotes from our research, you may have noticed that people remember specific phrases their secure bases said years, even decades, before. People don't remember rambling paragraphs: they remember pithy sentences that deliver the right message at the right time. We call these sentences "bull's eye transactions" because they carry tremendous power and impact that is right on target. Each of us authors remember key bull's eye transactions that influenced us:

Dan said to George, *"But George . . . I knew you could do it."*

Susan's grandfather told her, *"The bigger they are, the harder they fall."*

Duncan's spiritual teacher said to him: *"Every act is either an act of love or a call for love. Either way, the only response is love."*

Powerful words can alter the destiny of a transaction, a negotiation or even a life. Words can kill or words can cure. Words can belittle or words can inspire. Every word counts. Every gesture counts. You don't only impact people over months or years, but also in moments. Ten seconds of a bull's eye transaction can be more powerful than ten years of dull leadership. You can create hope and optimism with a single sentence:

When Karl was just 27 years old and had recently started a new job, an executive two levels above his boss approached him and said, "One day you will go for the chair I am sitting in." That notion just hadn't figured into Karl's outlook because the man was so far above him in the hierarchy. But those words planted the idea in Karl's mind that "at least I have a chance at this."

In potentially stressful situations, it's even more important to deliver a clear, powerful message. For instance, climbers and belayers use a very standard script:

Climber, when ready to climb, asks: "On belay?"
Belayer, when ready to belay, responds, "Belay on."
Climber confirms by asking, "OK to climb?"
Belayer responds, "Climb away."

Likewise, sailors use a certain language to prepare for a "tack," the maneuver that turns the boat into or out of the wind:

Captain announces, "Ready about."
Crew go to pre-determined positions and when ready respond, "Ready."
Captain calls, "Hard alee" or "Jibe Ho" (depending on the relationship to the wind) and then turns the boat.

An avid sailor translated this concept for his team at a major pharmaceutical company:

Stephen was becoming increasingly frustrated with his product development team. He would give them detailed directions and then they wouldn't deliver what he asked for. Then, one weekend, he skippered a boat. He found it so easy to use the standard calls, hear that the crew acknowledged them, and then do exactly what was needed. If only his team at work could do the same! Stephen then realized that the team's problem originated with him: his instructions had been too complicated and he hadn't asked if his team understood. So he spoke less and asked his team to repeat back what they had heard. Their deliverables then started to exceed his expectations. Knowing that they had understood a clear request, he found it easier to hold them accountable afterwards.

Powerful messages shine like a beacon in the fog of change. When fear, uncertainty and doubt permeate the environment, short, inspirational messages give people direction. They cut through negativity and focus the Mind's Eye on the positive.

Assess Your Secure Base Leadership Behaviors

On a scale of 1 to 5 (1 = never, 5 = always), rate how frequently you:

• Deliver powerful, memorable messages

• Speak clearly and succinctly

• Use non-verbal signals and gestures to accentuate your memorable messages

If you rated yourself less than a "3" for a particular behavior, make note of this characteristic as a development priority (see Chapter 8, Become a Secure Base for Others).

Tips to Develop Characteristic #5: "Delivers a Powerful Message"

1. **Pay attention to your non-verbal signals as well as your words.** Practice your tone and body language. Intensify your impact by combining the right words with an appropriate state and gestures.

2. **Don't let the moment pass.** Your "throw-away" sentences can be just as powerful as your carefully prepared presentations, so choose them carefully. Look for opportunities for bull's eye transactions.

3. **Deliver powerful messages clearly, succinctly and slowly.** Less is more when directing another person's Mind's Eye.

4. **Write powerful messages.** A few select words on a sticky note or on a card can become a secure base in themselves.

5. **Keep a notebook of powerful, short messages.** You may remember these from your past or you may hear or read them in your day-to-day activity. Look through the list regularly to build your repertoire of phrases you may want to use with others.

Key Learnings

- Grief is a natural emotion and occurs as an everyday part of life and work. People need to grieve organizational losses as well as personal ones.
- Grieving is a social process and cannot fully be done alone.
- Understand that grief is part of change. Loss activates the grief process.
- During times of change, give space for people to move through the grief curve.
- People have completed the grief curve when they can express forgiveness and gratitude.
- Rituals are an important part of working through change.
- Forgiveness is something you mostly do for yourself.
- Secure Base Leaders seek a greater truth by listening and asking questions.
- Active listening is fundamental to effectively managing change.
- Your words carry weight. Think about how you can inspire others and direct their Mind's Eye through powerful messages.

ॐ

"Getting over a painful experience is much like crossing monkey bars. You have to let go at some point in order to move forward."

–C.S. Lewis
1898–1963
Novelist, Poet, Academic, Literary Critic,
Essayist and Lay Theologian

ॐ

FREQUENTLY ASKED QUESTIONS

Q: Why can't people just accept change and get over it? Why do we have to do this grief stuff?

A: Grief cannot be avoided because employees are human beings and the bonding cycle is a naturally ocurring phenomenon. Once people care about something, they will have a grief reaction when they separate from it. When you view grief as natural rather than a problem, you will more effectively be able to lead your people through it.

Q: I can't "listen" all the time. Isn't it true that sometimes I have to tell people what to do?

A: We are suggesting a leadership style that is weighted towards listening—not composed only of listening. There will indeed be times when it will be helpful for you to share your view and to give immediate input. Our research suggests that telling people what to do should not be your habitual pattern.

Q: Do I need to be a psychologist as well as a leader?

A: You don't need to be a psychologist, but you do need to be aware of important psychological processes like bonding and grieving a loss. Being aware and sensitive to these issues does not require a degree in psychology. It simply requires tapping into the human elements of your leadership.

CHAPTER FIVE

FOCUS: BRINGING FORWARD THE POWER OF THE MIND'S EYE

On September 18, 2007, Randy Pausch, professor of computer science and human-computer interaction and design at Carnegie Mellon University, delivered "The Last Lecture: Really Achieving Your Childhood Dreams."[1] In his presentation, Randy told the audience of 400 people that he was dying of pancreatic cancer and had only a matter of months to live. He was 47 years old, married to the woman of his dreams and the father of three young children.

The talk was modeled after an ongoing series of lectures in which top academics are asked to think deeply about what matters to them and then give a hypothetical "final talk" answering the question, "What wisdom would you try to impart to the world if you knew it was your last chance?"

Randy took his lecture as an opportunity not to reflect on the tragedy of his situation but instead to focus on the positive. The speech offered warm reflections on achieving his seven childhood dreams, the importance of overcoming obstacles and his inspirational life lessons. He said that early in life you have to choose whether you're going to be a Tigger or an Eeyore.[2] "What I found is if you're an upbeat person, people

*will flock to help you and suddenly everything gets easier."
In a later interview on the Oprah Winfrey television show,
Randy commented that he saw life as being 10 percent
white, 10 percent black and 80 percent gray. "You can go
through life and say, 'Gee, that 80 percent gray part, that's
black, and life is a bad thing.' Or you can say, 'that 80 percent
gray part is part of the white, and it's the goodness and the
light.' I want to view life that way. It becomes a self-fulfilling
prophecy. That 80 percent in the middle really can go either
way, and if you decide you want to make it go good, not bad,
you have a lot more power to make that happen than you
might think."*

*With reference to how he dealt with obstacles, Randy used the
mantra, "The brick walls are there for a reason. They're not
there to keep us out. The brick walls are there to give us a
chance to show how badly we want something." He shared
how he used this mantra in his pursuit of his childhood dream
to be a Disney "Imagineer"—a dream that had taken him
more than two decades to achieve.*

*Randy understood that the national spirit at the time of his
childhood made an impression on him: "I was born in 1960.
When you are eight or nine years old and you look at the TV
set, men are landing on the moon, anything's possible. And
that's something we should not lose sight of . . . the inspiration
and the permission to dream is huge." Randy achieved his
seven childhood dreams in one way or another.*

*Randy's lecture became a worldwide phenomenon, watched by
over four million people on the internet. Randy went on to
co-author a book called* The Last Lecture, *which became a* New
York Times *best-seller. In May 2008, he was listed by* Time *as
one of the World's Top 100 Most Influential People.*

*Randy died on July 25, 2008, at his home in Chesapeake,
Virginia surrounded by his wife and children.*

Before his death Randy said, "It is not the things we do in life that we regret on our death bed. It is the things we do not. Find your passion and follow it . . . your passion must come from the things that fuel you from the inside. That passion will be grounded in people. It will be grounded in the relationships you have with people and what they think of you when your time comes."

This line from Randy's last lecture seems to stick with people the most: "I don't know how not to have fun." He continued, "I'm dying and I'm having fun. And I'm going to keep having fun every day I have left."

Imagine how easy it would have been for Randy to feel sorry for himself and withdraw from the world when he learned he was to die prematurely. Instead, Randy chose to step up, share what he was experiencing and attempt to inspire others. He created a different focus for the last weeks of his life: leaving a legacy. He demonstrated Secure Base Leadership by caring that his children would know who their father was and by daring to stand up and speak about death at this last lecture. His focus translated into a profound, inspirational impact on millions of people around the world who now have a role model for prioritizing the joy and possibility in life.

Randy's ability to remain positive in the face of illness and difficulty came from the power of his Mind's Eye, the part of the brain that is responsible for the way a person sees the world and directs his focus. Your Mind's Eye guides you to make sense of the events, experiences, challenges and opportunities in your life. While you cannot control what happens in your life, you always have choice as to how you react. William Ernest Henley wrote, "I am the master of my fate, I am the captain of my soul." The choice you exercise by being the master of your fate is determined by the focus of your Mind's Eye.

According to Einstein, "Is the universe hostile or friendly?" is the most fundamental question anyone can ask. Every day, you have a choice about how you answer—just as Randy had that choice. Your Mind's Eye is like a flashlight that shines where you direct its focus. You choose whether to focus your flashlight on the disappointment, pain, loss or other negative aspects of life or on the benefit, gain or other positive aspects of life.

Where you focus your flashlight determines how much you can accomplish at work and in life. High performers stay focused on a goal rather than on pain, frustration or discomfort. This focus gives them inspiration and confidence to take the risks necessary to achieve their potential. Marathon runners, for example, succeed when they focus on the benefit at the end of the event rather than the pain. If they did not, they would give into the pain and stop running.

One of the most important roles of a secure base is to help guide the Mind's Eye of other people. Your past secure bases shaped your Mind's Eye and, through bonding, they helped you to learn to care to dare. Behind your hopes, dreams and ambitions there are people, places, goals and experiences—positive and negative—that directed the shaping of your character, personality, beliefs and values. That shaping made you the unique individual you are. Through understanding how the experiences and people in your life shaped your Mind's Eye you can not only achieve more yourself, but you can also influence others to take risks, be creative, be innovative and seek greater challenges.

If bonding is the "heart" of leadership, the Mind's Eye is the "head" of leadership. Secure Base Leaders influence the Mind's Eye of others to maintain focus on the end game and thereby achieve goals, meet stretch targets and deliver results. Quite simply, through shaping a person's Mind's Eye, they open the doors of possibility and unleash his potential.

That's why a major part of becoming a Secure Base Leader is training your Mind's Eye as if it were a muscle. It's also why being a Secure Base Leader involves actively and constantly focusing the Mind's Eye of the people you want to influence and propel to high performance.

IS THE GLASS HALF EMPTY OR HALF FULL?

Do you think at its most primitive level the Mind's Eye in our brains is looking for danger and pain—the negative, the glass half empty? Or is it looking for pleasure and joy—the positive, the glass half full?

Take a moment and make a choice: do our brains more naturally focus on the positive or on the negative?

The correct answer is that the brain, at its most basic level, is fundamentally hardwired to look for danger, pain and the negative. Why? Our brains have one overriding goal beyond all others: survival. Survival starts with awareness of potential danger or threats. Only with that awareness can we avoid them. That is why our brains have an early warning system, a radar, that is always searching for what can go wrong.[3]

If our most basic drive is to survive by looking out for danger and what can hurt us, why aren't we all paranoid? Some people are indeed stuck in that place. We all know people who worry too much about anything, anywhere, anytime. Their Mind's Eye—their flashlight—stays focused on the negative, and they are always looking at the glass as half empty. These people have high levels of anxiety and stress and can often be quite "defensive" around others. As Figure 5.1 shows, these people end up "Playing Not to Lose" and go through life avoiding risks and often hiding their potential.

The fundamental principle behind secure base theory is that by connecting to somebody or something we each can achieve a feeling of safety that switches off the brain's search for danger. When we feel safe, we can open our minds to the most powerful forms of exploration. Explosions of creativity follow. Caring leads to daring as the focus turns to possibilities. With a secure base,

FIGURE 5.1 LEADING FROM THE MIND'S EYE

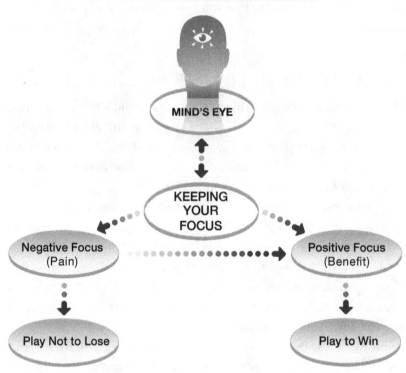

people reap myriad benefits which we describe later in this chapter. All in all, like Joe in this story, they achieve better results with less stress, and they tend to exude positive energy:

Joe often referred to the influence of his grandmother. She had lost her husband, sister and parents in the war and yet remained truly optimistic about life. He recalled a time as a child when he became frustrated while building a model plane at her kitchen table. She comforted him, telling him to remain calm and to focus his thoughts on the beauty of the finished product. Joe said that she was always helping him to see the positive side of events and to look for the learning in any given situation. She would also talk with fondness about Joe's grandfather, sharing stories from their lives so that Joe felt bonded to the grandfather he never met. She was truly a secure base who was always grateful for what she had rather than bitter about what she had lost. She was an important influence on how Joe was able to be a secure base to his family and his employees.

How Secure Bases Influence the Mind's Eye

The truth is that reality is both positive and negative. What you think about reality depends on where you choose to shine your flashlight. Our secure bases, the people and events and experiences that have shaped us through our Mind's Eye, influence much of what we think. What we think becomes a belief and we make choices based on those beliefs.

Everyone has both good and bad experiences in their lives. Leaders, teachers, doctors, colleagues, friends and others have the power to be secure bases and bring out the very best in people or to motivate them to turn defensive or aggressive. While not overruling the power of the self, secure bases help people make meaning out of both positive and negative experiences. They teach people about the benefits of focusing on the positive even amidst the pain.

Ask yourself:

- Do I approach problems from a positive stance or a negative stance?
- From what perspective do I make decisions?
- How do I bond with people I don't like?
- How do I view people with whom I have a conflict?
- How do I view people who are underperforming?

The way you answer each of these questions is based on how people throughout your past have influenced you in either a positive or negative way. The meaning you have made out of experiences you faced adds up to your self-esteem, character, personality, beliefs and values—all that makes you unique. As Figure 5.2 shows, your Mind's Eye makes meaning of your past experiences and uses them to create your future.

FIGURE 5.2 LEADING FROM THE MIND'S EYE

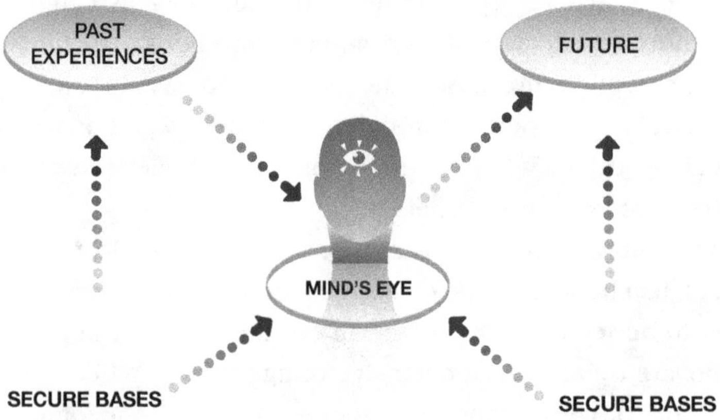

Consider these two anecdotes shared by leaders we know:

When Jane was four years old, her mother gave her a pair of adult dressmaking scissors and explained how to use them safely. Jane was surprised to find that all her friends had children's safety scissors. Jane felt a complete sense of trust and support from her mother who allowed her to take risks in a way that gave her confidence at an early age.

Julia was learning to ride her bicycle with her father's help. After several wobbly falls, Julia grazed her knee and began to cry. Her father, throwing his hands in the air with deep

frustration, shouted at Julia, "I give up! I can't teach you
anything" and walked away.

Julia feels insecure and unsupported by someone who should
have been a secure base to her. Julia's experience with her father
leads her to grow up with self-doubt, anxiety and a fear of failure;
she ends up in a low-level support job. Jane, on the other hand,
whose mother cared enough to dare, grows up with a confidence
and belief in her own ability. Jane's memory of her mother becomes
a powerful part of her Mind's Eye. She grows up to be a powerful
senior executive in a large multinational organization. Think of
how different Julia's perspective might have been if her father had
encouraged her when she fell off the bike by saying something
like, "I know you can do it. Try again. I'm with you. Together, we
will do this."

While one event can adversely affect a person's life, the cumula-
tive effect of a series of events generally leads to the viewpoint he
holds of himself, of others and of life itself. If, as you read this, you
start thinking about what you may have missed in early childhood,
don't worry. You do not have to be held hostage to your experiences. You can overcome virtually any negative experience in
the recent or distant past with the help of secure bases who lead
you through a "corrective experience" that brings forth a mindset
change.

For those people who lack awareness of the influences in their
lives, the future is nothing more than a memory of the past pro-
jected through the Mind's Eye. The future therefore can be a self-
fulfilling prophecy. You can take control of your future in two ways.
First, understand how past experiences affect the present. Second,
select the secure bases who will support your dreams and aspirations. While you were not able to choose the people who surrounded you as a child, you do have that choice as an adult. Chapter
7 details how you can shore up your tapestry of secure bases that
will fulfill your needs and teach you what you want to learn.

Tips for Influencing the Mind's Eye of Other People

When it comes to the Mind's Eye, your first step as a Secure Base Leader is to develop your ability to switch your focus as quickly as possible from the negative to the positive. Only when you are in that place will you be able to see the potential and possibilities of the people around you.

As a second step, you then help people to turn their own flashlights to the positive and away from the negative so that they can see the possibility and potential in any given situation. Start by empathizing with the person and saying:

- "It sounds like you're angry/frustrated/hurt about something."
- "If I were in your shoes, I might feel the same way."

Then ask questions to influence the way the person sees the situation:

- "What 'silver lining' can you see in this cloud?"
- "What new experience may this difficult situation open up?"

It is especially important to focus the Mind's Eye during times of "failure." You can lead by redirecting energy toward a constructive rather than destructive outcome. You do that by asking questions like these that help people learn from the experience:

- "What did you learn from this mistake?"
- "What would you do differently next time?"

Remind people that it is impossible to succeed without "stepping up to the plate" and risking failure. Failure is a step toward success. In the words of Wayne Gretsky, a top-scoring hockey player, "I miss 100% of the shots I don't take."

Secure bases shape the Mind's Eye of others in three main ways: they model positive focus, they influence self-theories and they actively help others improve self-control.

MODELING

If you are positive and optimistic, there were secure bases in your life—your mother, father, grandparent, sibling, teacher, boss, or someone else who inspired you—who modeled this attitude. Your mirror neurons simulate empathy with the actions of those people with whom you spent a lot of time. Remember, the healthy child does not want to stay only with a parent or caretaker. If the parent is relaxed and confident, the child wants to go out and explore. If, on the other hand, the parent is anxious or nervous, the child picks up on the anxiety and may be fearful and cling to the parent's side.

Ask yourself:

- If I have a negative outlook, who in my past modeled this approach?
- If I have a positive outlook, which role model(s) taught me this approach?

INFLUENCING SELF-THEORIES

Carol Dweck, a psychology professor at Stanford University, has studied motivation and achievement in children and young adults for nearly 40 years. Her signature insight is:

> "What people believe shapes what people achieve. Our self-theories can set the boundaries on what we are able to accomplish."[4]

According to Dweck, people can have either a fixed mindset or a growth mindset. People with fixed mindsets are likely to play it safe and not take risks. They "Play Not to Lose" because they view the world from a win/lose, right/wrong or pass/fail perspective. Their "view of self" is therefore defensive. If, on the other hand, people have a growth mindset, they are likely to "Play to Win" and view the world from a learning, potential and possibility perspective. Their "view of self" is therefore dynamic.

Secure bases help others focus their Mind's Eye toward a growth mindset and away from a fixed viewpoint. Many times a secure base gives a person a "view of self" or "self-theory" that sticks with him and may dramatically change his belief in himself. Sometimes, the secure base's influence comes through the powerful use of words. At other times, secure bases influence a person's belief through their actions.

A good belayer, for instance, who sees the climber hesitate or start to give up, encourages him by saying "You can do it" or "You're already most of the way there." Affirmations used in these coachable moments can help when people start to doubt themselves.

IMPROVE SELF-CONTROL

Secure bases are particularly useful in helping others direct their focus in a way that encourages self-control. Self-control is based on willpower and on how a person regulates the focus of his Mind's Eye to see the benefit beyond the pain and frustration. As we have noted, humans have built-in survival mechanisms that served our species eons ago but can get in the way of our self-actualization and growth. Each of us has to exhibit self-control to turn the flashlight from the instinctive negative to the positive. In fact, research psychologist Roy Baumeister cites self-control as the most important element for success.[5]

One example of self-control that is strongly influenced by secure bases is called "delayed gratification." Delayed gratification denotes a person's ability to wait in order to obtain something that she wants—the ability to focus on the benefit in the future rather than the pain and frustration of the moment. Research has demonstrated that secure bases strongly influence a person's ability to delay their gratification (see the "Secure Bases Influence Marshmallow Grabbers" box). Secure bases can use distraction to direct the person's focus away from the immediate frustration, temptation or perceived loss and toward other current or future benefits.

In the workplace, Secure Base Leaders put delayed gratification into action by describing a future opportunity and supporting the person's work toward it:

When Pierre did not receive a promotion, he was deeply disappointed and discouraged. Initially, he became so upset that his emotions affected his performance. He even started to think about leaving the company. Despite delivering the painful feedback that Pierre was not ready for the promotion, his boss remained a secure base. Through firm and clear guidance, he was able to remind Pierre to focus on the bigger picture, thereby helping him realize the value he added to the organization and motivating him to redirect his energy to the areas he could control and influence. After a year, Pierre's performance improved substantially and he realized he had not been ready for the anticipated promotion. Within another six months, he was back on track and ready for the next promotion opportunity. The good news is that this time around, armed with a new set of skills, he earned the promotion.

A Secure Base Leader knows when to be tough in order to be kind. As in Pierre's case, not getting what you want can actually be a blessing in the long run. Sometimes it is better to be slapped by the truth than kissed with a lie.

Secure Bases Influence Marshmallow Grabbers

In 1972, Stanford University Professor Walter Mischel conducted a landmark experiment about delayed gratification. He studied a group of four-year old children each of whom was seated in a room with one marshmallow placed in front of him. The researcher then promised a second marshmallow to each child who could wait 20 minutes before eating the first marshmallow. Imagine how hard that would have been for a child! The adult then stepped out of the room, leaving the child alone. Some children were able to wait the 20 minutes—usually by going to play with toys or reading books elsewhere in the room—and some could not distract themselves and gobbled up the marshmallow. The children who could wait were labeled "delayers" while the children who could not were called "grabbers."

The research team studied the developmental progress of some of these children as they moved through adolescence and into adulthood. Those children who had been "delayers" performed better through adulthood on a number of criteria including stress management and scholastic, social and financial success. The interpretation: the ability to delay gratification is clearly correlated with success.[6]

In an adaptation of the experiment, Mischel joined forces with Alberto Bandura and observed fourth- and fifth- graders in similar circumstances. They put some of the "grabbers" in contact with adults who modeled techniques to distract attention from the marshmallows. In a follow-up study, it was shown that these children had retained much of what they had learned in the modeling experiment. For these children, a single exposure to the adults was enough to integrate delayed gratification.[7]

STATE AND THE MIND'S EYE

A final fundamental aspect of the Mind's Eye is its relationship to state and results. Remember that by "state" we mean how a person "is" at any one moment in time—her physiology, attitude, emotions, mood, behavior and beliefs as they all come together, internally and externally.

The ability to manage your own state is directly related to achieving the results you want. In the words of Peter Meyers, actor, theatre director and leadership performance consultant:

> *"State is the most important part of communication and yet it is almost universally overlooked. Your state determines not only the quality of your communication but the quality of your thinking. The psychological and emotional condition you're in ultimately determines your ability to lead, bond and respond to what is happening around you."*[8]

And, as all good actors know, you can choose to change your state in a moment. You use your Mind's Eye to manage your state, positively or negatively.

Imagine the state you would be in if you rushed to the airport to catch a plane for a critical meeting, only to arrive and find the plane so delayed that you were certain to be late for the meeting. What state would you be in? Angry? Stressed? Frustrated? Ready to explode? Ready to yell at the airline representative? You may well experience an amygdala hijack (see Chapter 2).

That reaction is completely understandable: your Mind's Eye has taken you straight to the negative where you instinctively focus on the loss, pain and blame. As Figure 5.3 shows, this physical state carries your reaction and determines the "result" of your feeling stuck and missing the meeting.

However, by training your Mind's Eye, you can influence your mental and physical state to determine a better result. You

FIGURE 5.3 LEADING FROM THE MIND'S EYE

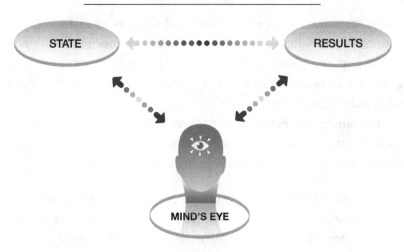

have a choice to shift your focus from the negative to the positive. The key is to ask yourself whether or not you have any possibility to control or influence the outcome of the situation. Can you change the fact that the plane is delayed? No. So shift your Mind's Eye from the pain of the delay to the gain of what you can do with the two hours you didn't plan to have. Can you do some extra research for the meeting, answer some emails, make some phone calls, read a book or even do some shopping?

By shifting your mental state, you automatically shift your physical state, too. The mind and body are connected; the brain does not necessarily distinguish fact (for example, bodily state) from fantasy or thought. So what you think affects how your body reacts. If you are a hostage to worry, fear or doubt, your brain, and therefore your body, will respond as if the threat really exists.

Dr. Craig Hassed, senior lecturer at Monash University, describes the link this way:

"It is important to note that the brain will activate the response when told to by the mind; it does not matter if the stressor does not exist or exists only in our imagination. Imagination, rumination, anticipation, exaggeration and dreaming—all can activate the fight/ flight response."[9]

So, when you use your Mind's Eye to shift your focus and thereby your thoughts, you change your physical state as well. You can even use your Mind's Eye to generate specific physical responses. Not convinced? Have someone read the prompts of this experiment to you and witness how your Mind's Eye can control your physical response:

Close your eyes and imagine that in front of you, between your thumb and your forefinger, you are holding a slice of lemon. You can see the tart, citric acid juices of the lemon sparkling in the sunlight. Now imagine a layer of white sugar sprinkled on top of the slice of lemon and watch as the white of the sweet sugar turns transparent as it absorbs those sour tart juices of the lemon. Now, slowly bring the slice of lemon up to your mouth, open up and bite down really hard on the slice of lemon. Feel the mingling of the sweet sugar juices with the tart, sour lemon juices as they trickle down your throat.

Open your eyes. Do you have more saliva in your mouth than you did before? You know there is no real slice of lemon. Merely thinking about a lemon was enough for your mind to send signals to your body to release saliva into your mouth. Your body does indeed respond to your mind's thoughts.

MIND'S EYE, EXPECTATIONS AND POSSIBILITIES

Figure 5.4 brings the various aspects of the Mind's Eye together to show what forces influence it and how it influences outcomes. Clearly, the way you focus the flashlight in your Mind's Eye will impact the expectations you have of yourself as well as others, and it will determine what you think is possible.

EXPECTATIONS DETERMINE RESULTS

What is fascinating about our Mind's Eye is the power we have to influence the result of any action through our own thoughts. Professor Jean-François Manzoni, author of *The Set-up to Fail Syndrome*,

FIGURE 5.4 LEADING FROM THE MIND'S EYE

demonstrates how our expectations can create the very outcome that we expect.[10] If we believe someone is a high performer and she is late for work, we are more likely to excuse the behavior, blaming an external event such as bad traffic. However, when we believe someone is a poor performer and she is late for work, then we are more likely to blame the person for being tardy. The set-up to fail syndrome is not necessarily related to actual performance because you selectively find negative evidence to support your view that the person is a poor performer. Psychologist Tali Sharot also found that negative expectations shape outcomes in a negative way. How? Expectations can become self-fulfilling when they impact our beliefs and subsequent actions which in turn affect the outcome.[11]

The following story shared by Terry Small, a brain expert, teacher and learning skills specialist, beautifully illustrates the power of expectations in relation to the Mind's Eye and results:

A first-grade teacher started a new job and among other information handed to her was the class list. When she looked at the sheet of paper, she saw the children's names and alongside each name was a number. "Wow," she thought. "They've given me all the smart kids—their IQ numbers are so high!" So, when she started to teach them, she stretched them as much as possible. When they complained that the work was too hard, she told them that she believed in them and knew they could do it. At the end of the year, the principal congratulated her on her amazing results. "Well, it's easy to teach when you have such a great group of kids," she said. "They were sharp, interested, motivated and all of them had IQ's of 150, 152, 153 and even higher." The principal asked how she knew the students had such high IQ scores, and she replied that the materials she had been given at the start of the year included a sheet of paper with the students' names and IQ scores on it. He smiled broadly and said, "Those were their locker numbers."[12]

Isn't it amazing that a teacher who confused locker numbers with IQ scores brought out the very best in her students? This teacher's perception of the children changed when she saw what she believed to be their IQ scores. Because of that her behavior changed. And because her behavior changed, the children's pictures of themselves changed, which led in turn to a change in *their* behavior. And all of this led to a change—an *improvement*—in the results. That is how her expectations changed the outcome.

The takeaway is that what you think affects the outcome. And often, through your thinking, you may limit yourself and others and not realize what may actually be possible.

Sometimes the power of that shift can be miraculous, as this story from business executive Alfonso illustrates:

At age seven, I had peritonitis and had to have surgery. The incision from the operation wouldn't close all the way, and the surgeon recommended that I pass a silver nitrate bar over it every day. That remedy created a burning sensation.[13] A year later, the incision was still open. While my parents took a week's vacation, my siblings and I went to stay with my grandmother. My uncle, Luis Alfredo, visited us. At the time, he was training in "mind control." He asked me how my scar was doing, and in frustration, I told him that after a year it was still open despite passing this bar over it every day. He then asked me to relax in bed and show him the scar, which I did. He put his hand over it and told me, "In one week it will be healed." "Really?" I asked. "Yes," he said. "And I don't need to use this silver bar any longer?" I asked. "Do as you want," he said. So I stopped using the bar immediately. When my parents returned from their vacation a week later, my incision had closed.

THE IMPOSSIBLE IS POSSIBLE

What is actually possible? How often do we let negative beliefs limit what we can achieve? How often do we, like the PhD student in the story below, achieve more because of our positive beliefs?

When he was a PhD student at Berkeley, George Dantzig arrived late one day for class. "On the blackboard there were two problems that I assumed had been assigned for homework. I copied them down. A few days later I apologized to the professor for taking so long to do the homework as the problems seemed a little harder than usual. I asked if he still wanted it. He told me to throw it on his desk. I did so reluctantly because his desk was covered with such a heap of papers that I feared my homework would be lost there forever. About six weeks later, one Sunday morning at 8:00 a.m., my wife and I were awakened by my professor banging on our front door. He explained that the problems I had solved, thinking they were homework, were actually two famous unsolved problems in statistics. That was the first inkling I had that there was anything special about them." Indeed, it was later suggested to Dantzig that had he known that the problems were not actually homework but two famous unsolved problems, he probably would not have tried to solve them.

Dantzig went on to have a distinguished academic career in mathematics and was awarded the National Medal of Science in 1975.

Irrespective of whatever crisis stands before them, people with a powerful Mind's Eye are able to switch it in the direction of opportunity, possibility and potential instead of being cynical, negative and destructive. Focus your Mind's Eye and you can overcome almost any obstacle in life.

Jamie Andrew lost both feet, both hands and parts of his arms and legs in a mountaineering accident. After recovering, he ran the London Marathon, climbed Kilimanjaro, and completed an Ironman Triathlon among other feats to raise funds for charity (www.jamieandrew.com). Here's how he describes the power of the Mind's Eye:

> *"It seems to me that our greatest limitations are the ones we impose on ourselves. I want to encourage others to*

throw out these misconceptions and to be all they can be. Remember, nothing is impossible. Follow your dreams!"

You unleash the deepest potential in yourself and in your people when you allow your Mind's Eye to focus on the powerful idea that the impossible is possible.

TWO SECURE BASE LEADERSHIP CHARACTERISTICS THAT HELP YOU FOCUS THE MIND'S EYE

All nine of the Secure Base Leader characteristics shape the Mind's Eye. Here, we shine the development spotlight on Characteristic #6: Focuses on the Positive and Characteristic #7: Encourages Risk Taking.

CHARACTERISTIC #6: FOCUSES ON THE POSITIVE

In our research, leaders repeatedly used expressions such as these to describe how Secure Base Leaders focus on the positive:

"You know this is painful, and it's a sign you are moving on to something new. And when she said that, it helped me to look toward the future."

"He always taught me not to be afraid of the unknown and basically to take the unknown as a potential opportunity."

"It's about being willing to give people the benefit of the doubt. Start out with the premise that the person's intention is to do something positive. When you challenge them and give them the opportunity, many people will respond in a very positive way."

"I know that right now you are dying of fear, but in three weeks you will be the champion."

This entire chapter has been about the Mind's Eye and how secure bases use the opportunity to guide the Mind's Eye of other people. In our research, we discovered that Secure Base Leaders are able to focus their own Mind's Eye on the positive and help direct the Mind's Eye of their followers toward the positive as well. They focus on benefits, create images of hope and possibility, and help people visualize the attainment of a goal. They set positive expectations that contribute to improved follower performance.

See how shifting the focus on to what can be influenced rather than on to what cannot be influenced opened up possibilities for this team:

The management team at a large multinational was facing "yet another" change as the company was going through a major reorganization. At a retreat, the managers indicated they were feeling demotivated and lost. There didn't seem to be any good news amidst the uncertainty. When Susan asked if they thought the new change was necessary, they all responded that yes, absolutely, the change was the right thing to do: the old structure clearly did not work and needed to be changed. Surprisingly, with that realization, they were then able to move on from complaining and instead focus their energy on the fact that this change was a positive. With this realization, the energy in the room visibly lifted and the team felt more empowered than before even though they were still facing exactly the same change process.

A positive Mind's Eye is linked to optimism. Look at almost any biography of an outstanding leader and you will notice that its subject was an optimist. Indeed, who would be motivated by a pessimist? Even though he wrote a book called *Only the Paranoid Survive*,[14] Andy Grove, former Intel CEO, was renowned for converting a negative situation into a positive one through resourcefulness. Optimism often comes out in the form of compelling visions, as organizational development researchers Popper and Mayseless explain:

"One of the consistent characteristics in descriptions of leaders is their ability to present a vision of the future, to point to a new way, and to transmit inspiring messages."[15]

Secure Base Leaders have a positive focus that is an integral part of who they are and this gives them authenticity. These "authentic leaders," as Bill George[16] calls them, create contagious optimism and confidence. When Secure Base Leaders start by taking care of their own Mind's Eye, they are able to take care of themselves and then direct the Mind's Eye of the whole organization toward the benefit, the potential and the opportunity that lies ahead.

Assess Your Secure Base Leadership Behaviors

On a scale of 1 to 5 (1 = never, 5 = always), rate how frequently you:

- Keep your team focused on the goal even when under pressure
- Focus on opportunity and possibility more than problems and difficulties
- Find and express the positive in situations

If you rated yourself less than a "3" for a particular behavior, make note of this characteristic as a development priority (see Chapter 8, Become a Secure Base for Others).

Tips to Develop Characteristic #6: "Focuses on the Positive"

1. **Check your own Mind's Eye.** Do all that you can to switch as quickly as possible from the natural negative to the positive:
   - When you run into a stressful situation, a negative person or a loss, take one deep breath before you say or do anything. With that breath, mentally tell yourself to focus your Mind's Eye on the positive.
   - Watch your state. You are more likely to slip to the negative or find it hard to switch to the positive if you are anxious, angry, frustrated or even hungry or tired.
   - At times when you find it difficult to retain a focus on the positive, take a few moments to remember the Secure Base Leaders in your life who have modeled a positive focus or

instilled a positive self-theory in you. Consider touching base with them to get a "booster shot" if you are really in a place of struggle.

2. **Fool your brain.** You can exercise your Mind's Eye by practicing doing something that you don't like. For instance, if you love swimming but hate cold water and you are confronted with a chilly pool, tell yourself that the feeling of cold water is exhilarating and feels wonderful. This "framing" enables you to go swimming even when the water is cold. You will still dislike cold water, but the way you focus your thinking enables you to take positive action, get beyond your dislike and enjoy a decent swim.

3. **Pick three people you want to influence to remain positive.** Each day, find at least one opportunity to plant a message of belief, confidence or optimism in their minds.

4. **Enroll others in a vision.** To keep your team members or organization focused on a positive future, work with them to formulate it in terms of a vision and to be convinced of its prospects for success. When you put enough energy behind that vision, you will inspire others to join in as well.

CHARACTERISTIC #7: ENCOURAGES RISK TAKING

In our research, leaders repeatedly used expressions such as these to describe how Secure Base Leaders encourage risk taking:

> *"He challenged me and pushed me regularly out of my comfort zone."*

> *"She really believed in me. She took me into the team even though I didn't have the experience, and she thought that I could do the job. She really trusted me. I would do anything not to let her down."*

> *"They gave me a $3 billion gas turbine deal. Their trust in me was the most important."*

> *"You should do it, you should try it out and if it doesn't work, then we can talk and find the best way forward."*

". . . what my father allowed me to do. We built a house together. He allowed me, as a 12-year old, to do substantial wood working, to work with big heavy stuff and all the construction."

A leader who does not encourage risk taking may be a comfort to others but would not fulfill the definition of a secure base. By encouraging risk taking, Secure Base Leaders move from acceptance and seeing potential to *action* based on their belief in others.

The action part of this characteristic is critical because it demonstrates that the Secure Base Leader is willing to take some personal risk. He may experience consequences if the person he is supporting fails. Yet, it is only through encouraging risk taking that the Secure Base Leader provides opportunities for others to fulfill their potential; with no risk, there is no way to know how far someone could go. Duncan experienced the power of having a secure base to influence his Mind's Eye when he and his wife visited a Six Senses Hotel in the Maldives. Without the secure base he met there, he would have been unlikely to take a risk and would have missed the experience of a lifetime:

When our seaplane landed at the island, Linda and I were met by a lady named Natsumi. A most gracious, warm and welcoming person, she was to be our host for our stay. She was clear, confident and friendly as she showed us around the island and explained how everything worked.

When we arrived at our room, I opened the doors and walked to the beach. As I stepped toward the water, I noticed a small shark swimming past. Alarmed, I called Natsumi. She very assuredly and confidently explained to me that only small baby sharks come inside the reef. "They pose no risk to humans," she said. She also assured me it was safe to assume that "mama shark" was not nearby.

Because I grew up in Africa, I tend to be wary of such assumptions. A mother hippo or lion would definitely have been nearby and ready to attack. But there was something about Natsumi's presence—her confidence and her warmth— that allowed me to trust her. So I went swimming, knowing there were baby sharks nearby. By acting as a secure base, Natsumi provided the comfort and assurance that helped me shift my Mind's Eye so I could challenge myself, take a perceived risk, and have an experience I will never forget.

Only by giving people chances do you learn when to bet on them and when not to. As Larry Bossidy, former CEO and Chairman of Allied Signal, says, "It's about betting on people not on strategies."[17] When Secure Base Leaders show this characteristic, they are clearly "Playing to Win" (effectively combining caring and daring) and with this approach, they are often tough and challenging in their feedback and encouragement to take risk.

When you combine a stretch opportunity with feedback, you provide "experiential learning." The idea behind this kind of learning is that taking action is necessary to fully integrate new knowledge. Encouraging risk taking and exploration furthers innovation as well. Researchers Jacqueline Byrd and Paul Brown make the case that risk taking is essential to innovation and creativity.[18]

Assess Your Secure Base Leadership Behaviors

On a scale of 1 to 5 (1 = never, 5 = always), rate how frequently you:

- Encourage those who work for you to take risks
- Provide real stretch assignments
- Give people freedom and responsibility (versus micromanaging)

If you rated yourself less than a "3" for a particular behavior, make note of this characteristic as a development priority (see Chapter 8, Become a Secure Base for Others).

Tips to Develop Characteristic #7: "Encourages Risk Taking"

1. **Role model risk taking.** People need to see that you are willing to stick your neck out, try new things, change, grow and yes, fail. When you fail and learn, you send a very strong signal to your followers.

2. **Be fair and clear about failure.** How you treat people who fail dictates other people's sense of whether or not it is okay to take risk. If you punish one person for failing, you may shut down many others. They will learn it is not safe to take risks around you, and even if you encourage them, they will hesitate or refuse. Instead of punishing failure, instill a growth mindset by asking questions about what people learned from an experience that didn't go well.

3. **Become aware of how consistently you give people the opportunity to take risks.** Where have you given people opportunities to put their potential into action, even when it involves the possible risk of failure? Make a list of the stretch assignments you have given the people who work for you. Consider these questions:

   • Have you demonstrated your belief in each and every one of your people through such assignments?

   • If you have not given some the opportunity for challenge, is it because you are concerned they can't handle it? What does that say about how you are viewing their potential? What kinds of assignments could be appropriate, or what feedback conversations do you need to have?

   • Are there some people you could challenge even more?

4. **Watch your state.** If you demonstrate through your words, gestures or body language that you are anxious about the risk you are encouraging someone to take, you are telling him that you don't believe in him. It would be like a belayer shaking in fear while the climber attempts a difficult move. Manage your state to manage your impact.

Key Learnings

- Managing your Mind's Eye is essential to managing yourself and is the root of all success. The focus of your Mind's Eye determines your results and what you achieve.
- Training your Mind's Eye involves daily practice to see opportunities.
- Modeling, influencing self-theories and improving self-control are all ways of impacting the Mind's Eye of others.
- Your beliefs about yourself are shaped by the people in your life, past and present.
- Secure bases focus the Mind's Eye on the benefit and gain rather than the loss and pain.
- You always have a choice about where you put your focus. Learning to use that choice is part of leadership development.
- Secure Base Leaders manage not only their Mind's Eye but also influence the Mind's Eye of others.

&

"Everything can be taken from a man or a woman but one thing: the last of human freedoms to choose one's attitude in any given set of circumstances, to choose one's own way."

-Viktor Frankl
1905-1997
Psychiatrist and Concentration Camp Survivor

&

FREQUENTLY ASKED QUESTIONS

Q: How much risk is appropriate? I can't bet the company on a person's development.

A: There is no simple answer to this question. You will have to weigh the specific situation and its context. Know that people tend to be able to take on more than expected. The most important element, however, is to have safety mechanisms built in to prevent a major downside problem. These could be regular feedback sessions, financial controls and other early warning measures that allow you to monitor the situation responsibly.

Q: Surely I can't be positive all the time . . . what about reality, what about the fact that bad things do happen? I don't want to be all "Pollyanna" about things.

A: Develop the discipline of constantly refocusing your Mind's Eye on possibility and opportunity. From time to time, things won't go your way and it will be important to acknowledge the disappointment. But then don't dwell on the negatives. Concentrate on your habitual pattern. A positive Mind's Eye refers to the habitual pattern of seeking to "Play to Win," even in difficult circumstances.

Q: My work is tiring. How can I be in a peak state all the time?

A: When you recognize that being in a peak state is about authentically expressing your "Playing to Win" approach, it is not tiring at all. Quite the opposite. Being in a peak state actually recharges your batteries.

Chapter Six

Achievement: Playing to Win

On August 29, 2009, Ted Kennedy Jr. delivered this moving eulogy at the funeral of his father, Senator Ted Kennedy Sr.:[1]

"When I was 12 years old, I was diagnosed with bone cancer. A few months after I lost my leg, there was a heavy snowfall over my childhood home outside of Washington, D.C. My father went to the garage to get the old Flexible Flyer sled and asked me if I wanted to go sledding down the steep driveway. I was trying to get used to my new artificial leg and the hill was covered with ice and snow and it wasn't easy for me to walk. And the hill was very slick and as I struggled to walk, I slipped and I fell on the ice and I started to cry and I said, 'I can't do this.' I said, 'I'll never be able to climb that hill.' And he lifted me in his strong, gentle arms and said something I'll never forget. 'I know you'll do it. There is nothing you can't do. We're going to climb that hill together, even if it takes us all day.'

Sure enough, he held me around my waist and we slowly made it to the top. You know, at age 12 losing a leg pretty much seems like the end of the world, but as I climbed onto his back and we flew down the hill that day, I knew he was right. I knew I was going to be OK. You see, my father taught me that even our most profound losses are survivable and it is what we do with that loss, our ability to transform it into a positive event. That is one of my father's greatest lessons. He taught me that nothing is impossible."

When we show the video clip of Ted Kennedy Jr. delivering this eulogy, we witness how profoundly it touches people, irrespective of their age, gender, nationality or political persuasion. The emotion comes not only from experiencing the deep and loving bond that enabled Ted Sr. to do and say exactly what his son needed on that momentous day but also from their longing to have someone who will do for them what Ted Sr. did for his son.

The profound truth is that we all want to have such a strong secure base in our lives. We all desire to bond and we all want to explore. It is human nature to desire both strong relationships through bonds and strong growth through challenges. When people like Ted Sr. stay connected and bonded to others *and* focus them to achieve stretch goals, we say that they are "Playing to Win."

When you Play to Win, you combine all of the components of Secure Base Leadership—the bonding, the processing of losses through grief, and the Mind's Eye—and put them in service of achievement. Not just any kind of achievement, but achievement that preserves and enhances relationships and takes people beyond what they felt was possible. You thereby unleash their potential. You care to dare. It is exactly the concept of the belayer remaining physically and emotionally connected to the climber as she scales the cliff. By working together, the belayer-climber team succeeds in getting to the top.

Because Playing to Win is inherently sustainable, it delivers healthy high performance. We define high performance as:

challenging yourself and others to see and achieve what is beyond normal expectation.

What do we mean by "healthy?" We mean achieving high performance in a sustainable way that is positive for the people involved.

In this chapter, we describe both what it means to Play to Win and what happens when you lead in a way that does not value relationships or provide adequate challenge to unleash potential. Your best lesson will come from envisioning the two Kennedys on the driveway that winter day. Recall how Ted Sr. simultaneously supported Ted Jr. and challenged him. Through his words, gestures and attitude, he was able to shape his son's thinking and help him to realize that "nothing is impossible." Was it likely that Ted Sr. was anxious for his son? Probably. Was there risk involved? Absolutely. Yet, he was able to manage his own anxiety while protecting his son from his fears, focusing their Mind's Eye together on the benefit and achievement.

Imagine how easy it would have been for Ted Sr. to say to his son, "Why don't we wait till next year when you have become more comfortable with your artificial leg and then we can sled together?" Instead of putting off or discounting the challenge, the father showed unwavering support and belief in his son, pushing him to succeed, "even if it takes all day." Think also of the way Ted Sr. celebrated their mutual achievement. He had his son climb on his back, and they both experienced the sheer exhilaration of sailing down that hill. Without this experience, Ted Jr. might forever have thought of himself as having very limited possibilities. Instead, he knew he could still achieve goals. And he knew without a doubt that his father would be there to support him.

Maintaining a Playing to Win approach as a parent, a leader or an individual takes work, especially when you are under great pressure and stress or when you face anxiety. As with all aspects of Secure Base Leadership, it is not about being perfect. It is about being self-aware and developing the tools to get yourself back on track.

FIGURE 6.1 FOUR LEADERSHIP APPROACHES

HIGH DARING

Playing to Dominate	**PLAYING TO WIN**
Playing to Avoid	Playing Not to Lose

LOW CARING ◀••••   ••••▶ **HIGH CARING**

LOW DARING

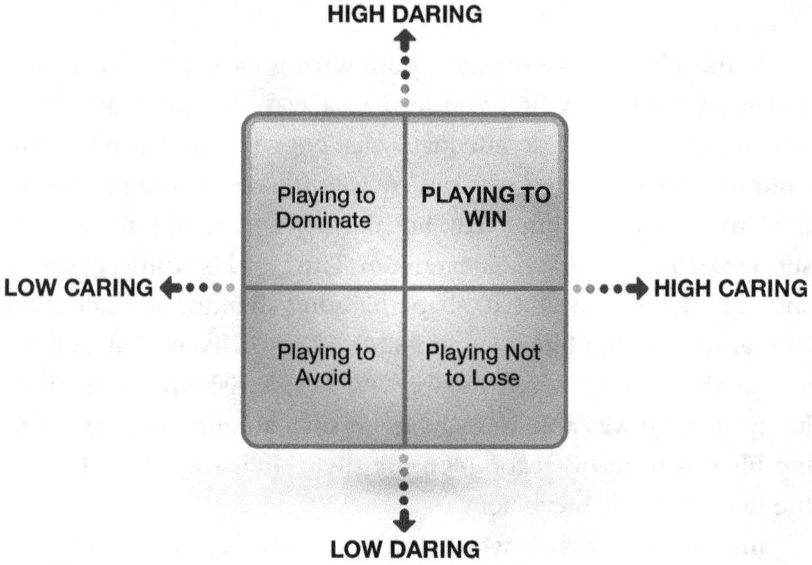

THE FOUR LEADERSHIP APPROACHES

Caring and daring are two trajectories of leadership that when combined in the correct balance deliver Secure Base Leadership (see Figure 6.1). This graphic shows how the intersection of varying levels of caring and daring creates four quadrants. The horizontal axis depicts "caring," how much a leader focuses on relationships; the vertical axis represents "daring," the level of challenge offered by the leader. The four quadrants represent four approaches to leadership.

We observe that depending on the context leaders may adopt any one of the approaches and may shift between approaches. In this way, we see this as a dynamic two-dimensional system within which leaders operate. Therefore, as you read the leadership approach descriptions, avoid trying to determine a fixed position for yourself. Instead, make note of the varying circumstances under which you tend to adopt each approach.

What is clear from our research is that sustainable high performers and Secure Base Leaders operate predominantly with a Playing to Win approach, with both bonding and Mind's Eye in full force.

Let's look at each approach in detail, starting with the approach you want to use most of the time.

PLAYING TO WIN

High Caring + High Daring
Inner Voice: "Together we can achieve great things"
C-theme: COURAGE

Playing to Win translates into your willingness to take the necessary risks to succeed. When you stay bonded to your people, while also focusing the team or organization on stretch goals, you are Playing to Win and, therefore, demonstrating Secure Base Leadership. When Playing to Win, you provide a high focus on relationships as well as a high level of challenge so that both you and your followers can reach the highest levels of performance. As much as possible, you take feelings of threat and defensiveness out of the equation. You are there to cover others' backs and, at the same time, you challenge your followers with tough feedback and high expectations. Since they feel both safe and challenged, they will feel free to explore, be creative and take the risks inherent in innovation. They will fully engage and follow you through change. Because caring is as important as daring, you will not pursue options that allow others to "lose."

Playing to Win is the approach that lets you lead at your best and have the deepest impact on others and on the business.

Many of the people profiled in this book who rose above personal challenges to give back to the world and pursue their own dreams are fantastic role models for Playing to Win. J.R. Martinez is one other such person:

Actor and Dancing with the Stars *Champion J.R. Martinez was a 19-year old infantryman in the U.S. Army serving in Iraq when his vehicle hit an anti-tank mine in April 2003. He suffered burns to more than 40 percent of his body and underwent more than 20 surgeries including six on his eyes. In an interview with* CBS News *correspondent David Martin he said, "A lot of guys just have one arm burned, and they would feel that it's over. You know, that there's no point of going on. And I would say, 'Man, you know, look at me. You know, I have more visible scars,' or, 'I catch more looks, and I've made it. I still go out. I still have fun. I still live life,'" he said. "I'm only 20 years old. You know, why am I gonna sit there and act like there's no point of living? There is."*

Martinez believes he was "chosen" so that he could help other soldiers deal with the trauma of burn injuries. He remains bonded to his colleagues, his dreams and his life. In 2008, he played the role of an Iraqi war veteran in the American soap opera All My Children *and, in 2011, he competed in the 13th season of the television show* Dancing with the Stars *and emerged as the winner. Martinez's success also marked the first win for his partner, dancer Karina Smirnoff, a professional who has competed with other partners in nine seasons of the show. J.R. credits her with pushing him to excel in routine after routine, leading him to the top of the competition.*

You will recognize that you are Playing to Win if these thoughts typically go through your head as you lead people:

- My relationships are key to my success.
- I can trust other people.
- People will support me when I need help.
- I am capable and good at what I do.
- I am ready to take appropriate risks.
- I enjoy leading others.
- I enjoy making decisions.

- I enjoy being with others.
- I value both the hard and soft aspects of leadership.
- I am a high performer and I expect high performance.
- Working together delivers the best results.

MYTH: Playing to Win means someone has to lose.

Not true. Playing to Win means that you achieve by meeting a significant challenge while also building a strong relationship. When you take a risk, you are competing against yourself rather than others and moving you and your team to a state of healthy high performance.

PLAYING NOT TO LOSE

High Caring + Low Daring
Inner Voice: "Let us be safe and not take too much risk."
C-theme: COCOON

If you are Playing Not to Lose, you are focused on failure, possible mistakes, worry and what could go wrong. Under stress, you may Play Not to Lose on the assumption that it is safer to get reassurance from others. When you maintain this attitude, you tend to be too cautious, are afraid of making decisions and avoid risk taking. Without the daring and the challenge, the close bonds you keep with your people may make you overprotective. You'll have a degree of engagement, but you will stifle creativity and innovation because you will want to avoid mistakes and failure at all costs. In short, you play defensively.

You will recognize that you are Playing Not to Lose if these thoughts and beliefs frequently go through your head as you lead people:

- I worry excessively about the outcome.
- I'm hesitant to make decisions by myself.

- Others may know better than I.
- I wish we had more information.
- Let's wait and see what happens.
- I need reassurance from others.
- I worry whether people will reject me.
- I'm afraid to make a mistake.
- I am concerned about being alone.
- I am concerned that people won't like my leadership.
- I avoid criticism and disapproval.

Your Opportunity:

To spend less time caught in this approach, develop ways to strengthen your Mind's Eye (Chapter 5) so that you can focus on the positive and encourage risk taking (see Figure 6.2).

FIGURE 6.2 THE MIND'S EYE DRIVES DARING

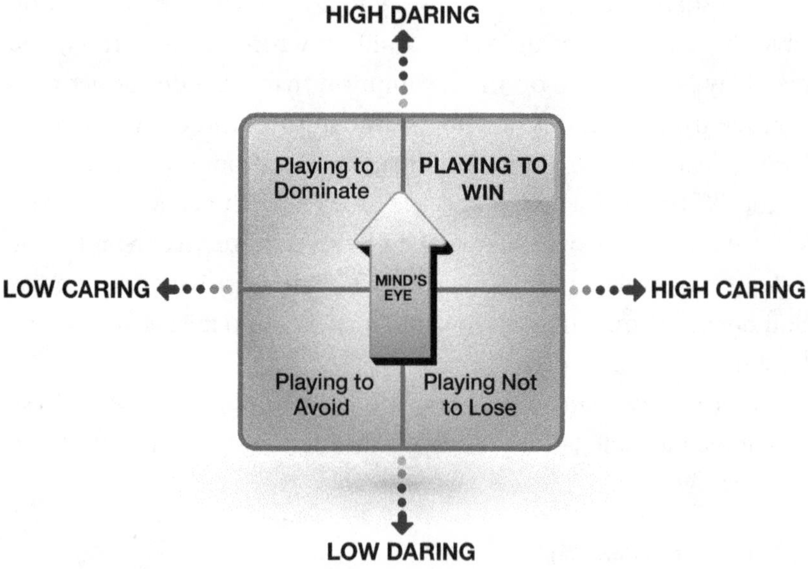

PLAYING TO DOMINATE

Low Caring + High Daring
Inner Voice: "Who needs others? I can do better by myself"
C-theme: CONTROL

Playing to Dominate means focusing on results at the expense of relationships. When you are under pressure, you may Play to Dominate because you believe "it is easier and quicker to do it myself." If you continue to use this approach, you can become detached from your people. In your isolation, you may find yourself making questionable decisions that do not take others' perspectives into account. You may replace all or most of your "people-focus" with a numbers-oriented "results focus." People may describe you as viewing the world in black and white terms. While you may be successful in achieving results in the short term, you are likely to create a negative "pacesetting" environment in which others struggle to keep up.

Your followers are likely to see you as an overly demanding boss they can never please. They will be very unlikely to want to engage with you since you are not reaching out to join them. And while they are likely to rise to certain challenges you put forward, they are unlikely to be creative because they are pushed into delivery rather than inspired to achieve through a sense of caring and engagement. With little care for the people you work with, you will be seen as pushing too aggressively.

You will recognize that you are Playing to Dominate if these thoughts and beliefs frequently go through your head as you lead people:

- At the end of the day, the only thing that counts is results.
- The soft stuff is nice to have but doesn't really matter.
- Business is not personal.
- People need to earn my trust.

- People must prove themselves repeatedly to me.
- People are generally not loyal.
- It is better to be independent.
- I prefer not to rely on others too much.
- At the end of the day, you come into the organization alone and you leave alone.
- People are only working for the money.
- You cannot truly depend on others.
- I deliver the best results when I work by myself.
- It's quicker and easier for me to do it myself.

Your Opportunity:

To spend less time using this approach, go back to the basic Secure Base Leadership component of bonding (Chapter 3). See Figure 6.3.

FIGURE 6.3 BONDING DRIVES CARING

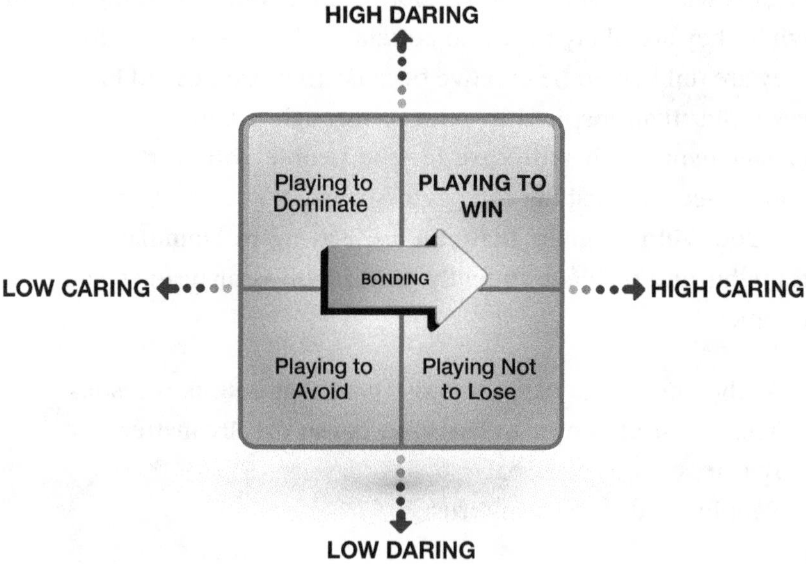

The Right Amount of Challenge

In his classic book *Flow*, Mihály Csikszentmihalyi says that "a state of flow" (in terms of optimal performance) can be achieved by creating enough challenge to demand complete attention to the task but not so much challenge that the person becomes paralyzed and overwhelmed with performance anxiety.[2]

If you Play to Dominate, you place so much focus on daring that you stretch individuals or your team too far. You knock them out of "flow" and they can easily become defensive and demoralized.

So, how do you provide the right amount of daring?

First, determine whether the person is asking for challenge. If she is, challenge her significantly. Set a high expectation on a stretch assignment and reiterate that you believe in her.

If the person is not asking for challenge but rather you as a Secure Base Leader have determined she needs to be challenged, divide a big challenge into small increments. Give one small increment and reiterate your belief in her ability to achieve this increment. If she does well and you see her confidence building, give her a second increment—maybe a little larger one this time. Chances are she will become more daring and ask for more herself.

What do you do if the person struggles with the amount of challenge you give? Say something like this to reinforce your confidence in the person and promote learning:

"I know you can do better. How can you work differently to achieve our goals? How can I support you?"

Playing to Avoid

Low Caring + Low Daring
Inner Voice: "I want to be left alone"
C-theme: CLOSET

When Playing to Avoid, you demonstrate the highest levels of defensiveness, risk avoidance, fear of making mistakes and even withdrawal. You may fall into using the Playing to Avoid approach when you opt out of both caring and daring. You will feel like you are just "clocking in and clocking out," and others will sense disinterest in your attitude. In other words, you will have disengaged and "checked out." You show up and do the minimum.

If you lead with this approach, your people are likely to be extremely demotivated as you are providing neither a relationship nor a challenge. There's nothing for them to engage with and no reason to take a risk on creativity or change. They, like you, will simply go through the motions while they try to avoid you just as you are trying to avoid them. This is simply a lonely and dismal situation for everyone.

You will recognize that you are Playing to Avoid if these thoughts and beliefs frequently go through your head as you lead people:

- I don't like people and people don't like me.
- There's no point in engaging—it's just a job.
- I show up and do the basics.
- I avoid taking risks.
- The people around me are incompetent.
- No one understands me.
- I am not appreciated.
- I wish people would leave me alone.
- My people can take care of themselves.
- No one looks after me, so why should I look after them?
- My job is not exciting or challenging.

Your Opportunity:

For the sake of your followers, your organization and mostly yourself, we encourage you to identify and grieve the losses you have experienced, using the process described in Chapter 4.

What does loss have to do with Playing to Avoid? We have observed that people who experience loss and do not grieve, for whatever reason, often resort to this approach in a futile attempt to retreat, find safety and avoid pain. Playing to Avoid reflects a state of detachment designed to protect you, consciously or unconsciously, from engaging with people or goals. Leaders are not immune from this pattern. If you recognize parts of yourself in this description, we recommend that you reflect on your past losses in life such as getting laid off, being passed over for a promotion or a bad breakup of a personal relationship. Assess what grieving you may still need to do to allow yourself to re-bond fully to life.

MOVEMENT UNDER PRESSURE

In our experience working with leaders, we have come to see that it is the *direction* of the "movement under pressure" or the ingrained habit of managing that is the most important take-away from this model.

There are two unhelpful directions in which you may move away from the Playing to Win approach:

Moving left: When you move left under pressure, you are essentially withdrawing from others, becoming more self-reliant and more of a loner.

Moving down: When you move down, you are essentially losing confidence in your own abilities and will tend to doubt your decision-making and judgment.

Assess yourself:

- Which approach do you tend to use most of the time?
- When you are under pressure, which approach do you tend to use?

> **Assess your organization as well:**
>
> • Which approaches do your boss, peers and direct reports use most of their time?
> • How could you be a better secure base for these people and help change their attitudes and approaches?
> • What is the culture of your company, your unit and your team? Are you focusing on both goals and people?

THE SIX LEADERSHIP STYLES

In his landmark article "Leadership that Gets Results," Dan Goleman summarized the six leadership styles as presented in Table 6.1.[3] He proposes that depending upon the situation different styles are useful in the short term. He suggests that leaders focus on the styles that have a positive impact on the organizational climate. However, he notes that in crisis or short deadline situations, a coercive or pacesetting style may be temporarily appropriate.

In Table 6.2 we summarize the four approaches identified in this chapter and compare them with the styles Goleman discusses. You will notice that Playing Not to Lose is reflected most in extreme Affiliative and Democratic styles. Those leadership styles do indeed create a positive feeling in the work environment, but without a high level of daring, they may not yield the best results over time. Similarly, Play to Dominate is reflected in the Coercive and Pacesetting styles. In our opinion, while either of these styles can be beneficial in the short term, they are both negative if sustained over a longer period of time. And yet many leaders tend to Play to Dominate much of the time, especially when under stress.

With Playing to Win's balance of caring and daring, Secure Base Leadership is the common thread linking the most sustainable and therefore effective leadership styles. Playing to Win most closely

Table 6.1 The Six Leadership Styles at a Glance

	COERCIVE	AUTHORITATIVE-VISIONARY	AFFILIATIVE	DEMOCRATIC	PACESETTING	COACHING
Overall impact on climate	Negative	Most Strongly Positive	Positive	Positive	Negative	Positive
The leader's modus operandi	Demands immediate compliance	Mobilizes people toward a vision	Creates harmony and builds emotional bonds	Forges consensus through participation	Sets high standards for performance	Develops people for the future
The style in a phrase	"Do what I tell you."	"Come with me."	"People come first."	"What do you think?"	"Do as I do, now!"	"Try this."
Underlying emotional intelligence competencies	Drive to achieve, initiative, self-control	Self-confidence, empathy, change catalyst	Empathy, building relationships, communication	Collaboration, team leadership, communication	Conscientiousness, drive to achieve, initiative	Developing others, empathy, self-awareness
When the style works best	In a crisis, to kick-start a turnaround or with problem employees	When changes require a new vision or when a clear direction is needed	To heal rifts in a team or to motivate people during stressful circumstances	To build buy-in or consensus or to get input from valuable employees	To get quick results from a highly motivated and competent team	To help an employee improve performance or develop long-term strengths

Source: Adapted from D. Goleman (2000)

TABLE 6.2 SECURE BASE LEADERSHIP AND EMOTIONAL INTELLIGENCE STYLES

SBL QUADRANTS	HIGH CARING	HIGH DARING	APPROACH	INNER VOICE	EI STYLE	SHORT-TERM IMPACT	LONG-TERM IMPACT
Playing to Win	Yes	Yes	Stretches self and others while keeping strong bond	"Together, we can achieve great things."	Authoritative-Visionary, Coaching	Strongly Positive	Strongly Positive
Playing Not to Lose	Yes	No	Keeps a strong bond but does not encourage enough risk	"Let's be safe and not take too much risk."	Overly Democratic or Affiliative	Somewhat Positive	Negative
Playing to Dominate	No	Yes	Remains fully focused on goal yet excludes other people	"Who needs others? It's quicker and easier to do it by myself."	Coercive, Pacesetting	Somewhat Positive	Negative
Playing to Avoid	No	No	Backs off of relationships with both people and goals	"I want to be left alone."		Negative	Negative

aligns with the Authoritative-Visionary style, though it can also be seen in a positive version of the Coaching style. The Authoritative-Visionary style best unleashes the potential of followers and is the best way for leaders to deliver high performance over the long term.

Two Secure Base Leadership Characteristics that Help You Play to Win

In many ways, Playing to Win is the outcome of a leader combining most, or all, of the nine Secure Base Leadership characteristics. However, two characteristics, "Inspires through Intrinsic Motivation" and "Signals Accessibility" come forth in the specific way a leader interacts with followers while Playing to Win. The first supports the challenge and the second supports the bond.

Characteristic #8: Inspires through Intrinsic Motivation

In our research, leaders repeatedly used expressions such as these to describe how Secure Base Leaders inspire through intrinsic motivation:

"He regularly asked me what I was learning as well as what I was accomplishing."

"It's the right thing to do. Don't worry about the profitability in the short term. It's the right thing to do."

"I want you to choose the job that plays to your strengths and will most satisfy you. Don't focus on the money at this stage of your career. The money will come if you are committed to pursuing your strengths."

"It's okay that you made a mistake and even that we lost some money. You learned an important lesson today

that will help you grow and develop as a person and as a leader."

"There's no point in being only the richest person in the graveyard. We must also enjoy ourselves along the way."

When we invited leaders to talk about the people and events that have influenced them, they did not reference money or financial reward at all. On the other hand, they did make multiple references to potential, learning, development, passion, contribution and meaning. In other words, Secure Base Leaders understand the importance of appealing to intrinsic motivation to get the best out of people rather than relying on extrinsic motivation.

Intrinsic motivation refers to a desire or drive to do something because it is inherently interesting or enjoyable. Extrinsic motivation applies to a scenario in which a person does something because it leads to an outcome that is separable from the task itself.[4] When intrinsically motivated, a person is moved to act for the fun or challenge involved rather than because of external pressures or rewards.[5]

Evidence suggests that financial reward, while being an element of motivation, is not the most important source of employee motivation.[6] What really motivates people is the ability to move toward self-actualization, the drive to fulfill their potential.

Secure Base Leaders find ways to tap into the self-actualization desires of their followers by providing rich experiences rather than rewards. A rich experience involves novelty, curiosity, discovery, playfulness, wonder and intrigue, and it draws on a wide array of skills. Rich experiences lead to learning because they contribute to the creation of new brain cells and they can stave off the onset of degenerative brain diseases such as Alzheimers.[7] In fact, numerous studies have shown that intrinsic motivation contributes positively to learning outcomes.[8]

Inspiring Others to Inspire Themselves

We often hear leaders question where they will find the money to motivate their people. After all, doesn't it cost money to build engagement and support innovation?

Our research shows that Secure Base Leaders succeed without spending extra money on salaries, incentives and bonuses. You may even say they succeed *because* they look for other ways to motivate their people.

Their secret lies in prioritizing "intrinsic" over "extrinsic" motivation. Because intrinsic motivation comes from within the person herself it costs you nothing. Extrinsic motivation, on the other hand, often comes in the form of a limited resource like money.

Examples of Intrinsic Motivation	Examples of Extrinsic Motivation
Learning	Money, Bonus
Challenge	Awards or Honors
Growth, Self-Development	Fame
Fun, Excitement or Novelty	Promotion
Desire to contribute or make a difference	Scores on tests

When you inspire someone by offering opportunities for intrinsic motivation, you build engagement without increasing costs.

Self-actualization can take forms other than learning. It can be manifested in deepening bonds, seizing opportunities and achieving stretch goals, as this anecdote demonstrates:

When Susan led a project team tasked with the creation of a new motto for the company, her boss inspired her by explaining the impact it would have on all aspects of the business as well as on consumers, customers and employees. This possibility of making a difference motivated her to dedicate considerable time to the project, working late into the evenings and on weekends while also doing her day job. When the motto "protects what's good" was finally launched, Susan was at the same time humbled and proud to see the results of the project team's work displayed on billions of the company's products worldwide. Many years later, the motto is still in use and she is still closely bonded to members of that team.

Self-actualization can also be linked to the idea of doing something good for others or for the world:

Duncan says that his work as a teacher and advisor to executives is so personally satisfying that the financial aspects of the work are irrelevant. "After a successful career in the corporate world in a variety of leadership roles, I am so pleased that I had the courage to change tracks and follow my calling to work more directly with the people-side of organizational life. I truly would not change my job for anything else in the world. There is nothing else I would rather be doing, no matter what you paid me. The most satisfying part is the knowledge that through my work I support other people in leading more successful and meaningful lives. It's a great feeling to make a difference."

The most successful people appear not to be motivated by being the richest people in the world. Instead, they are driven by the desire to achieve something. Money is a by-product of success as opposed to the goal in itself. We suspect that the times when you have been most inspired were times when your secure bases recognized your potential, your contribution and your strengths. Such inspiration propels you to Play to Win. You not only feel bonded and challenged, but you also have the capacity to bond with and challenge others.

Ask yourself:

- Did the people who most inspired and motivated me in my life use intrinsic or extrinsic motivation?

Assess Your Secure Base Leadership Behaviors:

On a scale of 1 to 5 (1 = never, 5 = always), rate how frequently you:

- Determine what is really important to people and use that insight to motivate them
- Stress the importance of learning, growth and development
- Focus people on achievement and fulfillment rather than financial reward

If you rated yourself less than a "3" for a particular behavior, make note of this characteristic as a development priority (see Chapter 8, Become a Secure Base for Others).

Tips to Develop Characteristic #8: "Inspires through Intrinsic Motivation"

1. **Do an inventory of the motivations you use.** Reflect upon how many of your speeches and conversations with your followers reflect intrinsic motivation versus extrinsic motivation. For example, during reviews, what is the primary mechanism whereby you seek to motivate people? Do you talk about financial reward or do you talk about learning, growth and development?
2. **Get to know your people as individuals.** Only when you know their aspirations and what makes them tick can you determine what kind of intrinsic motivation would be most effective for them.

3. **Build on the dual desires of people to both belong and achieve.** Invite people to be part of something bigger than themselves. Not only will this opportunity provide intrinsic motivation, it will also challenge them in the process. For example, give people projects or assignments outside of their job functions that contribute to the organization on a larger scale. Or, give them projects involving work with a not-for-profit.

CHARACTERISTIC #9: SIGNALS ACCESSIBILITY

In our research, leaders repeatedly used expressions such as these to describe how Secure Base Leaders signal accessibility:

"I knew they were always there and their support was, you know, a phone call now and again."

"I have this very good friend, I do not see her very often, but she has been part of my history all the way."

"He became a secure base for me . . . in fact still is, although he is dead."

"He always stepped in if you needed him, he was always available, always had his door open . . ."

The opposite of accessible is detached, and we have seen how a detached "independent loner" cannot be a secure base. The people we interviewed described how they believed that their secure bases were always accessible and available. What's interesting here is that their perception was not exactly the same as reality: secure bases were not in constant contact or necessarily nearby. Nor did they hold hour-long conversations. Instead, they were often far away and their conversations could be quite brief. Rest assured that being a Secure Base Leader does not mean a 24/7 open door/call-me-at-home-anytime policy.

Rather, what is important is the belief and perception that the secure base is available if needed. The idea of being supportive and accessible has more to do with a sense of the person and of the relationship, rather than of the actual amount of communication. Mary Ainsworth, whose work on Attachment Theory is critical to the secure base concept, studied how children interact with their secure bases. She found that separation was not the issue that upset children, but rather their *sense* of the unavailability of the secure base. In other words, a caregiver becomes a secure base not through constant physical proximity but through perceived availability in a time of need.[9]

One could almost think of accessibility as an "invisible" aspect of being a secure base; it has to do with the role you play even when you are not physically there. Someone who has died can be a secure base: his influence lives on and his messages can still be "accessed" through memory. Similarly, people you have never met, and never will meet, can be secure bases. Religious or political leaders, for instance, are accessible in terms of their key messages and teachings, even in the absence of their physical proximity. Actors and musicians can also be secure bases to people for the same reasons.

Nick Shreiber, former CEO of Tetra Pak, illustrated this characteristic perfectly:

When Nick became CEO, he implemented an email address called "CEOConnect" and committed to responding to questions from employees within 24 hours. Distinct from a whistle-blower process, CEOConnect was conceived as an interactive opportunity—a communications channel through which anyone could ask a question of the CEO. Interestingly, in his five-year tenure as CEO, Nick received only a handful of emails, but symbolically this email address sent a very powerful message that was greatly appreciated in the organization. At one stage, when discontinuing "CEOConnect" was proposed because it was used so infrequently, there was tremendous pushback because employees viewed it as a "safety

*line" to the CEO. In essence, through this simple action, Nick
had told the organization "I am available and accessible
should you want to communicate directly with me." On the
occasions when he did receive an email and responded within
the promised 24 hours, the person receiving the response
shared it with many others who in turn shared it with others,
and the story spread into company folklore.*

Your job therefore is not to be physically available to people
all the time. Instead, your job is to find ways to signal your accessibility and openness. You do so by showing that you care about
people. You reinforce the message by demonstrating vulnerability
and humanity that challenge the traditional messages that leaders
are to be seen but not contacted. You give people a real person to
engage with. When you do, you open up the possibility of bonding,
without which you cannot Play to Win or achieve enduring high
performance.

Assess Your Secure Base Leadership Behaviors

On a scale of 1 to 5 (1 = never, 5 = always), rate how
frequently you:

- Return calls or emails in a reasonable amount of time
- Remain supportive of people even when you have little
  direct contact
- Make yourself available to others when they have
  questions

If you rated yourself less than a "3" for a particular behavior,
make note of this characteristic as a development priority (see
Chapter 8, Become a Secure Base for Others).

Tips to Develop Characteristic #9: "Signals Accessibility"

1. **Concentrate on quality not quantity of time with your followers.** Every exchange matters. Some of the most important dialogues might be just a couple of sentences long or may even be as short as a symbolic gesture like a "thumbs up" sign.

2. **Lead by walking around.** If you stay holed up in your office, even with the door open, you send the message that you are somehow isolated or different. Portray accessibility by getting out and about. Visit people in their offices or workspaces. Remember to listen and ask questions as you interact with others.

3. **Keep interactions short.** Use "bull's eye transactions." When you do, you will set the expectation, in your mind and theirs, that it does not take a long time to provide a dose of caring or daring.

4. **Demonstrate that people can indeed contact you.** Make sure the people for whom you are a secure base do not have to jump through hoops to get in contact with you:

   • Provide an email address and phone number.
   • Instruct your administrative assistant to avoid acting like a gatekeeper who "protects" you from people.
   • Avoid talking about how busy or stressed you are. When you do, you are telling people that they are not as important as other items you are working on.
   • Get back to people when they contact you, even if it's to say, "When's a good time to talk next week?"

Key Learnings

- Playing to Win delivers healthy high performance for you, your team and your organization.
- Understanding how your attitude and approach change when you are under pressure can help you to self-regulate and keep Playing to Win.
- Playing to Win takes courage to risk caring and risk daring.
- Playing to Win involves managing your Mind's Eye and guiding that of others as well as practicing bonding.
- Playing to Win can create a sense of flow in which you perform at your best with the appropriate level of stress.
- You can inspire people to Play to Win through intrinsic motivation.
- Secure Base Leaders signal accessibility.

&

"Avoiding danger is no safer in the long run than outright exposure. Life is either a daring adventure or nothing."

–Helen Keller
1880-1968
American Author, Political Activist and Lecturer

&

FREQUENTLY ASKED QUESTIONS

Q: I see some very successful people in the world Playing to Dominate. If they can win that way, why can't I?

A: Yes, in the short term, it looks like people who Play to Dominate win. But they do not produce *sustainable* high performance. The pacesetting and domineering leader does not create the enduring loyalty and trust of followers. Eventually, those deficiencies will catch up with him.

Q: How can I be even more available? It's already 24/7 for me.

A: You don't necessarily need to be more accessible; you need to be perceived as accessible and actually be accessible when needed.

Q: We have a bonus structure in our organization. Are you saying it doesn't work and we should get rid of it?

A: No, incentive structures and bonus payments are indeed useful motivators to drive sales and commercial transactions. Yet, they are unlikely to drive enduring engagement. The research on pay is very clear: pay motivates up to a point, but only up to a point. Truly high performance—in any discipline—is not motivated by financial reward alone. It might draw people to the field or serve as an attraction and retention tool for a company, but money alone does not drive excellent performance.

PART III

CHAPTER SEVEN

STRENGTHEN YOUR OWN SECURE BASES

In his own words, Paul Rusesabagina was "an ordinary man"—a quiet manager of a luxury hotel in his native Rwanda.

But in the face of the genocide that all but destroyed his country, Paul became a hero to the 1,268 Tutsis and moderate Hutus he sheltered from the Interahamwe Militia at the Hôtel des Mille Collines. For three months, he used his influence and connections as acting manager to keep these lucky ones safe.

On April 6, 1994, mobs with machetes began the slaughter of 800,000 civilians in just 100 days. When the killing started, people turned up at Paul's home. "Why they thought I might be able to protect them was beyond me but it was my house they flocked to. We put the visitors up in the living room and kitchen and tried to stay quiet." Paul had a role model for this kind of hospitality, "It occurred to me later that I had seen this before. My father had opened our tiny hillside home to refugees during the Hutu Revolution of 1959. I had been a young boy then, a little older than my son, Tresor. My father's favorite proverb came back to me, 'If a man can keep a fierce lion under his roof, why can he not shelter another human being?'"

When the killing started, Paul, a former manager of Kigali's Hôtel des Diplomates, sheltered his family safely at the Hôtel des Mille Collines, where he had previously been employed. As other managers departed, Paul stayed put. He phoned the hotel's corporate owner, Sabena, and secured a letter appointing him Acting General Manager. Despite some difficulty in getting the staff to accept his authority, he was able to use his position to turn the hotel into a refuge. As the fighting escalated, those at his home and others arrived seeking safety. For protection against bullets and grenades, they put mattresses against the windows. For nourishment, they drank from the hotel's swimming pool and rationed the remaining food stocks.

Abandoned by international peacekeepers, Paul used his wits and a stock of liquor and cash to bribe the Rwandan Hutu soldiers, keeping the dangerous militia outside the gates during the hundred days of slaughter.

Paul's efforts were the basis of the Academy Award-nominated film Hotel Rwanda *(2004). Even though he took on a leadership role in the face of the unbearable genocide, remarkably, he believed he was simply continuing his role as a hotel manager. "Over and over, people kept telling me that what I did at the Mille Collines was heroic, but I never saw it that way, and I still don't. I was providing shelter. I was a hotel manager doing his job. That is the best thing anyone can say about me, and all I ever wanted. And that's really the best I have to give."*

In his book, An Ordinary Man,[1] *Paul recalls, "Words are the most effective weapons of death in man's arsenal. But they can also be powerful tools of life. They may be the only ones. Today, I am convinced that the only thing that saved those 1,268 people in my hotel was words. Not liquor, not money, not the U.N. Just ordinary words directed against the darkness.*

Words are the most powerful tools of all, and especially the words that we pass to those who come after us. I will never forget that favourite saying of my father's: 'Whoever does not talk to his father never knows what his grandfather said.'"

In fact, he credited his father with giving him his core values. He describes his father as "a man who taught me most of what I know about patience, tolerance and bravery." He continues, "Every New Year's Day, my father would give us all a verbal report card on our progress throughout the year, of becoming good men and women. Our father . . . showed us . . . compassion. His aim was never to embarrass us but to encourage us to do the right thing."

Paul Rusesabagina was a Secure Base Leader in every sense of the word. In a time of tragedy and chaos, he was able to calm, influence and inspire those around him through the powerful use of words. His secure base was his father, who not only role modelled the acceptance of responsibility for those in need, but also provided the magical combination of compassionate safety and intense stretch.

Ask yourself:

- Who were my secure bases growing up?
- Who cared about me and also dared me to attempt the impossible?
- Which experiences influenced the leader I am today? What are the "roots of my leadership"?

These questions are so important that in our High Performance Leadership program we spend a significant portion of our time discovering and uncovering those roots. It is a day filled with laughter, tears, reflection, emotion, grief, gratitude, "a-ha" moments and a tremendous amount of learning. Participants pull back the curtain hiding their past and become aware of just how much their leadership is impacted by the people and experiences of their life—positive experiences as well as negative experiences from which they learned. They become more fully aware of what—or more importantly—*who* they need, and who they can become.

In the words of IMD Professor Jack Wood:

> *"Learning about leadership takes practice, involvement and the willingness to question yourself. Work with a sense of freedom, willingness to take initiative, courage to explore, and openness to being surprised by what you might find. Skepticism, reluctance and defensiveness are as natural and spontaneous as courage, openness and risk-taking. As long as you are willing to explore what provokes your behavior, you will further your leadership capacity."*[2]

Self-awareness is in fact a key component of Secure Base Leadership. Through self-awareness you can strengthen your knowledge of your own secure bases, whether they are people from your present or past, goals or objects. You can even learn to become your own secure base.

YOUR CURRENT SECURE BASES

You need secure bases at all stages of your life. In fact, you need *multiple* secure bases in your life. Think of your constellation of secure bases as a foundation. Each secure base, whether a person, goal, object, event, experience, symbol or something else is a building block of your foundation. All these blocks fit together to create a strong base—one from which you interact with the world. Without a rich complement of secure bases, your foundation may be weakened, leaving you with a less stable version of yourself to show the world.

The danger of not having secure bases is that without the solid foundation they provide you become detached and isolated from your emotions. You will then veer toward Playing to Dominate (see

Chapter 6), an unsustainable leadership approach. Relying on secure bases to protect and inspire you is not a sign of weakness; others can stand on your shoulders precisely because you stand on someone else's. Consider that when a belayer is belaying a climber who is physically larger than he or when the climber is tackling a particularly challenging climb, the belayer will anchor himself. In some cases, the belayer will attach himself to the ground via a rope. At other times, one or more other people hold onto the back of the belayer's harness to keep him firmly grounded.

The two most important kinds of secure bases are people and goals. If you have people as secure bases but no secure base goals, you may feel very secure but you may play it too safe and not take the risks necessary to achieve success in life. You may feel a sense of belonging but may not feel as if you accomplish anything. If you have goals as secure bases but no secure base people, you are likely to experience considerable material success but be quite impoverished in terms of love and bonding to people. You may feel deeply lonely.

PEOPLE AS YOUR SECURE BASES

Start by identifying those people in each aspect of your life who give you both a sense of protection and inspire you to explore and grow.[3] Someone who fulfills just one of these roles may be a good friend or a hard-driving colleague but not a secure base. The friend may care deeply about you but not provide the challenge, and the colleague may dare you to take risks for the business but not provide a sense of security. Your secure bases will be those people who supported and encouraged you while you spread your wings and sought to reach your highest potential. They will be the people who uttered the most inspiring messages you ever heard.

Someone from your past who has since died may still be a secure base if her memory provides both the comfort and inspiration for you to go out into the world with confidence and high self-esteem as this anecdote shows:

When Manolo's father died in 1999, he felt a deep grief with his passing. Manolo recalls that his father always told him he could be anything he wanted to be and that his only limitations were within himself. Manolo says his father was his inspiration, "He protected my family and me during 15 years of civil war. A self-made man, he was successful, intelligent and yet remained humble and modest. Politicians and leaders still quote his words today." Even after his death, Manolo's father is still a secure base for him. "When I look in the mirror, sometimes I see his face. He still inspires me."

Once you have identified the people who are the secure bases in your life, consider thanking them if they are still alive for providing you with the support and energy to venture forth and succeed in your life. Doing so can be a powerful experience that strengthens and deepens the relationship.

Remember, a secure base is not perfect—nobody is! Avoid putting your secure bases, or anyone for that matter, on a pedestal as doing so will only lead to disappointment.

Ask yourself:

- Do I have enough people as secure bases?
- How many people in my life do I trust enough to really challenge me?
- Do I have people who are secure bases in both a personal and professional capacity?

GOALS AS SECURE BASES

Reflect on the goals you have set throughout your life. Why did you choose a particular goal? What motivated you to achieve it? How did you go about it? Many of the goals that become secure bases for us can take many years to achieve and also involve moments of failure along the way as well as success:

Jean-Pierre, an executive coach and close colleague of ours, set himself a goal of climbing all the peaks over 4,000m in Switzerland. At times, he has been close to reaching a summit and had to turn back due to changing weather conditions. After 24 years, he has climbed 39 of the 51 peaks and expects to fulfill his goal in 2019.

When a goal is a secure base, it gives you a source of energy and inspiration to pursue challenges in the present and future. Plus, when you reflect back on an achieved goal, you can draw energy from that past accomplishment. Goals provide a sense of safety for you in your daily life because they give a sense of meaning amidst the mundane and routine. They also provide what researcher Daniel Pink described as the "three factors for motivation": a sense of purpose, mastery and autonomy.[4]

Ask yourself:

- Do I have enough goals as secure bases in my life?
- Do I stretch myself enough to achieve or accomplish my goals?
- Do I break down my goals into small steps and enjoy the progress I make?

OTHER TYPES OF SECURE BASES

Table 7.1 shows various types of secure bases. In additon to people and goals, events (such as a wedding or graduation or sporting event), experiences (such as university life, a promotion or a holiday), places, beliefs and symbols can all be secure bases for people. For those who travel or live in different countries, their

TABLE 7.1 EXAMPLES OF SECURE BASES

PEOPLE	PLACES	EVENTS	EXPERIENCES	GOALS	OTHER
Mother	Country	Wedding	Childhood	Achieve a business target	Pets
Father	Home	Funeral	Adolescence	Get a promotion	Beliefs
Sibling	Nature	Sports	Being a student	Become a parent	Religion
Spouse	City	Disaster	Boarding school	Buy a house	Ideology
Teacher	Village	Accident	University life	Gain a qualification	Special objects
Coach	Town	Crisis	Being a parent	Run a marathon	Symbols
Boss	Park	Graduation	Marriage	Change a relationship	Memories
Authority figure	Sea	Birth of child	Having a family	Recover from an illness	Rituals
Peer	Mountains	Engagement	Employment		Prayers
Subordinate	Jungle	Promotion	Career		Work
Friend	Beach				Hobbies
Ancestors	Office				Money
					Music
					Poetry
					Books

motherland can be a secure base. If you have grown up in the mountains, or at the ocean, or in the jungle, or in farmland, your native topography will most likely be a secure base for you. Religion is a secure base for many people in the world. For Azim Khamisa, whose story we told in Chapter 4, his faith certainly was a secure base.

Objects can transform into secure bases. Children have special blankets or stuffed animals, tennis players may have a special racquet and many people have pieces of jewelry that give a sense of protection as well as a confidence that encourages exploration. In many cases, these items were given to people by their secure bases.

An activity that you repeat regularly can also become a secure base. If every day you go for a run or write in a journal or meditate, then any of these processes can give you both a sense of comfort and a feeling of energy and inspiration to face the world, as Sydney's story shows:

Sydney keeps a diary where she can express her thoughts and feelings on a daily basis. This act of reflection has helped her to become more self-aware. Her confidence in her own writing grew to such an extent that she has written and published a book. The very process of writing is a secure base for her.

For some people, a company logo becomes a secure base. In the words of a Johnson & Johnson employee, "When I cut myself, I bleed little J&Js."[5] Sadly, this kind of deep connection to a company is far less common than in the past.

Ask yourself:

- How many companies have I worked for where I identified strongly with the logo, symbol or brand?

CATALOGING AND EXPANDING YOUR SECURE BASES

To become more fully aware of the secure bases in your life, complete the chart in Table 7.2. Remember the definition of a secure base:

a person, place, goal or object that provides a sense of protection, safety and caring *and* offers a source of inspiration and energy for daring, exploration, risk taking and seeking challenge.

You are likely to have multiple secure bases. Be clear about your current portfolio of secure bases—and make sure that you always have both people and goals among your current secure bases. Note that secure bases may flow in and out of your life. Some may be short term and others long term; for example, in college, a professor may have been critical to your success, but you may have since moved on and now a boss takes that role.

During times of transition, like David in the story below, you will naturally lose some secure bases:

David, a successful senior manager who had been sent all over Europe to turn around divisions of a medical device company, left behind his native Paris to take a job running the U.S.

TABLE 7.2 YOUR SECURE BASES

People	Places
Events	Experiences
Beliefs	Goals
Symbols	Other

business unit of a large multinational company. David dived straight into getting to know the business, his colleagues and his direct reports. After six difficult months, he began to lose confidence as the unit's results started to slip. He had not developed close relationships within his new company and very much missed the structure and support of his old company. He also missed his former boss who had hired him straight out of business school and had encouraged him in his career. Overwhelmed with the stress of settling their young family into life in a new country, David's wife wasn't as available to him as she had been in their European assignments. David felt alone and didn't know where to turn for support and encouragement.

David lost the secure bases of his home town, his country, his company, his colleagues, his boss and, at least temporarily, his wife. He needed to develop a new collection of secure bases in order to keep his Mind's Eye focused and have the energy to see the possibilities of his new position. And he needed secure bases in order to become one for his new team. If you've lost your secure bases, take a look at the box for some tips on developing new ones.

Finding New Secure Bases

By identifying your secure bases, you develop a good idea of the traits of people who would be effective secure bases for you. That knowledge can help you find new secure bases in your life, be they friends, colleagues or partners. Remember, you cannot be an effective secure base if you do not have secure bases for yourself.

Here are some tips for developing new secure bases:

- Pick a secure base who furthers your dream. If you want to be a CEO, pick someone who understands what it takes to achieve that dream.
- When you have identified someone you would like to be a secure base, describe your situation and how they may be able to support you. Ask them to challenge you to achieve the goals you have set for yourself.
- Transform a desire into a goal that can be a secure base. If, in a transition, you've lost sight of your dream, we encourage you to devote time to reflection so that you can develop a new one. Dreams, in terms of things we want to achieve in the future, are powerful sources of motivation, joy and hope. You absolutely must have a dream in order to move forward in your life.

ROOTS OF YOUR LEADERSHIP

Your professional role is really just the tip of the iceberg of who you are. Behind every leader, there is a story that influences the decisions he makes today. You as a leader have a life history that carries many hidden gifts. At the same time, your story has crucibles of painful experiences from which you have learned valuable lessons. You are a tapestry of experiences and events and memories. Throughout your life you have learned, observed, experienced, perfected and developed habits that you have then repeated over and over again.

By understanding both the positive and negative aspects of your life and leadership stories or, as we call them, the "roots of your leadership," you become more aware of how secure bases have and will propel your performance. At the same time, learning about and changing ineffective patterns you have developed over time will liberate your leadership. You will then no longer be a hostage to your past.

PATTERNS YOU LEARN

Your current leadership is an extension of your life history. One of the most rewarding parts of working with executives is watching "tough leaders" come to realize that their toughness is rooted in their early life; it is not genetically predetermined. They begin to understand, often for the first time, that their negative pacesetting, hard driving, "take no prisoners" approach has been learned and is most likely directly linked to their early experiences. Until that point, they have been fooled by their own inner voices, convinced that their colleagues are underperforming, that the engineering/marketing/sales department is poor, and that people cannot be trusted—in each case placing blame for their pain outside of themselves. They have become independent loners, repeating patterns that they learned long ago to protect themselves.

Let's explore how these patterns come to be. You have developed mindsets, beliefs, perspectives and knowledge based on your experiences and the people you have encountered. New research in neuroscience has proven that past experiences become hardwired into the brain. Certain events become associated with specific states. An event in the present can trigger a state, like fear, from the past.[6]

For example, if you had a happy and empowered childhood, and you were well taken care of by your mother and father, grandparents or caretakers, you will see a benefit to being in close relationships. If on the other hand, for whatever reason, you did not have a positive childhood and did not get the kind of care and attention you wanted, you might have determined that you cannot rely on others and need to depend only on yourself. You may be an "independent loner."

You may then carry these beliefs about other people into your adult life, at home as a spouse or parent and at work as a leader or follower. These patterns are often represented by the "voice in your head," the voice that tells you that you can or cannot achieve something, that enables or disables you. They translate into a mindset deeply ingrained into your being.

Bowlby called these ingrained patterns "mental models." He emphasized that while there are indeed habits and patterns to our relationships, they are *learned* rather than genetic and ingrained from birth; they are based on life experience. And if something can be learned, then it can be un-learned. You have the power to do something about any pattern, no matter how deeply ingrained it may be. It's not easy but it is possible.

Often people excuse ineffective behavior by saying, "It's just the way I am," or "It's my personality," or "I've always been this way." Those justifications are simply not true. If you give away the responsibility for your action to an unseen, unknown force about which you can do nothing, you are allowing yourself to be a hostage to your past.

Consider this letter sent a few months after its writer participated in one of our programs. During the program he had shared how a teacher from his early school days had repeatedly told him he was not intelligent and would not amount to anything. Those words had led to a whole host of limiting beliefs about his ability, first in terms of overall intelligence and later in terms of his potential in the corporate world. During the program, he recognized how untrue this teacher's statements were and just how much they continued to limit his beliefs about himself. Through working with Duncan, he changed his beliefs about his true potential and ability, and he left the program determined to change some things at work:

Today I was appointed as one of the three members of the board of directors in our company. I write to you just to tell you that this has only happened because I have learned to control the little voice in my head telling me that I'm not good enough (the voice of my junior school teacher). When I was asked to take the position, the little voice again tried to pop up, but I calmed it down and told it that everything was under control and that I was appointed because of what I had already done and my true competence. I am ready and confident to take the position.

YOUR LEADERSHIP LIFELINE

What does all this have to do with secure bases and leadership? It has to do with answering the question "Are great leaders born that way or made?" We agree with research that proves that great leaders are *made*. Leadership is a culmination of life experiences and intentional development efforts. Secure Base Leaders recognize the power of their past and fully understand how the history of their beliefs, habits and relationship patterns impacts their leadership. The past includes both positive, rich experiences and negative experiences from which leaders have learned. Your life story brings your attention to the people, experiences and events that shaped you and it prepares you to make a conscious choice about the secure bases you want in your life going forward.

Secure Base Leaders develop an integrated understanding of how their past impacts the present and then, armed with this knowledge, they develop new habits and patterns that allow them to be successful in a different way. Two tools, the Leadership Lifeline and the Leadership Roots Questionnaire, will help you identify patterns so that you can build on the effective ones and liberate your leadership from those patterns that are holding you hostage. This work heightens your self-awareness and thereby builds a bridge not only to higher leadership performance but also to a great life. It can change your life if you are willing to go deep enough.

Tip: Sharing Your Lifeline

Find another person and work on your Lifelines together. When you share the experience and confide in someone else, you enhance the learning experience. Pick a spouse, a friend, a colleague or a family member.

As you talk through your Lifeline, telling the story of your life and discovering themes, you will gain deeper awareness about your life experience. The questions asked by the other person may prompt insights and "a-ha" moments. Plus, you will learn about the other person and create an opportunity for a deeper bond.

You will not gain the same depth of experience or insight by simply doing this exercise alone.

Plan to spend between 45 minutes and an hour creating your Leadership Lifeline as follows:

1. Take a large piece of paper and copy the template shown in Figure 7.1.

2. Divide the horizontal space into the years of your life and mark those years on this axis. Many people divide the Lifeline into decade-long sections.

3. Select the most important events in your life from your childhood to the present day, including both the positive ones

FIGURE 7.1 YOUR LEADERSHIP LIFELINE

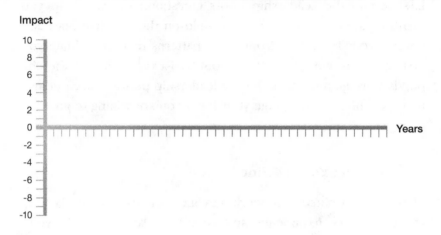

and the negative ones. You may want to write each event on a small sticky note along with the age at which it occurred and then sort these sticky notes according to time and importance. Most people find that a range of 15–20 events or experiences is both manageable and robust enough to identify patterns.

4. Assign a score to each event. Use a number up to +10 for positive experiences or a number as low as −10 for negative experiences. The rating is entirely your own perspective as to how you felt about the event or experience at the time. For example, some people would view being adopted as a +7, while others may view it as a −10.

5. Chart the events on your Lifeline, finding the coordinate between the age and the score. Place a dot and write the name of the event next to it.

6. Connect the dots to create your Leadership Lifeline.

7. Use the questions below as well as the Leadership Roots Questionnaire (see box) to think more deeply about the most

important personal and professional events that have had an impact on your life.

Secure Bases

Think about the most important people who have influenced your life—mother, father, grandparents, teachers and other important authority figures:

- How have they influenced you?
- In what ways are you similar to them?
- In what ways are you different?
- How did they inspire you and what did they say?
- How have they influenced your leadership?
- How have they influenced the way you bond to others?

Loss and Grief

Consider that deaths, relationship break-ups, significant health issues and previous physical, verbal or sexual abuse are all forms of significant loss (the loss of a person, opportunity and innocence, for example). Other events may have less impact but can also be losses: the departure of a favorite boss, a move or the lack of tools to do something you love.

- What losses have you experienced?
- Have you grieved these losses?
- Have you been able to re-attach to new secure bases?
- Who should have been a secure base for you and was not?

Conflict

- How has conflict been a factor in your life?
- Where did you learn about dealing with conflict?
- Who taught you about how to resolve conflict?

- What are some of your experiences with conflict? What beliefs about conflict did you learn from people or events?

8. Next, look at your Lifeline and notice any recurring themes. For example, does your clash with authority figures stem from an issue you had with your father? Does your avoidance of conflict link to your home environment as a child? Does your drive and ambition stem from the way you were rewarded as a child? What motivates you today is likely to be linked to your reaction to experiences in your past.

Here's an example of a pattern that emerged through the Lifeline experience:

Philip had difficulty bonding with people and he always attributed this to the fact that his father had died in an accident when Philip was young; therefore, he had grown up without a father figure. However, by going through his Lifeline and discussing it with others, he came to the realization that he was more affected by the relationship with his mother who, devastated by her husband's sudden death, was unable to cope with the grief and, in depression, sent her son away to boarding school. Through her action, Philip not only lost the secure base of his father, he lost his mother and his home, too. The anger he held inside for so long had manifested itself in a series of failed relationships with women and a tendency to remain aloof or detached in business. When he became aware of this destructive pattern, he was able to free himself from its power and to allow his childhood self to grieve the loss of his secure base and ultimately forgive both his mother and himself for the anger he had carried all those years.
Today, he is able to bond more effectively at work and in his private life.

Notice also what you have *not* included in your Lifeline. These omissions can provide data around some of the patterns that may have been established in your life.

9. To finish the exercise, write down the answers to these questions:

   - What are you most grateful for in your life?

   - What are you most inspired about?

   - What is your dream?

Leadership Roots Questionnaire

We developed this questionnaire to conduct the research reported in this book. Not only will it help you identify important events in your life for inclusion in your Lifeline, it will also help you become aware of the secure bases who helped you grow. That awareness may in turn provide you with support and stretch now and in the future.

Reflect on the questions and then write down your answers. Or, for greater impact, have a close colleague, friend, partner or secure base read the questions to you.

1. Starting with your childhood and youth, who were the people who both built your self-confidence and encouraged you to fulfill your potential?
2. Think of a story about a specific time or moment when the influence of one of these people was particularly significant . . . a moment that still impacts you today.
3. In what other ways have some of these people from your childhood and youth influenced you in your life?
4. Have any of these people influenced your leadership? If so, which people, and in what ways?

(Continued)

5. Turning now to your adulthood, have there been people in your professional life who have built your self-confidence and encouraged you to fulfill your potential?

6. Think of a story about a time or moment when one of these people was particularly influential. What did he or she say or do?

7. In your personal life as an adult, who are the people who have built your self-confidence and encouraged you to fulfill your potential? What is a story about one of these people that helps you better appreciate their influence?

8. Sometimes it is not a person who inspires us to be our best, but a goal, an idea, a dream, an event or a religious figure. Is this the case for you? How has a non-person secure base impacted your leadership?

9. Think about a time when you built another person's self-confidence and encouraged them to fulfill their potential? What did you say and do? How did they respond?

10. Think about a time of failure, loss or crisis in your personal or professional life. Who did you turn to and why? What did they say or do that was helpful at that time?

11. Was there a time in your professional life when you did not feel that you had anyone to turn to for support and encouragement? If so, what was the impact of not having such a person?

EXPECT AN INTENSE EXPERIENCE AND INTENSE RESULTS

Many leaders lead such busy and high-pressured lives that they rarely have the opportunity or take the time to reflect. However, in the words of management guru Peter Drucker, leaders "follow effective action with quiet reflection. From the quiet reflection will come even more effective action." We often find that the experience of doing the Lifeline is a powerful form of reflection because it is often the first time executives have given themselves the opportunity to identify the roots of their leadership. As a result, they realize that there may be some experiences from their past with which they have not come to terms. The process can be emotional and difficult, but ultimately cathartic and liberating.

It takes courage to look into your own past and accept the lessons that emerge. Many people are not willing to face this examination, dismissing it as psychobabble. Often, those people are resisting because they may not be ready to face what is there. Their fear of facing their past is actually so strong it stops them from experiencing the empowerment and release that awaits them after the work of this self-examination. However, in our experience, those courageous enough to look back and really understand how their past experiences influenced their behavior are able to liberate themselves from those patterns. Through daily practice and guidance, they are able to change their habits and, ultimately, their identity.

You may have unusually intense dreams the night after you complete the exercise as you may have awakened some subconscious memories. Call in a secure base if you want some support as you come to terms with patterns from your past that you may want to change.

Perhaps the best way to express why a Lifeline is worth the effort and courage is to consider success stories like this one. Mario is an executive who as a child was physically and verbally abused by his father. He repeated the pattern by becoming a bully at work. By working through his Lifeline, he was able to see the links to his childhood and was able to moderate his behavior.

During the last day at the Advanced High Performance Leadership program (AHPL), I discussed the option for me to see a psychologist. George recommended someone near my home. I went and saw him once a week for the first two or three months. We were able to hit two major points—breakthroughs that helped me to let go of "beliefs" that I was carrying with me for so long. I still remember how my AHPL coach Duncan said, "Nothing is wrong with you; there are just a couple of beliefs that you have to let go," and he was right. I started with the goal of becoming calm and secure. Well, that became one of the breakthroughs: what I was looking for was to become free—free from what I have carried with me for so long, the belief of being guilty for what happened or did not happen to me in my past. The amount of my inner hassle and nervousness was huge and created all kinds of stress, fear, aggression, etc. You can imagine how this breakthrough helped me to become an outstanding leader in my organization and a better father and husband. Another AHPL statement became clear and valid for me as well: "True happiness comes from giving up all hope to have had a better past." All those statements are easy to say and to repeat. More importantly, I am grateful for the work I did with the faculty and coaches as well as with my psychologist—only this work enabled me to understand the meaning of these words and how they related to me. I see the psychologist once or twice a month and we chat about all kinds of things. I enjoy these moments of reflection, his company and his advice.

Many leaders are fortunate and have not had such extreme experiences in their early childhoods. Even in those cases the Lifeline is beneficial in helping leaders better understand the influences on their life and their leadership.

BEING YOUR OWN SECURE BASE

If you have had a network of secure bases throughout your life, you may be able to internalize those experiences and ultimately become your own secure base. This does not mean you do not still need external secure bases. Indeed, if you do not have other secure bases, it is impossible to be a secure base for yourself. If you do not trust other people enough to be a secure base for you, then you are fooling yourself if you think that you are your own secure base. It is not about being isolated and doing things totally on your own; it is more about interdependence, knowing that you are not alone and drawing on the strength of others as well as your strength within.

A powerful history of secure bases, particularly in relation to people and goals, can build your own confidence and self-esteem to such a level that you have a deep internal resource from which you can draw support to deal with whatever life throws at you, as this story shows:

In 2008, 61-year old Alex Lenkei from Worthing, U.K. underwent surgery on his hand without the use of a general anesthetic. Alex sedated himself by using self-hypnosis. His orthopedic surgeon, David Lewewllyn-Clark, agreed to the procedure which involved removing some bone in the base of Alex's thumb and fusing some joints to improve his arthritis. Alex is a registered hypnotist who has been practicing since he was 16. "It took between 30 seconds to a minute for me to place myself under hypnosis, and from that point I felt a very deep relaxation. I was aware of everything around me, from people talking and at one stage a hammer and chisel was used as well as a surgical saw, but I felt no pain."[7]

Alex's belief in himself, his hypnotic skills and his ability to be his own secure base in the moment enabled him to undergo this surgery. He was not derailed by doubt, but rather he kept himself calm and focused on the goal. The surgeon's full support meant that he was also a secure base for Alex in the process.

Being your own secure base is a liberating experience and ensures that you are not hostage to your own or anyone else's fears.

How do you know if you are your own secure base? It is likely if you focus on the positive, remain calm in the face of adversity, and avoid judging other people. You are your own secure base if you have managed to tame the inner critic—that internal voice that makes you shrink from others and from yourself—and you have a sense of self that can withstand the stress and pressures of daily life. Take legendary free climber Catherine Destivelle as an example:

Catherine Destivelle spends her life scaling mountains and rock faces all over the world without ropes or other external safety devices. One slip in her concentration could lead to a long and deadly fall. In an interview, she said, "I don't think about the danger. I just concentrate on what I'm doing. If I do it, it's only because I am sure of myself." She defines the five most important ingredients for her success as:

- *A clear definition of success*
- *Being resilient enough to endure a great deal of pain and discomfort*
- *Disciplined preparation*
- *Developing the right support network*
- *Passion*

Although she climbs alone now without a partner on belay, she started out like most rock climbers. Catherine's father enjoyed climbing and was passionate about the outdoors. From a very early age, he took Catherine, his eldest child, to the Fontainebleau forest close to Paris where her passion for the outdoors grew. By 13, she had begun rock climbing.

Catherine's story shows how hours of practice, the right practice and the right model or coach can enable someone to become an expert who is no longer a hostage to fear. Having long-term secure bases in the form of people and goals allows her to become her own secure base when she is free climbing. Her strong support network, experience, self-confidence and goals replace a physical belay system or person.

If you had strong secure bases as a child or if you have strong secure bases at home, you may be able to be your own secure base in a new professional situation, for instance. The resilience and confidence you learned from your secure bases combined with secure base goals will provide you with a sense of comfort and the inspiration to grow into the new opportunity.

Key Learnings

- Self-awareness is a key component of Secure Base Leadership.
- You need multiple secure bases, including people and goals.
- Your current leadership is an extension of your life history.
- Your experiences will have created a set of habits and patterns.
- Secure bases can help you learn new habits or patterns.
- By understanding the roots of your leadership, you will no longer be a hostage to your past.
- Knowing and developing your secure bases can help you ultimately become a secure base for yourself.

&

"No man is an island, entire unto itself, every man is a piece of the continent, a part of the main . . ."

-John Donne
1572-1631
English Poet

&

FREQUENTLY ASKED QUESTIONS

Q: Why do I have to delve into my personal life at work?
A: Your work life is an extension of your full life. The two cannot be separated. You have one brain, one body, one belief system,

one life history and one set of important and influential life relationships. You cannot improve your self-awareness as a leader if you do not improve your self-awareness in totality. Since the roots of your leadership reside in your personal life, that is where you go to improve your current leadership.

Q: Should I see a therapist or counselor?

A: Not every leader needs to see a counselor. That said, if you know there are parts of your life story that are still unresolved and through reading this book you have come to realize that you are still hostage to some past event or person, then we strongly encourage you to seek professional support. Seeking support is a sign of real strength and commitment to excellence—not a sign of weakness. We know many high performing CEOs and executives who get some form of professional support that is absolutely essential to their ongoing professional success. You would be in very good company should you choose this route.

CHAPTER EIGHT

BECOME A SECURE BASE FOR OTHERS

Claude Heiniger was an instructor at a flight school located in Lausanne Blécherette, Switzerland. On January 29, 2001, he was on a flight with a trainee who had 1,300 hours of flight experience. As the plane took off, a locking pin from the right hand side landing gear fell from the aircraft, crippling the mechanism. Now airborne, Claude came to the conclusion that they would have to land the plane without properly functioning landing gear.

Claude's first instinct was to take over the controls. But then he had another idea. He asked the trainee questions to determine how he felt and to assess whether he was ready to fly the plane and land it in this emergency situation. The trainee agreed to take the controls, giving Claude the opportunity to concentrate on the big picture in a supervisory role. As Claude recounts, "The student actually did the whole flight. But I was right behind him in terms of providing input. We also divided up the work between the two of us in an efficient way. Geneva International Airport's main runway was actually closed for a couple of hours. We completed the flight lesson, exiting the concrete runway onto the grass with one collapsed landing gear. We walked away with very little damage to the aircraft."

Claude recalls, "It was not easy to let go of control. Later I discovered that this is very much an industry standard. When there are problems, the commander should not be the one having his head right in the situation. He should be able to step back and delegate as much as he can in order to keep an overview." He added, "The student needs to grow and I need to decrease. So it is actually a transfer of power, a transfer of know-how and a transfer of attitudes."

Can you imagine how easy it would have been in that moment, way up in the air, for Claude to take control of the plane? Claude's story describes the concept of Secure Base Leadership perfectly. On the one hand, Claude provided support and reassurance to his student and, on the other hand, he offered an opportunity for risk taking and learning—both for the student and for Claude himself. As he said, it was not easy to let go of control. This is what Secure Base Leaders do. They provide protection, safety and comfort *and* also encourage exploration and risk taking, even when that means changing their own mindset.

Note also that Claude's first reaction was to take control. He had to *consciously* tap into his role as a Secure Base Leader. Claude had learned the habit of being a secure base from his father, a missionary stationed in Laos, where Claude and his siblings were raised. Claude's father would encourage him to be involved in significant projects; he sent Claude off driving a jeep through the jungle when the boy was just 14. The memory of how his father trusted him and challenged him stayed with Claude and positively impacted his leadership. As an instructor, he would need to learn to control his state and be fully present for his students. You can imagine that an amygdala hijack (see Chapter 2) could happen in this stressful situation. You might even say that it would hijack any flight lesson.

You, too, can learn the "being" and "doing" associated with Secure Base Leadership, and this chapter provides additional guidance on how to pursue that learning. It begins with a self-assessment based on the nine Secure Base Leadership characteristics explored in Chapters 2 through 6. This assessment forms the basis for setting your development priorities. Then, we introduce you to three additional development opportunities that will help you connect better with others: developing a Secure Attachment Style, understanding the "signals" you are sending and receiving, and improving your capacity for dialogue. Each is fundamental not only to Secure Base Leadership but also to the way you interact with everyone at work and at home.

SET YOUR DEVELOPMENT PRIORITIES

No matter how much of a secure base you have been to date, you can always improve your skills and increase your effectiveness in creating your own personal form of caring and daring. Not every Secure Base Leader combines the "being" and "doing" in exactly the same way, and no individual leader embodies all nine of the Secure Base Leader characteristics.

Look back at your Secure Base Leadership behavior assessments from Chapters 2 through 6. Then, use the Characteristics Wheel in Figure 8.1 to assess your own areas of strength and areas for improvement. Gauge how often your actions display each characteristic by marking the corresponding point on the "spoke." Connect the dots to see the "shape" of your Secure Base Leadership and decide where you want to focus.[1]

Once you determine which characteristics you want to set as development priorities, go to the designated chapter (see Table 8.1) for specific guidance and tips.

Ask yourself:

- Which characteristics do I do well?
- Which characteristics could I improve upon?
- Which characteristics do I want to develop?
- Which improvement area would benefit me most as a leader?
- How would my team members rate me on the nine characteristics?

FIGURE 8.1 SECURE BASE LEADERSHIP SELF-ASSESSMENT

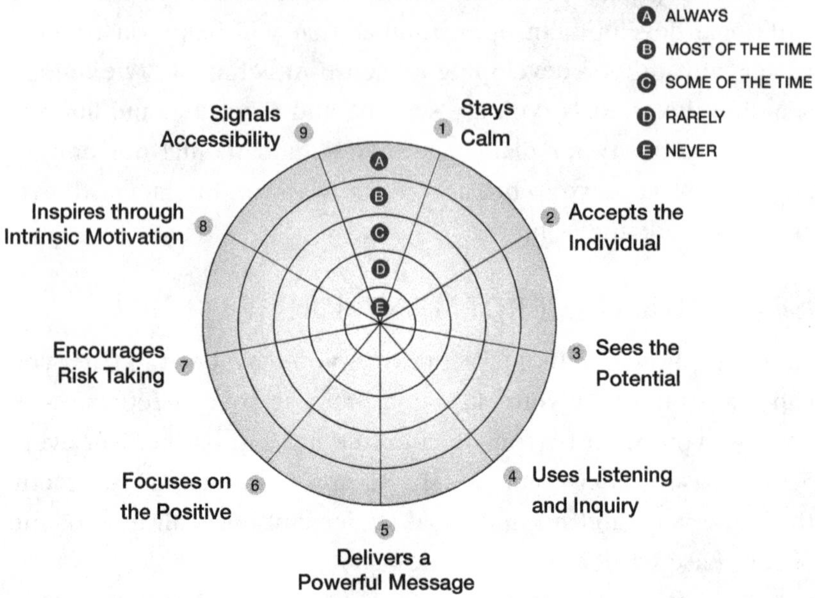

Becoming a Secure Base Leader is not a one-size-fits-all checklist certification process. It is a journey that you take over time. Sure, you can learn some techniques immediately, just as a belayer can learn the technical process of belaying in a matter of minutes. But to be really good, you have to belay repeatedly to develop the muscle memory. In other words, you have to develop new *patterns*. Your brain is infinitely capable of rewiring itself. All it takes is correct practice on a regular basis and the support of a mentor, coach or secure base to help you.

MYTH: Leadership is natural.

Not true. Leadership is a set of behaviors you learn, starting as a child and continuing throughout your life. You can break old patterns and build new ones.

TABLE 8.1 CHAPTER LOCATION OF CHARACTERISTICS

CHARACTERISTIC	CHAPTER WITH DEVELOPMENT TIPS
#1: Stays Calm	2
#2: Accepts the Individual	3
#3: Sees the Potential	3
#4: Uses Listening and Inquiry	4
#5: Delivers a Powerful Message	4
#6: Focuses on the Positive	5
#7: Encourages Risk Taking	5
#8: Inspires through Intrinsic Motivation	6
#9: Signals Accessibility	6

DEVELOP A SECURE ATTACHMENT STYLE

Part of the deep work of becoming a Secure Base Leader involves becoming aware of, and in some cases changing, very deeply ingrained patterns in the ways you interact with others. Some of these patterns are reflected in your "attachment style"—the way you connect to people and thereby bring the characteristics of Secure Base Leadership to life. Therefore, your journey to become an improved secure base for others at work and at home should include an understanding of your attachment styles.

You begin to gain this understanding by becoming aware of your natural attachment style and noticing how the way you connect with others tends to change when you are under pressure. Ultimately, your goal is to lead with a Secure Attachment Style most of the time and know how to return to that style if you slip out of it.

Research has shown that the attachment styles developed in early childhood often continue into adult life.[2] Kim Bartholomew, a leading researcher in this field, demonstrated that the models people hold in their minds about relationships have two dimensions: a "self" dimension and an "other" dimension. Each of these can have a positive or a negative pole. The "self" dimension relates to the thoughts and beliefs we have about ourselves (I am competent, I will succeed, I can do this) while the "other dimension" relates to our thoughts and beliefs about other people (Other people can be trusted, Other people will help me, Other people can be relied upon). Your attachment style in a given situation is the intersection between how you feel about yourself and how you feel about others.[3]

Adapted from Bartholomew's work, Figure 8.2 demonstrates how attachment theory works in the practice of Secure Base

FIGURE 8.2 ATTACHMENT STYLE QUADRANTS

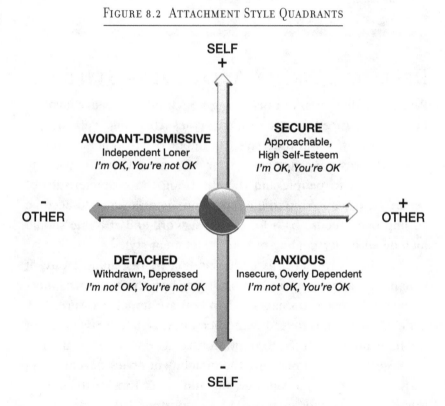

SELF
+

AVOIDANT-DISMISSIVE
Independent Loner
I'm OK, You're not OK

SECURE
Approachable,
High Self-Esteem
I'm OK, You're OK

-
OTHER

+
OTHER

DETACHED
Withdrawn, Depressed
I'm not OK, You're not OK

ANXIOUS
Insecure, Overly Dependent
I'm not OK, You're OK

-
SELF

Adapted from Bartholomew (1991) and Berne (1961)

Leadership. We have integrated Eric Berne's Transactional Analysis concepts into a model you can use to assess yourself and come to understand how and when you move across styles. Your shifts will depend on the external situation and your own internal patterns.

In the sections below, we describe the feelings, thoughts and behaviors common to each of the four attachment styles. As you read the descriptions and think of yourself within these quadrants, ask yourself:

What was the predominant style of the people around me during my childhood?

You are likely to repeat the predominant attachment styles of your mother and father. But remember, as with any pattern you have developed over time, you can learn to change your style if it is not serving you well. Without self-reflection and conscious work, your past will be driving your leadership style.

During times of great pressure and stress, which style do I tend to adopt?

Notice under which conditions you exhibit each of these styles and, very importantly, notice your habitual movement when under pressure. You may have a tendency to be in the Secure Attachment Style the majority of the time but find yourself slipping into one of the other styles when under stress. That's why in each attachment style description below we describe the feelings and behaviors of a leader on a good day and on a bad day.

Do I sometimes behave in ways consistent with styles other than my predominant style?

When you read these lists of feelings, thoughts and behaviors, keep in mind that we all exhibit elements of each style some of the time. Even a person with a Secure Attachment Style will have moments during which he exhibits a behavior associated with a different style.

1. THE SECURE STYLE: PLAYING TO WIN

As a leader, on a **good day**, are you:

- Focused on task, action and getting the job done?
- Focused on the people you work with—caring and daring, supporting and stretching them?
- Motivated to deliver results with and through the team?

As a leader, on a **bad day**, are you:

- Fully aware of what worked and what didn't work?
- Feeling frustrated or tired and allowing yourself the space for those feelings?
- Remaining aware that your attitude is a choice and turning to one of your secure bases for support?

If you answered "yes" to all or most of these questions, it is likely you have a Secure Attachment Style.

Linked to **Playing to Win**, the Secure Attachment Style is about providing support, comfort, security and confidence while also enabling risk taking, exploration, creativity and learning. You can imagine that Claude, the flight instructor introduced in the opening story of this chapter, must have connected with a Secure Attachment Style in order to keep his cool and turn the controls over to his student.

When you are operating in this quadrant, you:

- Are comfortable dealing with conflict
- Are willing to show vulnerability to others and are not afraid to ask for help when you need it
- Are not overly defensive and do not take things too personally
- Are open to changing your view when presented with arguments that make sense
- Tend to listen and reflect upon what others say
- Set yourself tough challenges but do not have unreasonable expectations of yourself or others

- Can remain calm in a crisis
- Are likely to have good communication skill and feel comfortable sharing information about yourself with others
- Have a growth mindset, remain curious and open minded, and are eager to learn
- Possess a healthy degree of self-confidence, high self-esteem and a strong sense of self-worth

If you recognize yourself in this description but want to hone your ability to remain here even under stress so that you can be a consistent secure base to others, consider these ways to develop:

- Continue to become more self-aware
- Work on emotional regulation and a Playing to Win mindset
- Allow yourself to be a role model for others and develop those around you
- Use your own secure bases as sounding boards and models

2. The Avoidant-Dismissive Style: Playing to Dominate

As a leader, on a **good day**, are you:

- Very focused on task, action and getting the job done?
- Motivated, self-reliant, autonomous?
- Able to deliver results?

As a leader, on a **bad day**, are you:

- Adopting a "Do as I do" pacesetting style?
- Exhibiting coercive, manipulative behavior?
- Withdrawing from others under pressure?

If you answered "yes" to all or most of these questions, you may be an "independent loner" with an Avoidant-Dismissive Attachment Style.

Don't worry. You are in very good company. Many people at the top of organizations get by for quite some time with this style, which you'll recognize as **Playing to Dominate**. It is about control.

If you had a childhood predominantly in this quadrant, you have a positive "self" model but a negative "other" model. As a leader, you:

- May well believe that it is better to do things by yourself than trust others
- May focus your Mind's Eye on others' faults while recognizing few of your own
- Will be seen as rational and matter of fact, and may be called a "cold fish"
- Are likely to judge the world around you, to divide things into black and white, right and wrong, good and bad
- Want to maintain your detachment and keep a distance in relationships
- May have only one or two very close friendships and those are likely to be based on a deep sense of loyalty and protection
- Follow a "My Way or the Highway" approach
- See yourself as self-reliant and totally independent in looking after yourself
- Are unlikely to display even appropriate emotion in front of others and avoid showing vulnerability in front of someone else
- Can be cynical and overly guarded in disclosing information about yourself

Moreover, you are unlikely to have secure bases in your life because you feel unable to trust others.

If you recognize aspects of yourself in this description, you may want to consider these development tips:

- Recognize that old patterns from your past are interfering with your leadership.
- Since you have developed a negative mindset about "others," deliberately shift your focus toward seeing the positive in other people. Work on letting go of your need to control by practicing delegation. Accept that others will undertake

projects differently than you and that their way can be "good enough."

- Balance your need to "get the job done" with increased emotional availability. Practice bonding by walking *toward* others. Ask people about their lives, their work and their dreams.
- Identify a mentor, coach or secure base with whom you can work.
- Follow the daily mantra of "practice bonding, practice bonding, practice bonding."

3. THE ANXIOUS STYLE: PLAYING NOT TO LOSE

As a leader, on a **good day**, are you:

- Using a consultative, democratic or affiliative leadership style? (See Chapter 6).
- Caring about others and taking enough time for them?
- Seeking out alternative views and options?

As a leader, on a **bad day**, are you:

- Overly anxious about your performance?
- Needing reassurance beyond normal feedback?
- Plagued by self-doubt and struggling to make decisions?

If you answered "yes" to all or most of these questions, you may be **Playing Not to Lose** with an Anxious Attachment Style.

You may focus on avoiding risk or loss and staying safe while remaining connected to other people.

If you had a childhood predominantly filled with anxiety, you may have a negative "self" model but a positive "other" model. As a leader, you:

- Put too much emphasis on relationships and tend to be overly sensitive to what others say and do

- Take criticism very personally
- Seek external validation and are highly dependent upon others for reassurance
- May become exhausted and prone to burnout because relationships with other people are too demanding
- Have low self-confidence and rely on other people to advise or support you
- Feel emotionally overwhelmed fairly frequently
- Rescue others too much and overly protect people from normal consequences
- Care more about the business and the people than others do
- Irritate other people and even drive them away because of your anxiety and insecurity
- Fail to separate the person from the problem. This trait may show up when you feel you are pushing others too far or giving them bad news, fearing that they won't like you anymore.

If you recognize aspects of yourself in this description, you may want to consider these development tips:

- Recognize that your leadership is influenced by your past relationships, particularly your childhood. Be aware that you have outgrown the subservient child position.
- When you find yourself turning to several others for input, you need to go back to your own decision-making and judgment. Listen to and respect your inner voice as much as you listen to others' opinions.
- Observe yourself and become aware of being needy, anxious or too demanding of others for support.
- Learn to trust yourself and your own judgment. Find a secure base to support you.
- Follow the daily mantra of "make a decision and take action, make a decision and take action, make a decision and take action."

4. THE DETACHED STYLE: PLAYING TO AVOID

As a leader, on a **good day**, are you:

- Taking time to reflect?
- Wanting to achieve a goal, even if you fear the outcome?
- Deeply desiring acceptance?

As a leader, on a **bad day**, are you:

- Freezing under pressure?
- Abdicating your authority?
- Blaming others?

If you answered "yes" to all or most of these questions, you may be **Playing to Avoid** with a Detached Attachment Style.

You experience conflicting emotions that may be a result of a stressful external situation over which you feel you have no control. Feeling like a hostage, you withdraw emotionally in order to protect yourself.

If you had a childhood predominantly in this quadrant, you may have a negative "self" model *and* a negative "other" model. As a leader, you:

- Feel you have no control over your life
- Want intimacy but, at the same time, avoid it for fear of rejection
- Worry that other people don't like you or are not interested in you and, therefore, you avoid contact with them
- Fear both success and failure. If you succeed, what will you lose and, have to leave behind? If you try and fail, how can you face other people who will then view you as a loser?
- Avoid having secure bases in your life because you fear the disclosure needed to create a deep enough bond. At the same time, you long for that kind of intimacy.

- Find it difficult to trust other people and are suspicious of their motives
- Experience feelings of jealousy and separation anxiety
- Avoid conflict and commitment. If you don't connect and commit, you can't be rejected and fail
- Tend to be overly shy in social settings and anxious about "getting it right"
- Have low self-confidence and low self-esteem. The fears you experience may become paralyzing to such an extent that you find yourself taking an observer role in life: you watch from the sidelines rather than participating actively. You may become a spectator at the show of your own life.

If you recognize aspects of yourself in this description, you may want to consider these development tips:

- Recognize that your leadership is heavily influenced by your past and potentially affected by pain from earlier relationships. Explore the impact of those relationships.
- Recognize that under pressure you lose self-confidence *and* withdraw from others—a losing combination. Work on staying present by focusing on the "now" rather than running from it. Distinguish fear associated with the past from the reality of the current situation.
- Focus on the problem, not on yourself or the other person.
- Allow others to care for you, support you and stretch you in your development.
- Practice the daily mantra of "build the bond and take action, build the bond and take action, build the bond and take action."

By better understanding your own attachment style and what it means to be in each quadrant, you can be more aware of your own tendencies. You can then focus on solidifying those tendencies that reinforce your Secure Attachment Style and minimizing those that steer you to other styles. You do this by changing your habitual reaction patterns and rewiring your brain. At the same time, remember that you are human and allow yourself a bad day here and there!

Learn about Your Signals and Read the Signals of Others

Connecting with others also involves picking up on the "signals" they are sending about themselves, their emotions and their needs. Signals are the verbal and non-verbal messages that confirm or deny the truth of a person's communications. They can send a quick and unambiguous message of truthfulness or dishonesty. At the most basic level, signals indicate whether a person is moving toward, moving against or moving away from someone else.[4] Signals can also communicate motivation—what someone is thinking and feeling.

Sometimes signals are as obvious as a hand indicating stop or go. However, most signals are far more subtle. Sometimes signals are conscious (applause that signals congratulations), and sometimes signals are unconscious (an eye twitch that signals "I'm nervous"). You—and everyone else—send signals unconsciously all of the time. In fact, it is impossible for you not to communicate signals in the presence of another person.

As discussed in Chapter 5, some of the signals you send communicate your state. That's why remaining calm is a fundamental part of being a Secure Base Leader. You generally cannot hide your anxiety because it is difficult to hold back signals sent through your unconscious behavior. However, in learning to take control of your emotions, you can "act" being calm and calm becomes your state. The old model of "fake it till you make it" does apply to a certain extent.

The big problem occurs when you are not aware of the signals you are sending. When you are aware, you can exert control over the signals. When you are calm, others' mirror neuron systems (see

Chapter 3) pick up on that calmness. If you are anxious, highly agitated or panicked, you may automatically incite those same states in the people around you.[5] That's why Claude had to control his state in order to keep his student calm and focused during their crisis.

The good news is that the people you are interacting with send signals as well. When you become a kind of "profiler" who is able to read conscious and unconscious signals accurately, you become able to determine another person's state and motivation. You then receive powerful clues that allow you to show caring and know exactly how much to dare someone to explore and seek challenge.

FOUR TYPES OF SIGNALS

Figure 8.3 captures the four main sources of human signals that are part of "transactions"—the verbal or non-verbal exchanges between people:

- Body
- Emotions
- Mind
- Spirit

The figure also demonstrates how the signals interact within an individual and within a system of two or more people. These four kinds of signals blend with the words people use to deliver and interpret a message—to talk with each other, to engage in a dialogue (see the "Improve Your Capacity for Deep Dialogue" section later in this chapter) and even to negotiate.[6] The other person interprets those words and the signals, sends signals of reaction, which you interpret, and so on.

B = Body

Signals are manifested to the outside world through the body. "Body language" includes gestures, posture, facial expressions and

FIGURE 8.3 TRANSACTIONS AND SIGNALS

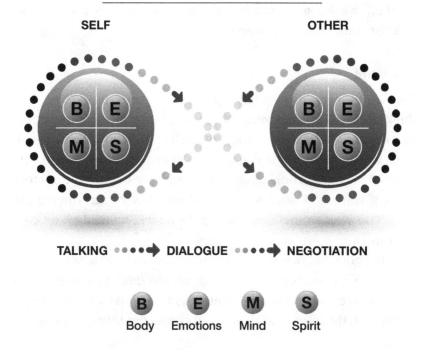

tone of voice. These can be conscious or unconscious, positive (a smile) or negative (a frown). The face alone has 27 muscles that contract or relax in response to emotions or intention. Body language can be obvious, as in the case of crossed arms or legs or a yawn, or it can be more subtle as in the case of a change in pupil size or the slightest hand movement.

E = Emotions

According to respected psychologist Paul Ekman, examples of basic emotions are anger, fear, joy, sadness, disgust and surprise[7]. These emotions activate the body, which in turn sends out signals. Whether you are happy or sad, your energy displays your emotional state and reflects what you are feeling. We are, after all, feeling as well as thinking beings. Rarely do we feel neutral about a situation.

We may act neutrally but, invariably, inside we feel one way or another. We *transmit* our emotions—what we feel about somebody or something—through our signals.

M = Mind

You send signals about what is going on in your mind. What you think becomes a signal, often (but not always) through the words that you use. For instance, you may think you want to leave a room. Your words say, "I want to go now." Your body leans toward the door. This combination sends a consistent message. On the other hand, if you say "I want to stay" and your body leans toward the door, you send an incongruent signal that will be read either consciously or unconsciously by others.

Thoughts and beliefs are closely connected. What you believe about the other person affects the signals you send. Your signals will reveal where you are focusing your attention with your Mind's Eye. In the end, the intention of the mind comes out through the body.

S = Spirit

"Spirit" indicates the intention that is behind all other signals: your purpose, your motivation—why you are taking action—and your end goal. Signals from the spirit convey a sense of judgment. Was an act intentional or unintentional? If the side effect is seen as good, people tend to attribute positive intentions to the act. If the side effect is deemed bad, then people tend to attribute negative intentions to it. It is your job to determine whether a person has positive intentions or negative intentions. Her underlying motivation may be expressed through her body language.

Sometimes people try to control their body language or words in an effort to send a different message than the one that they have inside. Studies show that in cases where a message is inconsistent and based on emotions, the words only count for 7%, the tone for 38% and the body language for 55% of the message that is received.[8] Without realizing it, we are all body language experts and are tuning in or tuning out the signals that we pick up from those around us.

Moreover, the mirror neuron system links us to intention, not just action.[9] Leaders who ask "Does anyone have any questions?" with their arms and legs crossed are actually sending a very different signal ("I'm not really open to your input") than their actual words. They should not then be surprised when nobody asks a question!

BECOME A PROFILER

With practice, you will be able to read signals in order to understand another person's goals and motivation. You will then have powerful information as to how best to respond to those signals.

Observe for Intention

Signals will let you know if people mean what they say. Your job is to add up the clues to see if the words are consistent with other signals or if there is incongruence. Consider especially the energy around the words. Eyes will often communicate motivation, and that is why someone who is lying resists looking you in the eye. If someone looks you directly in the eye and says, "I'll finish that task before noon," you can understand that her full intention is to do just that. On the other hand, if she does not look you in the eye, then you may want to follow up with other questions to confirm her commitment.

Listen for Covert Meaning

People will often communicate their motivation through their choice of words. Compare these sets of questions:

Have you seen the report I dropped off?

vs

Shall I assume you didn't read the report I dropped off?

Why were you late for the meeting?

vs

Why are you always late for my meetings?

In both cases, the second question communicates a motivation of blame. The words people use are often signals of how they truly feel. In some cases, they may reveal people's innermost concerns or fears.

Observe for Emotions

People are driven primarily through emotion. Conscious and subconscious body language displays people's feelings and therefore their likely motivation. See Table 8.2 for signals of common emotions.

TABLE 8.2 SIGNALS OF EMOTIONS

EMOTION	SIGNALS
Joy	Smiling, enthusiastic gestures, shining eyes, expressions of gratitude
Surprise	Dropped jaw, opened mouth, raised eyebrows, wide-opened eyes, astonished voice
Fear	Contracted body state, hands in protective position, shaking, flinching, wide-opened eyes, energized in a non-goal directed way, paleness in face and extremities
Anger	Excessive sarcasm, irritability, agitation, reddened face, clenched jaw or fist, puffed-up chest, tense muscles
Sadness	Crying, pouting mouth, downward gaze, drooping eyelids, brows drawn together, contracted body state
Disappointment	Reddened face, lack of enthusiasm, contracted body state, passive and/or passive-aggressive behavior

Secure Base Leaders need to be skilled at picking up the signals of negative emotions as well as positive ones. When you sense anger, sadness or disappointment, consider what kind of frustration or loss the person may be facing. You can then express your interest, concern and caring in order to bond more deeply. The person may then feel able to vent negative feelings in a safe environment. After that emotional release, you will be more able to redirect the person's Mind's Eye toward the positive.

IMPROVE YOUR CAPACITY FOR DEEP DIALOGUE

An extension of sensing, interpreting and reacting to signals, the ability to dialogue is a connection skill that can be developed relatively easily and delivers powerful results. Essential to both bonding and directing the Mind's Eye of others, dialogue allows people to influence each other as they work toward a deeper understanding of each other and the task at hand. A true dialogue reflects a feeling of togetherness—a sense of unity because you speak and you are understood and you listen and you understand. Deep dialogue is about seeking a greater truth by thinking and talking *together*; in that way, it drives connection. In deep dialogue, no one person owns the "truth."

Deep dialogue involves a powerful combination of listening, inquiry and talking. It is about shared exploration and is a way of thinking and reflecting. To have a deep dialogue, you have to suspend judgment and open yourself up to the process of discovery.

When your words do not have the impact you desire, in one way or another, you are blocking the impact of what you intended. For some reason, others misread what you mean to say. For instance, if you try to express your trust in someone's potential to undertake a challenge and you are perceived as crossing a line of intimacy or pushing him too far too soon, you may be missing deep dialogue skills. More precisely, you may be using one or more "blocks to dialogue."

KEY BLOCKS TO DIALOGUE

Every day, we all use blocks to dialogue without being fully conscious of what we are doing. Our responses can become habitual and can derail the opportunity for a powerful and effective dialogue. There are four primary blocks to effective and deep dialogue: discounting, passivity, redefining and overdetailing.

Discounting

When you minimize, maximize, disrespect, or put down another person in some way, you are discounting. The phrase "Yes, but" usually discounts what was said before. Phrases like "You don't get it" or "You couldn't possibly understand" and "I can't" or "I could never" are also discounts that will block an effective dialogue. Many habitual responses involve unconscious or partially unconscious discounts. The opposite of discounting is giving full recognition to self, other people or the situation.

Ask yourself:

- When and how do I use discounts?
- In what ways do others around me block dialogue through discounts?

Ban "Yes, but!"

"Yes, but" is another way of saying, "My idea is better than your idea and I may not even have my idea yet." That's why "Yes, but . . ." is a subtle sign of discounting and disrespect.

To promote dramatic improvement in dialogue in your teams or at meetings, ban the words, "Yes, but . . ." Instead, encourage people to say either:

"No, I disagree. Here's why . . ."

or

"Yes, I see your point and I think . . ."

Removing "Yes, but" from dialogues will lead to quicker and more effective communication and results.

Passivity

When you or another person refuse to engage in a dialogue, preferring to withdraw or be non-responsive, passivity occurs. Often the outgrowth of some type of fear response, the focus is on protecting oneself rather than on engaging with another. If you find yourself resisting dialogues, ask yourself "What am I afraid of?" If you have passive people in your team, create a safe environment, a space where they feel comfortable contributing, that will encourage them to speak and have their voices heard. The opposite of passivity is asserting and expressing your opinion and your thoughts.

Ask yourself:

- When and how am I passive in dialogues?
- In what ways do people around me demonstrate passivity in dialogues?

Redefining

When you change the focus of a discussion or dialogue to maintain control or to avoid something that may be uncomfortable for you, you have redefined. Or, you may use redefining to avoid engaging with the other person. Expressing your opinion can feel risky. When you redefine, you "defend" yourself and thereby maintain your own view of yourself without threat from an external source. When asked a direct question like "What do you think of the quality of your work?", if you answer "The team is happy with my work," you have redefined. Sure, you answered, but you answered a different question—one that allows you to avoid giving your opinion of your own work. Redefining is a subtle block and is one people often use without realizing it. The opposite of redefining is responding directly to a question and expressing what you feel, think or believe.

Ask yourself:

- Do I answer questions directly? (Did you answer this one directly with a "yes" or "no?")
- How often do you redefine questions?
- Do I know people who avoid answering questions directly?

Overdetailing

When you give too many details instead of using direct, clear and simple speech, you have engaged in overdetailing. You can fall into overdetailing when you are in a tense or awkward situation. The tendency to talk too much robs space from the other person and restricts her ability to insert what she wants to say. The point of the discussion is lost amidst all the details. To promote deep dialogue, practice using the **four-sentence rule**: say what you have to say in four sentences or less. Then, ask a question to engage the other person. This approach ensures that your dialogue remains direct and engaged. The opposite of overdetailing is to say what you have to say in a concise, clear and caring way.

Ask yourself:

- Do I talk too much? (Did I feel compelled to reply to this question with more than a simple "yes" or "no?")
- Do all the details I give really add value?
- Do I know others who talk too much? How does this habit affect others?

We encourage you to practice recognizing how you inadvertently use these blocks to dialogue and then to become aware of how they derail deep dialogue in your team or family. Weeding them out will improve the quality of your dialogue so that you can develop the emotional connection essential for bonding.

Practical Skills for Developing Deep Dialogue

Just as you would plan a written report or formal presentation, you can plan for deep dialogue by thinking of these questions in advance and as the dialogue progresses:

- What is my **state**?
- What is the **outcome** I want to achieve?
- What **choices** can I give?
- What **concessions** can I make?
- *And perhaps most importantly:* What **questions** will I ask?

These questions take you through the "SOCCQ" model of dialogue skills: State, Outcome, Choice, Concession Making and Questions. This model is particularly useful for role plays (see box).

Role Playing

When you are facing a difficult dialogue, increase your chances of success by doing a role play to prepare yourself. Remember how an expert becomes an expert through hours of deliberate practice? Your brain responds to rehearsal (practice) and the actual event in the same way. Practice will lead to a better outcome if you practice correctly.

In addition to preparing what you want to say (and how you want to avoid using blocks to dialogue), rehearse playing the other person's role. When you put yourself in the place of the other person and into the emotional state of the other person you increase your empathy and better understand his position.

State

The first skill is to be aware of your state. How do you feel? Are you feeling anxious or aggressive? Or are you feeling calm and grounded? Remember, you will send signals of your authentic state and your intent. Those signals can stimulate a similar response in the other person. If you are anxious about a dialogue, it is likely that the other person will sense that feeling in you and become anxious or defensive. The key to any successful dialogue is to get yourself into as calm and grounded a state as possible before you start. Then, keep checking in with your state. If you find yourself becoming frustrated, afraid or angry, pause and take a few deep breaths or stand up and move around in order to change your state. There is nothing wrong with silence. It will serve you better than acting out an unproductive state.

Outcome

The next skill is about becoming clear on your ideal outcome *before* you begin the dialogue or continue through a longer dialogue. If you know what you want to achieve, then you are better able to manage the conversation toward this result. If you have no idea of the outcome you are seeking, then you can easily become a hostage during the conversation. However, it is also important to remain flexible when actually in dialogue, in case some new information comes forward. At that point, you may wish to adapt your desired outcome.

Choice

When in conversation, wherever possible, give other people choice. Do not *tell* them what they need to do; you will create compliance but not commitment. They will do what you ask only because they have to. By giving choice, you create commitment because the people *choose* to do what you are asking within the boundaries that you define. Here is a simple (and all-too familiar) example from dealing with children. In the morning you tell your child to get dressed, she says "No," you say, "Get dressed now!," she says "No!" The intensity escalates and the volume increases but the result is the same: frustration on both sides and a child in pajamas. Instead, ask your child, "Do you want to get dressed before or after breakfast?" "Do you want to wear the red shirt or the blue shirt?" "Do you want to get dressed by yourself, or do you want me to help you?"

It is the same with adults. People tend to choose from the options they are given. In most cases, they do not like being told what to do. Giving choice, even in difficult situations, is a powerful tool. Remember the story of Sam from Chapter 1. George asked Sam if he wanted to be handcuffed in the front or the back. Either way, he ended up handcuffed. By giving choice, you create respect and engagement.

Concession Making

The next skill, and possibly one of the most difficult, is concession making through the use of words. When you make a concession, you invoke the universal law of reciprocity: you give something and you get something in return. However, in the middle of a dialogue, you have to really listen and stay calm in order to recognize the subtlety of a concession from the other person. Then, you need to "reward" that concession. For example, if you give tough feedback and the other person acknowledges it, thank them for that recognition before moving onto the next point. Words like "thank you" or "I appreciate that" are concessions that can defuse a tense atmosphere. If you make the first verbal concession, it is more likely that the other person will follow suit and give you a concession. This technique not only improves your concession-making skills, it also improves your ability to listen actively—both vital skills for deep dialogue.

Questions

The fifth skill, and the most powerful of all, is asking the right question at the right time. Remember how Claude began guiding his flight student by asking questions. Questions can be open- or closed-ended. A dialogue should be an exchange between two people with the goal of seeking a greater truth. In order to keep the exchange a dialogue as opposed to a monologue, your most powerful tool is the open-ended question. State what you want to say in clear yet respectful terms. Then, ask a question. For example:

"I am concerned that the production quality slipped this week. Our raw material cost has gone up and output has gone down. *What is your view of what happened?*"

Or at home:

"I understood that we agreed that you could play computer games after you had finished your homework, taken the dog for a walk, and made your bed. *How did you understand our agreement?*"

After every transaction, ask a question. This method keeps both parties in a dialogue and, in a difficult situation, it reduces tension and emotion. After asking a question, remember to pause and wait for a response. Do not fill the silence with more words; instead, wait patiently for the other person to reply.

Never underestimate the power of deep dialogue. By practicing these skills and by avoiding the basic blocks to dialogue, you can ensure that you model secure base behaviors and characteristics.

Remember, when you try something new such as asking more open-ended questions, you are likely to feel a little awkward, if not uncomfortable, at first. However, the more you practice, the easier and more natural the new behavior becomes. You will learn the nuances of when it is most important to ask questions or when to bring forward one Secure Base Leadership characteristic over another. Even the technically-proficient belayer takes years to really learn the nuances about how much slack to give, when to give verbal coaching, and exactly what to say to the climber. You will know what to do by reading signals to understand others' intent and needs.

By assessing where you stand on the nine characteristics, working on your attachment style, becoming better attuned to the signals you and others send, and developing the skills for deep dialogue, you can learn new ways to connect more deeply with others and thereby make significant progress on your Secure Base Leadership journey.

What are you waiting for? Start today.

Key Learnings

- Being clear about where you stand on the nine characteristics can help you determine where you need to focus to improve in your role as a Secure Base Leader.
- Being aware of your attachment style under normal circumstances and your attachment style under pressure can help you become a Secure Base Leader.
- Regardless of your early attachment style, you can rewire your brain and practice using more of the Secure Attachment Style.
- Be a Profiler. Notice both the signals you are sending and the signals you are receiving from others. Learning to read those will enable you to be a more effective leader.
- Signals involve the body, the emotions, the mind and the spirit.
- Eliminating the blocks to dialogue between yourself and others will improve your effectiveness at work and at home.
- Practice the use of choice, making concessions and asking targeted questions in order to improve your conversations.

&

"Before you are a leader, success is all about growing yourself. When you become a leader, success is all about growing others."

–Jack Welch

1935–

Former Chairman and CEO, General Electric

&

Frequently Asked Questions

Q: For how many people can I truly be a great Secure Base Leader? Is it better to do a really good job with two or three people, or to try to change my approach with everyone?

A: It is perfectly natural to have varying levels of relationships with your colleagues and direct reports. At minimum, though, you should be on the positive side of neutral with everyone who reports to you. You cannot afford to have a broken bond with anyone in your team. Remember that being a secure base is not hard work. It requires some deliberate practice, but the benefits make it a rewarding process.

Q: What do I do when someone is sending me negative signals and not wanting me to bond with him?

A: This situation happens from time to time, and you will need confidence and resilience at your end. Stay focused on some common ground and don't get taken hostage by their signals. You can be sure that the situation will deteriorate if you join them with negative signals. Do your best to maintain the bond and stay focused on your goal. If you think about it, there really is no downside to bonding. The worst thing that could happen is that people may not reciprocate or respond immediately.

Q: What should I do when a colleague has a challenge in his personal life? Should I talk to him about it?

A: We believe that with a caring attitude it is absolutely acceptable to acknowledge something that is going on in a colleague's personal life. It is appropriate to ask if he or she needs any support from you. Then, read his or her signals to judge whether to go further with the conversation. Let him or her dictate the depth of the conversation.

CHAPTER NINE

TRANSFORM YOUR ORGANIZATION INTO A SECURE BASE

Hendrik du Toit, CEO of Investec Asset Management, knew that while his firm had been extremely successful throughout its first 15 years, it needed to develop further in order to achieve enduring success on the global stage. The firm placed huge importance on consistent, strong investment performance results for its clients. While it was undeniably successful, the leadership group realized that it was not developing talent broadly enough. It was struggling to retain young talent who found the environment excessively challenging and not sufficiently supportive. Leaders were proud to describe Investec Asset Management as a "lion's den." In the language of Secure Base Leadership, the firm "Played to Dominate." It achieved strong results, sometimes at the expense of relationships and emotional bonds. While this approach worked to deliver short-term results, Hendrik knew that in the long term, there needed to be a stronger talent pipeline.

When brought in as a consultant to address this issue, Duncan introduced the idea of "results and relationships"[1] to value both dimensions of Secure Base Leadership explicitly. To take the notion of Secure Base Leadership deep into the organization, Hendrik invested in a comprehensive leadership training program that reached every single team leader in the organization. Hendrik says, "Funnily enough I used to be very skeptical of these types of initiatives—especially leadership training. I much preferred the idea that the best people would naturally find a way to the top and would excel because of their determination and results. But I came to realize that we were never going to reach our true potential as a global organization if we didn't take a more systematic approach to the development of our people." The sessions introduced the concept of Secure Base Leadership and emphasized the importance of understanding loss, separation and grief as well as developing good dialogue skills. Duncan used their lion's den metaphor to remind them that even lions look after their cubs. In this way, the firm maintained its cherished "performance" approach and metaphor, and it also added a relational bonding aspect.

After the training, Investec Asset Management incorporated relationship building and maintenance into their annual performance process. Employees who did not do well with relationships were given clear feedback and told what was expected of them in the future. The company built in financial rewards as well. Through these and other steps the firm has developed a stronger culture—one that values relationships in more explicit ways—and systems that provide the necessary development and support structures for a more successful approach to talent development.

The idea of being a secure base started from the very top with Hendrik, who embodied Secure Base Leadership. He manages to combine the elements of support and challenge in extraordinary ways. He is demanding, relentless, seldom satisfied and always stretching his people. He also brings humanity to his leadership; he consistently exhibits concern for the well-being of all staff. He is an example of a care to dare leader.

There is now a palpable sense of family and concern alongside the real sense of performance and achievement. While the culture still pushes people to strive to do better, people also feel supported. Engagement is at an all-time high.

In 2011, Investec Asset Management celebrated 20 years of success in the highly competitive global asset management industry. The company was named European Asset Manager of the year and Hendrik was recognized as the investment industry's European CEO of the Year.[2]

At Investec Asset Management, a program that began as a talent development program ended up strengthening the very culture of the organization. We would go as far as to say that the company itself became a secure base, not only for its employees, but also for its clients.

What do we mean by an organization becoming a secure base? Remember that in addition to people other entities can also be secure bases when they provide a sense of protection and a feeling of comfort as well as offer a source of energy and inspiration to explore, take risks and seek challenge. When a company like Investec Asset Management provides that combination of safety and stretch, it becomes a secure base to any employee or external stakeholder who feels those benefits.

Your ultimate success as a Secure Base Leader comes when you influence not only a handful of individuals but also the very culture of your organization. When all the "puzzle pieces" of your organization—the vision, mission, values and strategy as well as the structural elements like policies, procedures and human resource systems—come together in the spirit of providing both security and stretch, the organization becomes a secure base. And, of course, Secure Base Leaders are like puzzle makers who put all of the pieces in the right place.

Transforming your organization into a secure base will eventually lead to a change in its culture. Your experience has probably taught you that managing organizational change is no easy task. As evidence that change is hard and fails more often than it succeeds, researchers often point to the fact that up to 90% of merger and acquisition deals do not achieve their objectives.[3]

What if you started the transformation process by applying Secure Base Leadership concepts to the change process? Specifically, this requires you to:

- Remember that any change involves loss. People need to grieve that loss. Build time and energy into your plan so that you can incorporate the steps in Chapter 4.
- Focus on the learning you can achieve along the way, not just on the end goal. Any failure is an opportunity to learn. Understanding failure allows you to adapt and influence the future.
- Work with what you can change rather than worrying about those pieces you can't change. If you're not "the big boss," just start by working within your sphere of influence.
- Strive for excellence not for perfection. When working on your must-win battles, as recommended by authors Peter Killing and Tom Malnight,[4] make establishing Secure Base Leadership one of them. Set your goal to make the organization a secure base as much of the time as possible.
- Break the big challenge down into small steps. Approach change systematically and make changes on a daily basis to maximize your chances of success.

The starting point we recommend is inspired by Systems Thinking expert Peter Senge, whose landmark work on "learning organizations" (see box) reinforces the role of the organization as a secure base: "In essence, every organization is a product of how its members think and interact."[5]

Essentially, if you want to transform the organization into a secure base, you need to work on people's mindsets. You will be most successful in that pursuit by concentrating your efforts in these areas:

- Inspiring Secure Base Leadership at every level
- Incorporating Secure Base Leadership concepts into human resource processes
- Clarifying goals, vision, missions and other "desired-achievement statements"

The Learning Organization

Harvard Business Review rated Peter Senge's 1990 book, *The Fifth Discipline*, as one of the most important management books of all time. In it, Senge popularized the notion of the "learning organization." Our research suggests that Secure Base Leadership is a strong foundation for organizational learning.

Senge describes learning organizations as places where "people continually expand their capacity to create the results they truly desire, where new and expansive patterns of thinking are nurtured, where collective aspiration is set free, and where people are continually learning to see the whole together."[6]

Within that definition, there are five "disciplines" in Senge's learning organization:

1. **Systems thinking:** a concern for the whole and the interrelationships between the parts of the whole
2. **Personal mastery:** a deep commitment to a lifelong journey of personal learning and development
3. **Mental models:** a commitment to reflect upon individual and organizational beliefs and mindsets

(Continued)

4. **Building shared vision:** envisioning and sharing common images of a possible future
5. **Team learning:** learning together which has exponential benefits to individuals and organizations

Senge's focus implies the strong ability to take a risk. Taking risks is about daring and the foundation necessary for daring is caring.

Finally, embedded in Senge's notion of the learning organization is an emphasis on the importance of dialogue. He argues that good dialogue unlocks the learning and potential of individuals and teams, and it generates the possibility for discovering creative, meaningful and relevant solutions to challenges.

These five disciplines and the emphasis on dialogue clearly resonate with Secure Base Leadership and its nine characteristics. When you focus on the learning, self-awareness, personal growth, bonding, Mind's Eye and deep dialogue inherent in Secure Base Leadership, you will also be investing in building a learning organization that will engage and inspire your people to achieve great results.

INSPIRING LEADERSHIP

It will come as no surprise that you will begin the transformation process by encouraging as many leaders as possible to integrate secure base concepts into their approaches and attitudes. If the only leader you can influence is you, then you start there with the work we proposed in Chapters 7 and 8.

According to IMD Professor Ginka Toegel, the success of an organizational change program is directly related to the level and breadth of senior leadership involvement. The three of us co-authors have been involved in numerous leadership development initiatives over the years, both through IMD Business School and on our own. Our experience mirrors Professor Toegel's findings. We have learned that the most powerful organizational transformations occur when the most senior leaders have been personally involved in the transformation journey and, in particular, when the leadership team undertakes that journey together. "Taking part" doesn't mean showing up for the kick-off and debrief. It means that the leaders are directly involved in the training, share their own stories and challenges, and make themselves vulnerable and open to personal change. They approach the journey with the idea that they too will change as individuals rather than seeing the process as a leadership program for "the others." We see higher levels of traction and commitment to the initiative from the other leaders when the top leader gets personally involved in the process in this way. Others are then more willing to participate themselves and take the initiative into their teams.

On an IMD leadership program for Neste Oil, CEO Matti Lievonen insisted that he take part in the full program. He wanted to go through it in the same way as all the other managers. While not without its challenges, this commitment demonstrated that Matti was serious about the changes needed and that he would not ask his people to do something that he would not do himself. Matti powerfully modeled leadership for the managers and inspired considerable respect in the process.

Leaders play an enormous modeling role. Leaders' actions transmit messages throughout their sphere of influence. You may have noticed how people model the behaviors and even the language of their leaders. The more leaders you can get to be secure bases, the more people will be inspired to be secure bases and the more likely the broader organization will become a secure base.

ENROLLING OTHER LEADERS

Executive education program participants inspired by secure base concepts often instantly want to enroll others in their organizations. In the same spirit, you may be eager to pass this book on to your colleagues.

A leader who attended one of our High Performance Leadership programs had tremendous success in taking this material into his organization by introducing it to his Board:

The Board of SNV, the Dutch development agency, arranged a series of sessions around the world for teams to explore the concepts of Secure Base Leadership.

During this process, participants completed all of the reflection exercises described in this book including the Lifeline. There is no doubt that doing this work together benefitted the individuals in terms of increasing their own self-awareness and also building the strength of their teams. After hearing each other's Lifelines, participants had a far greater sense of appreciation and understanding for their teammates as people. The process allowed them to have much more direct and challenging work conversations that in turn led to a deeper sense of trust and compassion.

The SNV case demonstrates what is possible and how beneficial it can be when leaders get to know more about the human beings they work alongside. Note that this process involved a facilitator and enough time to prepare and debrief fully. If you choose to take this idea forward in your organization, be sure to manage the process professionally and devote adequate time to it.

Ask yourself:

• How can I enroll colleagues to become Secure Base Leaders?
• How well do I know my close work colleagues?

Introducing Secure Base Leadership to Your Colleagues

Executives sometimes ask us if it is appropriate to take this material back into their organizations and teams. They are concerned that asking about their colleagues' personal lives and leadership histories would be a breach of privacy. They are concerned that the work required to become a Secure Base Leader is perhaps too personal and emotional for the workplace.

These concerns would certainly be valid if the work was done in a way that left people feeling exposed or vulnerable or if the information shared was used against people.

Make sure you don't cross a line by following these guidelines:

- Include yourself in the process and do all of the exercises with the group.
- Use a facilitator so that you can be a participant rather than the group's teacher.
- Plan sufficient time to develop trust, build understanding, do the work and then fully debrief and close.
- Develop a contract of shared confidentiality within the group.
- Remind everyone of the reason and purpose for doing this exercise. Direct their Mind's Eye to the benefit and positive outcome.
- Always give people a choice as to what they want to disclose. Never force people to share.

LEADING WHEN IT IS NOT POSSIBLE TO ENROLL OTHERS

What do you do if it is not possible to get sufficient participation from senior leadership? Concentrate instead on transforming your teams or sphere of influence. Set your goal to make just one slice of your organization a secure base.

If you give up because you feel you do not have the position or access to drive organizational transformation, ask yourself if you are simply making an excuse not to take responsibility for what you can change. Remember that you can break down any big challenge into smaller pieces.

INCORPORATE SECURE BASE LEADERSHIP INTO HUMAN RESOURCE PROCESSES

The second area to investigate in your organizational change process is your organization's human resource processes. You can integrate the core ideas of Secure Base Leadership into every human resource process. It is important to see Secure Base Leadership as a set of behaviors that can be identified, taught, learned, encouraged, assessed and rewarded. If your formal organizational processes encourage behaviors that are not consistent with Secure Base Leadership, you will not succeed in transforming your organization.

JOB DESCRIPTIONS AND RECRUITMENT

Can you find a way to incorporate elements of both caring and daring into a person's job description? For example, instead of only focusing on the "hard" elements of a job description, can you explicitly include the nine characteristics of Secure Base Leadership or at least the ones that most resonate with your organization?

Think also about interview questions that give a candidate an opportunity to talk about his experience of being a Secure Base Leader. Questions like these let candidates for even the most junior positions tell you about how they balance relationships and results:

- Can you tell me about a time when you encouraged a person to do something she thought impossible?

- How do you keep a team engaged while also pushing for a result?
- What techniques do you use to learn and remember people's names?
- How much time each day (or each week) would you spend talking informally with colleagues?

Also remember to ask questions about their secure bases:

- Who has been the most inspiring person in your life?
- Can you tell me about a teacher or coach who really challenged you to go above and beyond what you thought possible?
- When did you achieve more than you thought possible? Who or what supported you in that quest?

Remember that when you interview candidates you are representing the culture of your organization. If you only speak about process and results, you send the signal that people don't matter. Conversely, after the candidate has settled in to the interview, if you do not challenge her with some tough questions, you will not demonstrate that your organization has high expectations.

COMPETENCY MODELS

Competency models have become increasingly popular in organizations because they provide a standardized way to assess employees against a benchmark of performance. They provide clarity on the *elements* of high performance. While we did not develop the characteristics of Secure Base Leadership as a competency model, they provide a very powerful framework to develop the specific competencies you expect in your organization. If your organization already uses competencies, compare them to the nine characteristics. See if there are any obvious gaps or inconsistencies in your existing approach.

Individual Objectives

As with job descriptions, we are amazed at how individual objectives often ignore the caring aspect of leadership. Often the objectives are very clear on the numbers and targets but unclear on the relational aspects of performance. Sometimes we see vague objective statements like "improve communication with key stakeholders." You will better integrate Secure Base Leadership when you write objectives that are more clearly focused on both caring and daring. See Table 9.1 for some examples.

Performance Reviews

Job descriptions, competencies and objectives come together in a robust review of performance. If you do not review the elements of Secure Base Leadership during an annual performance review, you will miss a critical aspect of the "reinforcement loop." In other words, you will not have a way to indicate formally that someone has achieved the objective, fulfilled the job description or demonstrated the competency. When you acknowledge that someone has done what was asked, he is more likely to continue and even improve his behavior.

Secure Base Leaders who set forth challenges hold people accountable for achieving or at least attempting to achieve them. When you do not hold someone accountable, you send the subtle signal that you do not care or that you do not really think he is up to the challenge. Performance reviews are a perfect way to hold people accountable in a systematic way which demonstrates that the organization itself is serious about the objectives and goals it sets.

We are surprised at how often the formal review process is left out of important organizational change initiatives. Companies spend huge amounts of money and time on a change initiative and then revert to the previous year's measures of success in the actual performance review. We cannot overstate the importance

TABLE 9.1 CARING AND DARING OBJECTIVES FOR INDIVIDUALS

CARING OBJECTIVES	DARING OBJECTIVES
Consistently seek to understand the underlying reasons for team members' behavior	Seek to understand the hopes and ambitions of team members
Seek to understand the intrinsic motivations of team members	Seek out concrete opportunities for team members to take on challenges that fulfill their ambitions
Provide concrete support and assurance when team members face challenging times, professionally or personally	Consistently challenge team members to elevate their performance beyond expectations
Ensure team members have the necessary training and skill development to complete their tasks	Consistently focus team members on their underlying strengths and potentialities
Provide encouragement and coaching to team members when they have a task that is new and challenging	Provide challenging and direct feedback on performance of team members
Demonstrate an ability to move on from a negative situation and give team members a true opportunity to start afresh	Allow team members to find their own solutions to problems, even if this approach causes some anxiety and stress
Consistently demonstrate awareness and appreciation for the human dimensions of change	Demonstrate ability to say "no" confidently to team members when appropriate; be able to explain reasons behind that decision
Provide communication and feedback loops with team members to ensure clarity and responsiveness	Demonstrate willingness to delegate important tasks to team members

of analyzing your performance review process to see if it supports or negates aspects of Secure Base Leadership.

While intrinsic motivation is at the heart of high performance, remuneration matters are also very important to people. Whether used as carrot or stick, the incentive structure does indeed make a difference. Secure Base Leaders can be evaluated on expectations linked to the remuneration equation. Organizations like Investec Asset Management have found a way to measure Secure Base Leadership performance through a formal and fair process.

TALENT DEVELOPMENT

Because talent development systems allow you to set expectations and invest in teaching people how to meet them, these processes are wonderful places to integrate Secure Base Leadership concepts.

MYTH: Talent development is for high potentials only.

Not true. When you see the potential in individuals and tell them you believe in them, they are more likely to reach higher and achieve greater success.

Talent development revolves around seeing the potential in individuals to improve their skills and behaviors. It means the development of every individual's talents and considering what he needs to learn as well as what he likes to do. A Secure Base Leader believes that all employees have "high potential." Based on the research we presented in Chapter 2, she understands that all human beings have much more potential than anyone realizes. There are people in your organization—including perhaps yourself—who are only skimming the surface of what is really possible for them to learn to do.

Translating the Nine Characteristics into Objectives

To go even further with integrating Secure Base Leadership into your organization, consider encouraging behavior change by setting development objectives like these that are based specifically on the nine characteristics:

Characteristic	Sample Objective
Stays Calm	Consistently react in a calm manner when under pressure and use effective stress management with self and others.
Accepts the Individual	Demonstrate appreciation for the fundamental value of team members as people, even when short-term performance does not meet expectations.
Sees the Potential	Consistently consider how team members could develop and grow into new roles and responsibilities.
Uses Listening and Inquiry	Ask questions of others more than tell people what to do.
Delivers a Powerful Message	Deliver concise and deliberate communication with team members.
Focuses on the Positive	Focus on opportunities, possibilities and benefits, even in challenging moments.
Encourages Risk Taking	Provide team members with concrete opportunities to take on new challenges beyond their existing responsibilities.
Inspires through Intrinsic Motivation	Motivate others based on the desire to learn, develop, grow and fulfill potential.
Signals Accessibility	Demonstrate accessibility to team members through being responsive, approachable and available in their times of need.

Stretch people by including no more than two of these objectives at a time and remember to give support in addition to the challenge. Provide the development tips in Chapters 2 through 6 along with the objectives so that people have a place to start their individual work.

People do not achieve the pinnacle of their performance alone. High performers have supportive relationships, whether with a coach, a teacher, a mentor, a friend, a boss or another type of person. If your organization develops everyone, it will reap the benefits of a critical mass of people achieving their highest potential.

As you look at how your organization views talent, consider the words of organizational development professor Herb Shepard: "We are born as a life-loving bundle of energy with a marvelous array of potentialities."

Your opportunity is to seek out the "marvelous array of potentialities," the unique "genius" of the people in your organization.

Could You Swim Across the Atlantic Ocean?

We often ask executives in our programs "Could you swim across the Atlantic Ocean?" We are impressed if even one person raises his hand. We then share the story of Ben Lecomte who swam across the Atlantic Ocean to honor his deceased father, to raise money for cancer research and to propose to his girlfriend. He swam 5,980 km in 74 days. You can look up the full story online or read it in *Hostage at the Table*.

After telling the story of Ben's amazing achievement, we ask the question again, this time clarifying, "We're not asking whether you *want* to swim across the Atlantic Ocean, we are only asking if you *could*." This time, many hands go up.

You expand your influence by working to change the way your organization views talent. If the basic assumption in your organization is that people are limited and have reached their ceiling, you and other leaders will give up on them. You—and by extension, your organization—will not be demonstrating Secure Base Leadership.

Instead, when your organization supports you and other leaders to step up and be a coach—a Secure Base Leader—who brings out the potential in others, you and other leaders will:

- **Accept the human being.** People are able to express themselves fully when they feel welcome, accepted and valued rather than judged and evaluated only in a negative way.
- **See the potential.** Often an individual is not able to see his potential and the contribution he could make. As a Secure Base Leader, your job is to be constantly seeking to explore the untapped potential of your people. When enough leaders take this approach, your organization unleashes the combined astonishing potential of its workforce.
- **Provide the opportunity for risk taking.** Your organization needs ways to give people the chance to get in their 10,000 hours of practice (see Chapter 2). They need to be given leadership responsibilities, projects and stretch assignments that allow them to realize their potential.

Does this approach mean that your company should not have high potential programs? No, of course not. There will indeed be differences in the way you choose to develop people and the amount of resources you invest in each person. The important point is that your organization can only become a secure base if the shared underlying assumption is that everyone has astonishing potential. Employees then are expected to show and develop their talent and put some "skin in the game." Talent development is a reciprocal process where both employee and employer are expected to contribute and invest for mutual benefit. The company is expected to invest in its employees and the employees are also expected to take responsibility for their own development.

Ask yourself:

- What is my organization's current approach to talent development?
- Does my organization view people as fundamentally limited or limitless in potential?
- Is talent development for a small group of high potentials or is it for everyone?
- What does my organization expect in return for talent development?

Talent Development on a National Level

This story is a great example of an organization that showed humanity, generosity and spirit in its approach to collective talent development:

Led by its Managing Director Tan Sri Azman, Khazanah Nasional Berhad is the investment holding arm of the Government of Malaysia. This stand-alone organization worked with the Malaysian government on a large leadership and talent development project that has been a great example of organization-wide Secure Base Leadership. Rather than fight each other for talent, 20 different government-linked organizations have come together to develop the total pool of talent. In the words of Tan Sri Azman, the idea is to "create an archipelago of talent rather than islands of talent."

It was, of course, no easy task to persuade the various sub-organizations to participate in this joint initiative and effectively share their talent with other organizations. The CEOs had to work together to create a basis for trust and shared rules about how it would work. They had to commit to sharing their best and brightest talent with each other.

(Continued)

A common goal they could agree upon was that of developing the talent of Malaysia. As explained by Mohamad Kamal Haji Nawawi, who at the time was Senior Vice President of Strategic Human Capital Management at Khazanah, "It was a way of building talent in the country of Malaysia and speaking to that vision. Twenty CEOs sitting together was a watershed in terms of developing talent for our own organizations. We can't afford to be selfish about talent anymore. If we develop a big enough talent pool, it doesn't matter if we lose individuals because we have an enriched talent pool for the nation. We need a large pool to develop talent for the country."

They also agreed that the best way to develop talent was through experiential learning and that the movement of individuals would be a way to provide such opportunities. As Tan Sri said, "Most learning comes from experiential learning —being given stretch assignments, being thrown in at the deep end and being outside your comfort zone. With a secure base, more learning occurs. This experience can be extremely transformational."

YOUR SPHERE OF INFLUENCE

If you are working in a large multinational organization with a centralized HR system, these processes may be well outside of your influence. We do not recommend you take on your global HR system! Rather, work within your existing system and apply the concepts of Secure Base Leadership to your team's people, practices and culture. For instance:

- Include all or some of the nine characteristics in job descriptions you write.

- Set objectives for individuals that encourage development of one or more of the characteristics.
- Include Secure Base Leadership behaviors in the feedback you give or in coaching conversations.
- Propose performance-based incentives within your budget to reward Secure Base Leadership behaviors.

CLARITY OF GOALS, VISION AND MISSION

In order to transform your organization into a secure base you need to address a third area: its goals, vision and mission. People need to bond to other people *and* to goals. The goals, vision and mission of an organization can infuse a deep sense of caring and daring into all employees and even other stakeholders.[7]

ORGANIZATIONAL STATEMENTS AND THEIR SECURE BASE ROLE

People can bond with short-term annual goals, with longer-term visions or with the mission of the organization. Because the definitions of these often-used terms vary, let's group them together as "desired-achievement statements." No matter what label is given to a statement about what an organization is trying to achieve, if it is focused on Playing to Win (high caring plus high daring), the organization is signaling its intent to be a secure base to employees.

In most cases, desired-achievement statements focus on the results aspects of goals:

- "10:10:10—10% growth by 2010 in 10 regions"
- "5005"—50% growth by 2005
- "To be number one in all chosen categories"

While these statements create clarity about the desired results, they do not explicitly incorporate the caring aspect of Secure Base

Leadership. The best desired-achievement statements will incorporate caring *and* daring. Take for example this story about the vision Tetra Pak developed in 2002:

Susan was part of the team that worked on Tetra Pak's new vision in 2002, one that is still in place today. The previous vision was more like a statement about the industry in which the company operated: "To become and remain the leading liquid food processing and packaging company." Driven by a request from within the organization to have a vision that better represented the spirit and passion of the company, CEO Nick Shreiber assembled a small project team to create a new vision. In an intense, collaborative process, the team engaged hundreds of people from across the company in defining the components of the vision. The result was a new vision statement which everyone in the company could identify with, remember and stand proudly behind, a vision that has also stood the test of time: "We commit to making food safe and available, everywhere."[8]

Note that by incorporating the word "we" the vision includes all 20,000+ employees in a way that taps into individual potential and expresses a caring spirit toward a very daring challenge.

Mission statements tend to incorporate the caring aspect more than shorter-term goal statements because missions tend to focus on longer timelines and a wider group of stakeholders. For example:

Patagonia, a clothing manufacturer:
Build the best product, cause no unnecessary harm, use business to inspire and implement solutions to the environmental crisis.

Fairmount Minerals:
We, the Fairmount Minerals family, are united in our commitment to exceed all expectations while fulfilling our economic, social and environmental responsibilities.

Whole Foods Grocery Stores:

Whole Foods. Whole People. Whole Planet.

Starbucks:

To inspire and nurture the human spirit—one person, one cup and one neighborhood at a time.

ENROLLING YOUR PEOPLE IN YOUR DESIRED-ACHIEVEMENT STATEMENTS

Most companies will have some version of these lofty statements. Even companies embroiled in engagement-destroying scandals have these kinds of statements. Having a vision or mission statement alone is not enough to make your organization a secure base. The statement needs to be authentic and resonate with the employees as a part of their daily lives. How do you achieve such deep integration?

Hands-down the most important step is the direct and personal involvement of senior leadership. If leaders in the organizations pay only lip-service to any kind of desired-achievement statement, the statement will be ignored. However, if leaders reference the concepts in daily interaction and actively use them as a source of guidance in decision making, the statements become truly useful.

Bringing others along with the statements is an ongoing process. A single presentation, email, town hall meeting or corporate video is not sufficient. Integration deep enough to make the organization itself a secure base requires repetition, patience and persistence. In fact, one senior executive recounts that this need for repetition was perhaps his biggest learning upon becoming the CEO of a large multinational:

"I was struck daily by the requirement to repeat the key messages. Even when I thought the messages were conveyed, I learned time after time that it could almost never be repeated enough—especially the important messages about our vision, mission and values."

Remember to incorporate into your HR processes the spirit and desired actions that flow from your broad statements. This step will ensure higher levels of visibility and accountability and demonstrate that you are serious about what you have said you want to achieve.

Celebrating Achievements

Just as a Secure Base Leader congratulates someone for achieving a personal or stretch goal, your organization should celebrate its achievements. Especially in the case of visions and missions, which are extremely long-term and aspirational, take the time to celebrate small successes along the way instead of waiting for the end. If upon achieving a goal your leadership team members simply declare the next stretch target, they will be operating as pacesetters who are Playing to Dominate.

Visions and missions become more powerful and compelling when people believe that they are possible, even if they are not at all easy. By highlighting success and achievement along the way, your leadership team will be reminding people of that sense of possibility. This affirmation creates a positive, self-reinforcing cycle of "I see the goal, I achieve the goal, I see the next goal," and it encourages people to see the organization itself as an active secure base.

The Results

Sonu and Eva Shivdasani have created one of the most prestigious hotel groups in the world, Six Senses Resorts and Spas. With locations primarily in the Maldives and South East Asia, Six Senses is consistently recognized by publications such as Condé Nast Traveler *as running some of the most desirable hotels in the world. Duncan has worked with the global senior leadership team and also with team leaders at hotel locations.*

What is most striking about Six Senses is the strong sense of loyalty among the staff. There is no doubt that Sonu and Eva are secure bases as individuals. As is often the case with founder-led businesses, their personalities and style are very much reflected in the culture of the organization which they work hard to develop.

Deeply loved by the staff, Sonu and Eva are seen as caring and supportive but also as unrelenting in their commitment to their mission and service delivery. They empower people. For example, all staff members have a personal budget for "recovery." When an inevitable mistake is made, the person serving the guest is able to make the situation better immediately by providing a free drink or some other compensation. This system demonstrates trust and empowerment of the front line staff. At the same time, it serves as a useful control function that indicates where there may be a systemic problem in service delivery. Through this program the staff members have to assume greater accountability for ensuring a fantastic guest experience even when things go wrong.

As a guest, you feel the palpable sense of high engagement. It is as if every person is directly empowered, accountable and responsible, and there is no distinction between senior and junior staff. The result is that you feel taken care of by everyone.

Sonu and Eva are Secure Base Leaders themselves. They have integrated the concept into the very culture of the organization, through role modeling, expectation setting and specific processes. They have created an organization that is a secure base to the staff and to clients. In so doing, they have developed a team that performs at a high level, delivering spectacular results in a very competitive and dynamic industry.

When you transform your team or your organization into a secure base, your influence reaches far beyond the people you interact with. You help drive systemic engagement and create the conditions for innovation.

ENGAGEMENT

When the organization consists of a network of people bonded together and to the organization, engagement becomes ingrained and long-lasting. People are therefore more resilient in difficult times. Because they want to keep the bond with the secure base that is the organization, employees are less likely to underperform or leave. When the organization expresses a full belief in the potential of its people, they will be inspired to stretch not only to achieve personal goals but also to fulfill the very mission of the organization. They will believe that anything is possible; they will see the organization's vision as their goal.

INNOVATION

Innovation emerges from curiosity, openness, fascination, learning, creativity, teamwork, collaboration, pattern recognition, psychological safety, experimentation and, of course, acceptance of failure in that experimentation process. A secure base, whether in the form of a person or an organization, creates all of these inputs. Innovation is not about technology; it is about ideas and ideas come from people. Through its relationship-focus, your organization provides the support and safety that people need to innovate; they will know they are supported even through the necessary failures. Plus, the goals and possibility of the organization will provide the opportunity for everyone to focus on the benefits of the change inherent in the innovation process, rather than on all the risks and costs.

We have seen that some organizations are able to create a culture and philosophy that are closely aligned with the key ideas of Secure Base Leadership. We see caring and daring ingrained in daily behavior from the most senior leaders to the most junior employees. We see it expressed in different ways and often with no direct or explicit link to the words "Secure Base Leadership." Organizations that commit to both daring and caring—to Playing to Win by valuing both challenge and support—display the very best of Secure Base Leadership. These organizations have managed to transform into a secure base that provides safety, inspiration and energy.

Key Learnings

- When an organization prioritizes both relationships and results, it can be a secure base to employees.
- If you do so with sensitivity and care, you can introduce the Secure Base Leadership concept to your team and organization.
- As you seek to develop an organization as a secure base, you need to focus your efforts in three main areas:
  - Leadership engagement in the initiative
  - Human resource processes
  - Goals, vision and mission
- The results of your efforts will be an organization or team that can Play to Win together in a culture of caring and daring.

℘

"A company is stronger when bound by love rather than fear."

-Herb Kelleher
1931-
Co-founder, Chairman Emeritus and
former CEO of Southwest Airlines

℘

Frequently Asked Questions

Q: What do I do if my organization doesn't work this way?

A: Don't try to fight against the policies and culture of your organization. You will enter a painful and fruitless exercise if you don't have the requisite seniority within the organization to make systemic changes. Instead, focus on the areas where you have influence and take responsibility for the behavior of yourself and your team.

Q: You should meet some of the people I have to work with! How can you say that everyone has potential?

A: We believe that every person has unrealized potential in some untapped domain. That point of view does not mean that every person is well-suited to be the CEO, but it does mean that every person could do more if given the opportunity to express his or her unique talents and strengths.

Q: Should I treat everyone exactly the same? We don't have the resources to send everyone on expensive development programs.

A: You approach everyone with "unconditional positive regard," but then you can still have tailored development plans. Every person should have some kind of development plan because the alternative is an acknowledgment that he or she has reached a ceiling. If she has indeed reached a ceiling in a particular area, then your job as a leader is to help find some other domain where she can develop and contribute.

CHAPTER TEN

HUMANIZE YOUR LEADERSHIP AND YOUR ORGANIZATION

Alberto C. Vollmer is a Venezuelan businessman who runs his family-owned company, Santa Teresa Rum Distillery. In February 2000, when President Hugo Chávez had just changed the constitution, had started speaking out against private property and land owners, and was encouraging his followers to take land, almost 500 families moved onto a portion of Alberto's 18,300-acre hacienda and established compounds. Demanding that they leave or calling the police would have been pointless because these activities, at the time, were encouraged by the President himself. Instead, Alberto put an unusual proposal to them: ". . . OK, so you invade my land and I'll invade your minds." As Alberto put it, "If you resort to violence or being reactive or defensive, you're at an enormous disadvantage. Plus, I was vastly outnumbered." Following negotiations with the leader of the invading families, Alberto approached the state government, which was solidly behind Chávez's plan. Alberto offered to provide land and a housing plan for 100 families if the state government agreed to finance those homes and if the land invaders agreed to build the homes. Also, Alberto asked the State to agree to find homes for the other families. Says Alberto, "I wanted to reach an acceptable agreement and that meant finding a common ground for negotiation. That common ground was 'dignified homes.' They couldn't say 'no' to that but it wasn't going to be easy, either."

The community has become known as the Royal Way neighborhood. "We fought to have a home, and thanks to God, we have a dignified home that we can leave for our children," said Yumila Aquino, one of the first squatters. Alberto also offered people the opportunity to participate in job-training programs sponsored by the distillery. An unexpected outcome emerged from this agreement. A few years later, the leader of the invading families asked Alberto to be his son's godfather and several years later, the man was hired by the company's foundation and trained as a community projects manager.

In 2003, Alberto faced another challenge. Local gang members stole a guard's gun, nearly killed him, and were then arrested by the distillery's security staff. Alberto intervened, instructing the guards to remove the handcuffs. He then spoke with the gang members and gave them a choice: be handed over to the local police or agree to move onto the hacienda and work for the distillery with no salary but with free meals and on-the-job training.

The boys chose to accept the second option and eventually became productive members of the community. Alberto recalls, "We had to be much more ambitious and think, 'How are you going to change the reality of these people so they're productive for themselves?'" He explained, "It's not a handout. It's about giving something sustainable." Alberto was asked by the gang leader to expand the program to others and was astonished when 22 additional gang members showed up.

This unofficial pilot program developed into Project Alcatraz, a highly successful endeavor that identifies gang members, recruits them and then redirects their energy into constructive initiatives that benefit the youth involved and their communities. Project Alcatraz's ambitious mission is the eradication of crime without violence. Says Alberto, "One of the things we do is give them rugby training, not because rugby is particularly big in Venezuela, but because it teaches the right values. It is a contact sport with a gentleman's attitude."

The participants learn different crafts. They build conventional and alternative homes and work in the production of gourmet coffee. Five have become certified rugby coaches who have recruited over 500 new players from the community. Others have become security guards and two have become professional bodyguards for ministers. The three-month program also includes psychological sessions, community service and training in civic values. Through it participants come to espouse the project's philosophy: violence brings violence and trust breeds trust.

"The reason young people come to Project Alcatraz is that they see male role models, in myself and my colleague Jimin, who they can aspire to follow. We work to develop hard-core gang leaders by saying, 'Redirect your leadership to something useful. Violence just shows you're weak. Turn violence into virtue. That takes real guts.'"

Can you imagine how easy it would have been for Alberto to respond with force and aggression toward the people who invaded his land? Or for him to respond with a sense of retribution for the mindless acts of local youth? Instead of reacting to either of these situations in what many may see as a reasonable, conventional way, Alberto chose an innovative and, some may argue, "unreasonable" path.

As with other Secure Base Leaders, Alberto recognizes the influence and impact of his parents:

"My mother always read us stories about heroes—the Men of Iron, Ivanhoe, Robin Hood—and I was inspired by them. Both my mother and father always talked about 'doing your duty.' My father had a saying. 'Whatever happens to this country, good or bad, it is your responsibility.' This phrase has always been a benchmark in my life."

He also talked about the influence of his family's forbearers:

"They were actually able to prevail in all the rough conditions, dealing with any hardships that they had with a long-term philosophy."

Alberto's story shows that with inspiration one leader can stand on the shoulders of his ancestors and have an enormous influence on the lives of individuals, an organization and even society. With courage, he Plays to Win by creating challenge while collaborating and building strong bonds. Certainly, Alberto demonstrates the full possibility of a Secure Base Leader.

Yet, what is most striking is that Alberto began by seeing the humanity of the people involved in the situations he encountered. In his mind, the squatters were people instead of a problem. The gang members were youth full of potential instead of criminals needing to be prosecuted. He exemplifies the advice of Walter Bettinger, CEO of Charles Schwab: "As a leader it is essential to be focused on the goodness of human beings."

In both of the situations described in this story, Alberto also linked what was happening on his property with the needs of society. He brought a broader perspective—one far bigger than himself or his company—to bear on his decisions. In short, Alberto took Secure Base Leadership to the next level. He *humanized* his leadership and his organization. Your most significant opportunity is to do the same.

When we ask senior leaders to reflect on their learning experience with us, they often tell us that they "feel human" again. Or they say they have "gotten back in touch with their humanity."

Somehow, their very nature as people had become hidden over their years of corporate life. In the supportive and challenging environment provided by our programs, they are able to fully experience their dreams, their hopes, their emotions, their unresolved grief and their family relationships. And they describe themselves as "feeling alive again" or say "it has been life-changing," or say that they have "rediscovered a part of myself I had lost."

That experience of feeling alive again represents the essence of our mission to humanize organizations. We want as many people as possible to feel alive at work. That is why we are dedicated to promoting, teaching and writing about those aspects of organizational life that allow people not just to achieve organizational goals but to do so in a way that allows for human flourishing.

We do not need to tell you that we all operate in a fast moving, ever-changing world that is full of crisis and upheaval. You see that world each day on the news and in your email inbox. The acronym VUCA (Volatility, Uncertainty, Complexity, Ambiguity) describes this state of affairs. If you are like most of the executives we encounter, you are living in a VUCA world and know all about it!

We recognize the tough realities of business in the 21st century. We know that organizations need to change to survive and thrive. What concerns us is the way that change is often implemented. We notice the dehumanization of the workplace happening in parallel with, or perhaps as a response to, the state of markets, competition and economies. Everywhere we look, we see more focus on efficiency and survival and less focus on people. The human cost of VUCA is huge and deserves more attention.

Our research and experience supports the critical and current need for Secure Base Leadership. It is ideally suited to navigating VUCA environments. Secure Base Leadership provides the safety and risk, trust and exploration—the caring *and* daring—necessary for organizations in today's tumultuous world.

Depending on your starting point, humanizing your organization may be a big challenge. You start by humanizing your leadership and influencing others, either directly or indirectly, through modeling and being an example.

HUMANIZE YOUR LEADERSHIP

You begin humanizing your organization by opening yourself up to the humanity of others, and you begin that process by first attending to your own humanity. By reading this book, asking yourself the questions highlighted throughout it, and completing the various exercises, you have begun your personal journey.

ELEVATE YOUR HOPES AND DREAMS

To feel more alive and get in touch with your humanity, find a way to elevate your hopes and dreams, your passion and joy, your conviction and determination, and your spontaneous enthusiasm for your work and for your life. These are precisely the positive forces we have encouraged you to inspire in others by being a Secure Base Leader for them. Remember also to inspire yourself.

One of the most common ways that these forces get blocked is through unresolved loss and grief. We cannot stress enough the importance of focusing on this personal work. If you are struggling with the humanizing challenge, pay special attention to the Lifeline exercise in Chapter 7. Exploring the secure bases of your life will be one of the most direct ways to get in touch with the joy inherent in your own humanity.

SHOW VULNERABILITY

Remember that showing emotion is a sign of strength. Tears are small badges of courage. Don't be afraid to expose your vulnerability. In your vulnerability is your humanity and in your humanity is your strength.

We have seen time and time again that when a leader opens up others open up too. In the moment when the leader shows emotion, he becomes more accessible as a human being and people therefore want to bond with him. Through showing a deeper part of himself he gives others something to connect with and the relationship dynamic changes. People who were previously detached and distant become willing to cooperate and bond. While they may still disagree with a leader's decision, they agree that the leader has good intent and is simply doing his best.

Uplift People around You

You will achieve truly sustainable high performance when you intentionally seek to uplift the potential and talent of the people around you. In the language of Secure Base Leadership, this means focusing on developing strong, enduring bonds with people while also maintaining a challenging and opportunity-focused mindset. The Mind's Eye is always focused on Playing to Win.

Humanize How You Organize Work

Ever-flattening hierarchal structures and the dominance of the knowledge economy mean that the old systems of command-and-control, top-down management, employment-for-life, climbing the corporate ladder and staying at the top are diminishing day by day. The way companies organize work—or, to be more precise, the way that *leaders* organize work—can either support or block people's very humanity. You can help humanize your organization by changing some of the traditional and even newer ways work is organized.

24/7 Contact

Does your organization allow people to have downtime to live a full non-work life in the evenings, early mornings and weekends? Are you, as a leader, taking sufficient breaks from work to keep yourself creative and energized? Or are you making issues for your team and your organization by sending emails or calling employees

Your Next Steps: The Four D's of Success

It's one thing to talk about inspirational goals. It's another to put them into action. Be openly ambitious and hopeful about what can be achieved, but also recognize that having a substantial positive impact takes work and discipline. That's why in this and the next box we offer some suggestions to help you at a practical level as you make a firm commitment to humanize your organization.

Think about the four D's of Success (Desire, Discipline, Determination and Development). As you answer these four questions, reflect on your level of seriousness about achieving your goal:

- Do you really have the **desire**—the burning commitment and the focus—to achieve your goal?
- Are you willing to apply the necessary **discipline** to succeed? What will you sacrifice to do things differently? What daily steps will you take?
- Do you have the **determination** to continue when you meet your first obstacle? How will you cope with failure and setbacks along the way?
- Who will help you, challenge you and keep you on track with your continuous **development**? How will you celebrate success and measure your milestones along the way?

at all times of the day and night in non-emergency situations? Recent neuroscientific research shows that people can become addicted to checking emails: each time they do, they receive a small dose of dopamine (our brain's "happy chemical") that can give a boost of pleasure.

The brain works more effectively and efficiently when it has regular breaks. Wean yourself off any email addiction you may have and encourage your people and teams to do the same. Be aware of the signals you are sending.

Ask yourself:

- Can I turn off my phone and computer for extended periods of time in the evening and on weekends so that I can connect back to my humanity and let others do the same?

MAKE TIME TO BUILD RELATIONSHIPS

Does your organization schedule work—whether on the production floor or in executive meetings—in ways that enable people to get to know each other as people, talk about themselves and build bonds? Or does your organization set a relentless pace that leaves no time for relationships?

Day by day, the pace you and other leaders set sends a strong signal as to what you value. Is it people or simply the job they have to get done? See what you can do within your sphere of influence to create time for bonding.

RECOGNIZE THE HUMAN COST OF VIRTUAL TEAMS

As technology allows for more virtual work options, organizations are increasingly fragmented and project-based with people more attached to their work and their direct colleagues than to the company. Even the very humanistic-sounding programs like "working from home" and "flex time" further fragment the workplace community. Though positive in many ways, these trends make person-to-person bonding at work harder.

The solution may be right in front of your nose in the form of a "Generation Y" employee. This generation has grown up in the age of the internet. Recent research conducted by Ashridge Business School and the Institute of Leadership and Management has identified a number of interesting features of Generation Y employees. They want:

- Freedom and independence
- A relationship with a boss who is more of a coach and friend than a manager in the traditional sense
- Work-life balance

The study's recommendations for how to deal with Generation Y employees can help you humanize your organization to everyone's benefit:

- Accept characteristics like those of Generation Y employees as authentic expressions of a person's needs and expectations rather than as character flaws to be screened out.
- Emphasize communication. Hold regular, open conversations about each employee's personal expectations and ambitions and how to better align these to her job and to the organizations goals. Do what you can to grant autonomy and empowerment without abdicating responsibility.
- Use a coaching style of leadership rather than seeking to control and direct.[1]

HUMANIZE YOUR SOLUTIONS TO REAL PROBLEMS

The more you lead, the more complexity you will face in making decisions and implementing solutions to real problems. Some of the challenges cannot be escaped or passed on to someone else. When you take people into consideration in your decision making and then implement solutions that protect their very humanity, you

Your Next Steps: Action Planning

Take a few minutes to translate your commitment to becoming a Secure Base Leader into goals and action plans.

Remember to break down any big goal into small steps. When you decide to run a marathon, for example, you don't just go out and run the 26.2 miles or 42 km. You start by doing short runs and build up over a period of weeks and months. The same approach applies to achieving any target, including becoming a Secure Base Leader. Think about the small daily steps you can take and focus on those as well as the end goal.

Follow these instructions to take the first steps on your personal journey:

- **Draft your top three goals and define your next-step actions**

  Think about:

  - How specific and meaningful are the goals for you? Who will be affected by your goals? How will they react when you achieve these goals?
  - How attractive and challenging are the goals?
  - How will you measure progress and results? How will you celebrate goal achievements?
  - To whom will you communicate these goals?
  - What timeframe will you set to achieve each action and goal?

    Tips:

    - *Remember to make your goals SMART—specific, measurable, actionable, realistic and time-stamped.*
    - *Write your future goals in the present tense. The brain takes action based on the present state not the future.*

- **Present your goals and actions to someone you trust**
  Describe how you want to monitor progress until the goals are achieved.

- **Get feedback and refine your goals as you learn and develop** take a big step toward humanizing your organization. And when you neglect people and their human needs in times of crisis, you rob the organization of its potential humanity.

HUMANIZE YOUR RESPONSE TO LAYOFFS

Layoffs, redundancies, right-sizing, reorganizations: so many words for one of the most destructive sources of dehumanization. Often leaders turn a layoff into a legal exercise rather than a human one that considers the impact on real people. The human aspects are increasingly driven solely by the HR function rather than by the line managers directly involved. In too many cases, tightly controlled scripts and centralized scheduling have replaced honest dialogue and customized plans.

A recent case in the United States involved a person who was laid off on the day he returned to work after his son had died. As if the timing was not bad enough, the communication method was worse: there was no conversation, just a pink slip on his desk. Where was the humanity in that approach?

People feel more aggrieved by the dehumanizing ways in which a layoff is handled than by the actual decision to lay them off. When people feel dehumanized, they resort to solutions such as lawsuits.

There are other ways to handle layoffs, as Roger's story shows:

When a large European multinational announced significant layoffs at a factory in the U.S., Roger, a member of the management team, flew from Switzerland to explain the reasons behind the decision and why it was necessary for a successful, profitable company to take this action. While employees were clearly unhappy at losing their jobs, they thanked Roger for having the courage and decency to fly over, stand in front of them and be accountable. The fact that he respected them enough to make the trip and have an open dialogue enabled them to keep their dignity.

Grievances, Harassment and Violence

Organizations need grievance and harassment committees: they provide a necessary level of protection and they can be a secure base for employees. However, in our experience, when Secure Base Leadership becomes pervasive throughout an organization, its employees tend not to use these committees.

Leaders who dialogue and solve conflicts in a respectful, bonded, caring and humanizing manner take care of issues well before the committee stage. Addressing issues in a personal and direct way maintains bonding and results in people feeling supported rather than ignored, disrespected or excluded.

When issues are ignored or avoided, either by the line manager or the organization, emotions can escalate. The aggrieved party then feels increasingly isolated and detached, and they may act out in an aggressive and sometimes violent way. There have been numerous examples of employees carrying out extreme acts of violence in the workplace. Such acts are almost always preceded by disrespect, loss or grief. Hans Toch identified the three stages of any violent act:

1. The person first feels disrespected and views others with disrespect.
2. The person then acts on that feeling of disrespect.
3. The other party then responds in a defensive way.[2]

When Secure Base Leaders remain calm and empathetic and maintain a mindset of respect toward others, they can stop potential issues at the first stage. Companies that invest in building the people skills involved in Secure Base Leadership humanize their organizations and may reduce the cases of grievance, harassment and aggression in their workplaces.

HUMANIZE HOW YOU HANDLE MERGERS

Mergers and acquisitions can also disrupt people's jobs and self-esteem. They can be handled poorly or, as in Glen's case described below, with a Playing to Win approach that values the humanity of everyone involved. This story shows what is possible when a leader seeks out a human solution to a very real financial challenge:

As a large multinational company refined its strategy after a merger, a significant part of its combined sales force was no longer needed. Any layoffs could have created a huge issue because one of the merged companies—the one where I worked as Head of Commercial Development, Europe—had a culture of long-term employment. One solution was to sell the unwanted business to another party.

The CEO and financial controller were both skeptical that a deal could be made. After three complete breakdowns in negotiations over a three-month period, there was no solution on the table. My manager gave me a shot at leading a team to structure a deal. He had always had faith in me and often let me push new and innovative boundaries like exploring new business models.

By managing my Mind's Eye to find a positive solution against all odds and knowing that my boss had faith in me and the team, we came up with a deal that had never before been attempted in our industry. This deal allowed the company to do the correct thing for employees who had given so much over many years. Specifically, it guaranteed each member of the combined sales force a job for three years, with current seniority and benefits in their same territories and the opportunity to launch three new products. It was also a "win" for the new company: it gained a ready-made and experienced European sales organization.

*Almost 1,000 employees benefitted from this deal. I am
extremely proud. It had been hard because we had to convince
our management team and the workers' councils and unions
of all the countries involved. The best moment for me was
when the General Manager of our division in Germany
announced the changes and 250 people gave him a standing
ovation because they knew that the company had done the
right thing by them and they were able to maintain their jobs.*

Consider also this example of Secure Base Leadership in action:

*When Marie, a member of our book project team, visited a
branch of the U.K.-based financial institution Northern Rock, the
manager told her how Richard Branson was handling Virgin
Money's takeover of Northern Rock. He told her that Branson
had sent a personalized letter to each employee along with a
copy of his autobiography. He also shared that Branson was
traveling around the country on his motorbike to visit every
branch that Virgin was taking over to personally meet with the
staff. He had reportedly also assured Northern Rock employees
that he guaranteed them jobs for the next three years.*

Not only did Branson's actions calm and motivate affected
employees, they also initiated a ripple effect that reached thousands of customers and other stakeholders. By taking care of
employees in his own distinctive style, Branson demonstrated his
own humanity as well as that of his organization.

Ask yourself:

• How can I humanize my own leadership?

Humanize Your Mission

One of the greatest and most promising shifts happening today is
the increased focus on social and environmental responsibility in

the mission and purpose of organizations. When the mission is related to a broader societal responsibility, some organizations manage to develop a tremendous sense of affinity and connection among their employees and, in some cases, even customers. Such missions invite people to use the vehicle of the organization to have a positive impact on the world. In providing this opportunity, organizations access a core aspect of their employees' humanity: the genuine desire to make a contribution and to make the world a better place. Consider how the managing director in this story gave his communications manager an outlet for his humanity at work:

James Neville, managing director of U.K.-based dairy nutrition company Volac, thinks big. His family-owned company may be small by some standards, but its variety of highly successful businesses links it to each main step of the dairy supply chain. "We are probably the only company that buys milk products that originate from farms and sells products back to farmers as well as international food manufacturers." In 2010, with this position of influence in mind, he articulated a new company mission: to lead a sustainable U.K. dairy industry. "The opportunities to reduce the environmental impact of dairy production are real. But so are the nutritional, rural and economic needs of our nation. We want to help the industry become sustainable not just in environmental terms but also in business terms. A viable dairy farm failing means a small business going under and a rural landscape becoming vulnerable to decay. I wanted to use Volac's position of influence to ensure the industry's future."

After more than a year of research and planning, Volac chose to pursue its mission as part of the Dairy 2020 coalition, of which it is a founding member. Stakeholders in the dairy supply chain have come together in an unprecedented way to

define what a sustainable dairy industry looks like
and to agree about the contribution it can make to a
sustainable world.

James gave his corporate communications manager, Andy
Richardson, the stretch assignment of taking on the
responsibility not only for Volac's role within Dairy 2020 but
also the additional responsibility of coordinating Dairy 2020
communications. "It has been a ton of work," says Andy. "But
it's also given me an incredible opportunity to contribute not
just to our industry, but to our nation as well, at a level I
could never do on my own. With Dairy 2020, I've met with
government ministers and the leaders of our industry. I feel
very proud of what I've achieved, of what James has achieved
through his leadership for Volac and our industry, and of the
direction our industry is now headed."

We have noticed that strong Secure Base Leaders like James
tend to have a perspective broader than their own department,
division, company or even industry. Many set society-level goals
that inspire not only employees but also other stakeholders. Think
of all of the Secure Base Leaders we have profiled throughout this
book and remember how Richard Branson, Christa Brelsford, Azim
Khamisa, Irina Lucidi, Randy Pausch, Ted Kennedy Sr., Paul Rusesabagina and Alberto Vollmer have all had a powerful impact on
society.

We believe that this tendency comes naturally from the Secure
Base Leader's Mind's Eye, which focuses on the positive and the
potential to such an extent that even the impossible becomes possible. Like the belayer, who from her position on the ground can
scan the rock face and see it in a broader perspective than the
climber who is inches from it, the Secure Base Leader gives followers opportunities to stretch beyond what they can see themselves.
The belayer can say, for instance, "There's a hand hold about two
feet from your right hand, at 2 o'clock," and she keeps reminding

the climber of the big picture by saying, "Just 10 more feet and you're at the top!" Likewise, the Secure Base Leader reminds followers of their contribution to a greater community:

Robert Swan, OBE, is a polar explorer and environmentalist who describes himself as "the first person stupid enough to walk to both poles." Swan has dedicated his life to the preservation of Antarctica through the promotion of recycling, renewable energy and sustainability in order to combat the effects of climate change. Passionate about Mission 2041 (www.2041.com), his quest to engage people in saving Antarctica, Robert shares his message and leadership lessons with companies and governments all over the world. As the last unspoiled wilderness on earth, "Antarctica is," in his words, "currently protected by a treaty prohibiting drilling and mining until 2041. Decisions made by today's youth will impact our entire planet's ecosystem and the future of life on earth." He works closely with companies organizing sustainable Antarctic expeditions in which selected executives can develop their leadership talents while at the same time doing something constructive for the planet.

Robert says it is vital to inspire trust in others. People become more efficient and get on with what needs doing when you trust them. "Leadership is not always leading," he says. "Sometimes it is about support." When selecting a team, it is important to choose strong people who will challenge, push and stretch you. You may not necessarily like them.

With his focus firmly on ensuring the preservation of Antarctica, Robert implores all of us to "Think BIG: you only have one life. Focus on sustainable inspiration."

We believe that humanizing your organization is an opportunity to realize the positive role your business could play in society. To many, seeing social involvement as an opportunity means shifting a deeply-held belief about the fundamental role of business. The shift is about connecting to future generations and the legacy and resources we will leave for them; it is about bonding to the earth in the knowledge that destroying our very nest is a threat to our survival. It is also about being satisfied with less, knowing that we can never get enough of what we don't need, and focusing on what author Diana Coyle calls the "economics of enough."[3]

You can think of social responsibility along the two dimensions of the bonding cycle and the Mind's Eye. In terms of bonding, we see social responsibility as a way into a deeper and more concerned relationship with a wider group of stakeholders. This broader set of stakeholders could represent the natural environment, the full supply chain of production or the broader communities in which the organization operates. Bonding with these groups means shifting from pure self-interest to a broader sense of "other-interest." As in bonding with an individual, bonding with stakeholders requires being curious, being accepting of others' values and different points of view, developing deep dialogue and approaching issues with an inquiring mind. When you embrace the opportunity to improve the quality of your relationships with a broader set of interested parties, you enhance the humanity of your organization.

In terms of the Mind's Eye, the important aspect is to see the possibility within the realm of social responsibility. There is a benefit to every change. Your role is to get the Mind's Eye of the team or organization focused on that benefit. In the case of social responsibility, the benefit goes way beyond simple shareholder value. By including a concern for a wider set of stakeholders, you can add an inspirational and motivating human dimension to your organization.

Ask yourself:

• How can I humanize my organization?

YOUR MOST ENDURING LEADERSHIP OPPORTUNITY

The rapidly changing nature of today's world is here to stay. We have no doubt that in the short term the adaptability and survival instincts of organizations will allow many organizations to succeed. They will succeed by becoming ever more efficient, ever more flexible and ever more adaptable. But at what cost? Specifically, at what cost to the human beings inside those organizations? Our concern is that in the drive to be efficient, lean, adaptable and innovative, the human dimension of organizations may be ignored or minimized. When a dominant mindset of "Well, we've got to do what we've got to do to survive" becomes embedded in organizations, people will lose.

The question is: What can you do about it?

You can care to dare. If you choose to act as a Secure Base Leader and adopt a Playing to Win approach, you will respond to challenges by seeking both survival *and* great relationships. You won't allow bonds to break just because you are under pressure. You won't cut headcount just because that's the easiest thing to do. You will always be asking yourself, "How can we win *and* keep the human dimension thriving?"

Will it be easy to maintain the Playing to Win approach? No. Will you still have to make some difficult decisions that negatively impact the lives of your employees or other stakeholders? Yes, you will.

Maintaining the Playing to Win approach comes down to your intent and your core beliefs, to your basic approach to leadership and, in fact, to life. If your starting point is that people are a cost to be minimized, your organization might survive but it won't thrive. If, on the other hand, you fundamentally believe that human beings are valuable and a source of goodness, a true asset not in financial terms but in their very essence, you will make your decisions with an entirely different perspective. In your attitude, in your state and

A Place Where You Can Be You

Linden Lab, the company that created the virtual online world "Second Life," is a powerful example of a company that appears to embody the notion of humanizing an organization. If you go to its website, you will find a full description of its culture. One element really caught our attention:

"There's love in the spirit of our mission, the enjoyment we take in each other's company, the style and humor we have at our best. We're here because we're open to all the wonders of the world and the goodness in each other; even the cynics among us harbor the begrudging belief that all things are possible. This is a place where you can be you, and we ask you to make the choices that enable your colleagues to bring out the best in themselves."

The company also has an internal feedback mechanism called the "Love Machine" which is an intranet-based system that allows people to send appreciation notes to each other. These notes are then collected, used as part of the performance review and can result in a small financial reward.

While an idea like a Love Machine might not fit your corporate culture in terms of style or language, it demonstrates that the organization is making an explicit effort to enhance and promote the human spirit.

What can you do within your organization to enhance and promote the human spirit?

in your authenticity, you will be operating as a secure base. From that position, even your difficult decisions will be understood and received with a higher degree of acceptance and appreciation. You will achieve results in a way that also elevates the contribution and value of the human beings inside your organization.

People spend the majority of their waking lives at work. Each organization is potentially a place of thriving, flourishing and growth. It can also be a place where human beings are devalued. The turning point is leadership. And within leadership, the essence is Secure Base Leadership. Secure Base Leaders like you provide others with the example of what is possible in our changing world.

We are deeply committed to the mission of humanizing organizations through Secure Base Leadership. When you take the journey to become a Secure Base Leader, you enhance first your own human spirit, then the human spirit of others, and finally the humanity of your organization. Enjoy the journey.

ℬ

"Do not go where the path may lead. Go instead where there is no path and leave a trail."

–Ralph Waldo Emerson
1803–1882
American Essayist, Lecturer and Poet

ℬ

About the Research

Between 2006 and 2010, we conducted a two-part research study that validated the Secure Base Leadership theory and reinforced our conviction about its value in organizations.

Prior to our formal research, all three authors had personal experience that led us to a number of practical and real world insights. We have a combined 60 years of working with the concepts for what we now term Secure Base Leadership. Much of that experience came from teaching and working with thousands of executives from around the world across industries. We knew from direct experience with senior executives that the material works on the ground. In our formal feedback process at the end of our programs and in our follow-up programs, we heard success story after success story. However, while this anecdotal evidence inspired us, we wanted something more definitive around which to structure the Secure Base Leadership concept. We therefore embarked on a multi-year research journey that involved numerous members of our team around the world. With significant input and support from George Kohlrieser and IMD, the research project culminated in Duncan Coombe's PhD thesis in Organizational Behavior from Case Western Reserve University.

The research included two main studies: an initial qualitative study to develop the characteristics of Secure Base Leadership and then a large-scale quantitative study to measure its impact on important organizational outcomes.

STUDY ONE: DEVELOPMENT OF THE CHARACTERISTICS

Description

An inductive, qualitative research study aimed at identifying the dimensions of Secure Base Leadership.

Objective

To bring greater insight into the behaviors and characteristics associated with Secure Base Leadership within the organizational context.

Participants

60 organizational leaders identified by our research team:

- Predominantly from Europe, the U.S. and Asia
- Average age: 48 years old
- 70% male and 30% female

These individuals were chosen by the research team as representative of real-world high performing leaders we encounter in our daily work. In order to ensure maximum resonance with our target audience, we purposefully did not want the bulk of our interviewees to be famous CEOs.

Interview Process

The team conducted the interviews following a semi-structured interview protocol. An important part of the interviews was therefore the series of additional explorative sub-questions asked in response to answers. Those sub-questions allowed us to obtain depth and richness of data. These questions were focused on language, phrases, actions, stories, applications and insights.

Interviews were recorded and subsequently transcribed. The focus was on stories of secure bases and Secure Base Leadership that illuminated our inquiry.

Questions included:

- Who were the people in your childhood and youth that helped you the most—who built your self-confidence and encouraged you to explore, create and achieve?
- Can you tell me a story about a specific time or moment when one of these individuals' influence was particularly significant? What did they say? What did they do? What did you learn?
- Apart from parents and immediate family members, who were some of the other people who were most influential when you were growing up?
- Can you tell me a story about a specific time or moment when one of these individuals' influence was particularly significant? What did they say? What did they do? What did you learn?
- Who were the people who have been most influential and helpful to you as an adult and as a leader? Why? How?
- Can you tell me a story about a specific time or moment when one of these individuals' influence was particularly significant? What did they say? What did they do? What did you learn?
- Please tell me about a time of failure, loss or crisis. Who did you turn to and why? What did he or she say or do that was helpful at that time?
- Please tell me about a time when you, as a leader, helped another person. How did you help build someone's self-confidence and encourage them to explore, create or achieve? What did you say and do? What was his or her response?

Analysis

The interviews were analyzed in a rigorous multi-step process according to a Grounded Theory approach based on the work of researchers Glaser and Strauss.

First, ten of the interviews were read multiple times. This step allowed the researchers to become immersed in the data and create first order codes. During the reading of the interviews, notes were recorded around specific behaviors and actions. In this initial reading of the interviews, 37 first order behaviors were recorded. These 37 first order behaviors were then sorted to create second order groupings of behaviors. Examples of these second order groupings were:

- Inquiry and listening
- Acceptance of the person
- Positive mindset

The interviews were then re-read to check the validity of these groupings to ensure that all behaviors described in the interviews could be grouped into these categories.

The second order groupings were then described more fully. A description of each was developed and accompanying sample evidence was collected. This information was then shared verbally and in writing with three co-researchers. The co-researchers then read the interviews with the intention of performing an inter-rater reliability analysis. Two of the co-researchers read all 60 interviews and one of the co-researchers read five of the interviews.

Conclusion

Through this process, the groupings were qualitatively confirmed as being representative. Following this process, the characteristics of Secure Base Leadership described in *Care to Dare* were established.

Study Two: Testing the Characteristics

Having established the characteristics of Secure Base Leadership, the research team then wanted to know whether they could be used to predict elements of organizational performance. In other words, does Secure Base Leadership have a positive relationship to organizational outcomes?

Description

A deductive, quantitative research study aimed at examining the relationship between Secure Base Leadership and other organizational outcome variables.

Objective

To show that a leader displaying the characteristics of Secure Base Leadership will produce beneficial leadership outcomes.

Participants

Attendees of selected executive education programs at IMD.

Participants were identified through an online survey administered in advance of the leadership program as part of their preparatory work. In addition to participating themselves, participants were asked to invite their direct reports and their manager to participate in the study.

Therefore, there were three separate groups of participants:

- Leaders (participants in the leadership program)
- Followers (direct reports of the leaders)
- Managers (the managers of the leaders)

We conducted the research over multiple programs, piloting and refining our approach to recruiting survey participants.

Over the course of our research, we surveyed almost 1,000 people. The leaders themselves were overwhelmingly male (85%) which is a reflection of the demographics of senior leaders in large multinational organizations. There was a higher proportion of female "followers" (30%), again a reflection of the demographics of large multinational organizations.

Survey Design

As a first step we created an instrument that would measure the characteristics of Secure Base Leadership. This was based on the findings, words and phrases of the previous study, and it was refined through a series of pilot studies. The aggregated measure of Secure Base Leadership was the independent variable in the study.

As a second step, we tested whether Secure Base Leadership had a positive relationship to other existing and well-established organizational variables. We chose three primary dependent variables for this study:

- A measure of Leader Effectiveness (measuring the extent to which the leader was perceived to be effective as a leader by his manager and direct reports)
- A measure of Job Satisfaction (measuring the job satisfaction of the direct reports)
- A measure of Psychological Safety (measuring the extent to which direct reports felt that it was safe to try new things, make mistakes and share their opinions)

Analysis

Analysis involved a number of different quantitative methods that extended from basic correlations and regression analyses to more advanced structural equation modeling.

Results

Through this analysis we discovered a positive relationship between the characteristics of Secure Base Leadership and the outcome variables of Leadership Effectiveness, Job Satisfaction and Psychological Safety. The behaviors of Secure Base Leadership contribute to these three outcomes.

Clearly, Secure Base Leadership is not the only input into these three outcomes. However, our research makes a compelling case that if a leader consistently displays the characteristics of Secure Base Leadership, he or she will be more likely to achieve these outcomes.

Conclusion

Our direct experience of working with executives in real situations and our anecdotal evidence of the success of Secure Base Leadership were supported by our research. The studies described in this overview provided an initial rich description of the characteristics of Secure Base Leadership as well as the evidence to support their positive impact on important outcomes such as leader effectiveness and job satisfaction.

NOTES

Preface
1. Richard Branson, *Losing my Virginity. How I Survived, Had Fun, and Made a Fortune Doing Business My Way* (London: Ebury Press, 2009).
2. Richard Branson, *Screw Business as Usual* (New York: Penguin, 2011). Quote from http://www.virgin.com under Richard Branson.

Chapter One
1. We know the word "comfort" may not be clear in English or other languages. By comfort we mean the calming effect that the presence of a leader gives.
2. John Bowlby, *A Secure Base: Clinical Applications of Attachment Therapy* (London: Tavistock/Routledge, 1988), 11.
3. J. W. Anderson, "Attachment Behavior Out of Doors," in *Ethological Studies of Child Behavior*, ed. N. Blurton Jones (Cambridge: Cambridge University Press, 1972), 199–215.
4. John Bowlby, *A Secure Base*, 11.
5. We recognize that there may be negative secure bases: people who make you feel safe and who encourage you to explore and take risks, but for a negative outcome or to harm others. Think of historical leaders who have been able to convince large groups of people to take actions that were against the best interest of themselves or others. For example, in 1978 in Jonestown, Guyana, Jim Jones convinced his followers to commit suicide resulting in 909 deaths. For the purposes of this book, we are focusing on the secure bases that influence us to achieve positive things in our lives.

6. Warren Bennis, "Learning to Lead," *Executive Excellence* 13 (1996): 7.

7. Micha Popper and Ofra Mayseless, "Back to Basics: Applying a Parenting Perspective to Transformational Leadership," *The Leadership Quarterly* 14 (2003): 48.

8. Micha Popper and Ofra Mayseless, "Back to basics," 50.

9. Time Specials, "The Top 10 Everything of 2011, Top 10 Nonfiction Books, 2. Steve Jobs by Walter Isaacson," by Lev Grossman, http://www.time.com/time/specials/packages/article/0,28804,2 101344_2101108_2101118,00.html #ixzz1jERQAHFQ, accessed January 12, 2012.

10. "Gallup on Engagement and Trust. What Followers Want From Leaders. The 'vision thing' pales in comparison to instilling trust, compassion, stability, and hope. A GMJ Q&A with Tom Rath and Barry Conchie, authors of Strengths Based Leadership," *The Gallup Management Journal* August 2009.

Chapter Two

1. Oren Harari, *The Powell Principles: 24 Lessons from Colin Powell, a Battle-Proven Leader* (New York: McGraw-Hill, 2004), 1.

2. Daniel Goleman, *Emotional Intelligence: Why It Can Matter More than IQ* (New York: Bantam, 1995), 15–32.

3. Carl R. Rogers, *A Way of Being* (Boston: Houghton Mifflin Company, 1980), 116.

4. Jim Collins, *Good to Great: Why Some Companies Make the Leap . . . and Others Don't* (London: Random House, 2001), 197–204.

5. Daniel Pink, *Drive: The Surprising Truth About What Motivates Us* (New York: Riverhead Books, 2009), 23.

6. Eric Berne, *Transactional Analysis in Psychotherapy* (New York: Grove Press, 1961), 13.

7. Paul Ekman, *Emotions Revealed* (London: Orion Books, 2004), 51–52.

8. Craig Hassed, "Mindfulness, Well-Being and Performance," *Neuroleadership Journal* 1 (2008): 1–7.

9. S. I. Dworkin, S. Mirkis, and J. E. Smith, "Response-Dependent Versus Response-Independent Presentation of Cocaine: Differences in the Lethal Effects of the Drug," *Psychopharmacology* 117/3 (1995): 262–266.

10. Robert M. Sapolsky, "Stressed-Out Memories. A Little Stress Sharpens Memory. But After Prolonged Stress, the Mental Picture Isn't Pretty," *Scientific American Mind*, September–October 2011.

11. Ernesto Rossi, *The Psychobiology of Gene Expression: Neuroscience and Neurogenesis in Therapeutic Hypnosis and the Healing Arts* (New York: W. W. Norton Professional Books, 2002).

12. Craig Hassed, *Know Thyself: Stress Relief Program* (Melbourne: Michelle Anderson Publishing, 2002).

13. Anders K. Ericsson, Michael J. Prietula, and Edward T. Cokely, "The Making of an Expert," *Harvard Business Review*, July–August 2007

14. Benjamin Bloom, *Developing Talent in Young People* (New York: Ballantine, 1985).

Chapter Three

1. Bill Fischer and Andy Boynton, *The Idea Hunter: How to Find the Best Ideas and Make Them Happen* (San Francisco: Jossey-Bass, 2011), 25.

2. Duane P. Schultz and Sydney Ellen Schultz, *Theories of Personality*, Ninth Edition (Belmont, CA: Wadsworth Publishing, 2008), 166.

3. Joseph Chilton Pearce, *Magical Child: Rediscovering Nature's Plan for Our Children* (New York: Dutton, 1977), 72.

4. Nova Science Now, "Mirror Neurons," online video directed by Julia Cort, http://www.youtube.com/watch?v=XzMqPYfeA-s (Part 1); http://www.youtube.com/watch?v=xmEsGQ3JmKg (Part 2), accessed January 12, 2012.

5. Vilayanur S. Ramachandran, *The Tell-Tale Brain: A Neuroscientist's Quest for What Makes Us Human. A Brief Tour of Human Consciousness* (New York: W. W. Norton & Co, 2011), 134–135.

6. Daniel Goleman, *Primal Leadership: Realizing the Power of Emotional Intelligence* (Boston: Harvard Business Review Press, 2002), 327–332.
7. Dennis Reina and Michelle L. Reina, *Trust and Betrayal in the Workplace: Building Effective Relationships in Your Organization*, revised and expanded, 2nd edition (San Francisco: Berrett Koehler, 2006).
8. Gallup Study, "Poll Reveals Germans Are Just Working to Live," January 21, 2004, http://www.dw-world.de/dw/article/0,1094681,00.html, accessed January 12, 2012.
9. John H. Fleming and Jim Apslund, *Human Sigma: Managing the Employee-Customer Encounter* (New York: Gallup Press, 2007), 151–170.
10. Carl R. Rogers, *A Way of Being*, 116.
11. Bill Clinton, *My Life* (New York: Knopf, 2004), 25.
12. Indra Nooyi, "The Best Advice I Ever Got," CNN Money, http://money.cnn.com/galleries/2008/fortune/0804/gallery.bestadvice.fortune/7.html, accessed January 12, 2012.
13. Marianne Williamson, *Return to Love: Reflections on the Principles of a Course in Miracles* (New York: Harper Collins, 1992), 165.
14. Joel Raphaelson, ed. *The Unpublished David Ogilvy* (New York: Crown, 1986).

Chapter Four

1. Michael Lee Stallard, *The Heart of Starbucks' CEO*, www.michael-leestallard.com/howard-schultzs-broken-heart, accessed March 30, 2012.
2. The Grief Recovery Institute Educational Foundation, "Grief Index: The Hidden Annual Costs of Grief in America's Workplace," 2003, http://grief.net/Articles/The_Grief_Index_2003.pdf, accessed January 12, 2012.
3. In the words of one of them: "Losses loom larger than gains. This asymmetry between the power of positive and negative expectations or experiences has an evolutionary history. Organisms that treat threats as more urgent than opportunities have a better chance to survive and reproduce." Daniel Kahneman, *Thinking, Fast and Slow* (New York: Farrar, Straus and Giroux, 2011), 282.

4. BBC News, "Inseparable Twin Friars Die Hours Apart, age 92, 3 June 2011," http://www.bbc.co.uk/news/world-us-canada-13651149, accessed January 12, 2012.

5. James Lynch, *The Broken Heart: The Medical Consequences of Loneliness* (New York: Basic Books, 1977).

6. Elizabeth J. Carter and Kevin A. Pelphrey, "Friend or foe? Brain Systems Involved in the Perception of Dynamic Signals of Menacing and Friendly Social Approaches," *Journal of Social Neuroscience* 3 (2008): 151–163.

7. David Rock, "SCARF: A Brain-Based Model for Collaborating with and Influencing Others," *NeuroLeadership Journal*, 1 (2008), also available at http://www.davidrock.net/files/NLJ_SCARFUS. pdf, accessed January 12, 2012.

8. Matthew D. Lieberman and Naomi I. Eisenberger, "The Pains and Pleasures of Social Life," *NeuroLeadership Journal* 1 (2008).

9. Elizabeth Kübler-Ross and David Kessler, *On Grief and Grieving: Finding the Meaning of Grief through the Five Stages of Loss* (New York: Scribner, 2006).

10. "Grief Index: The Hidden Annual Costs of Grief in America's Workplace," 2003.

11. Matthew D. Lieberman, "Why Symbolic Processing of Affect Can Disrupt Negative Affect: Social Cognitive and Affective Neuroscience Investigations," in *Social Neuroscience: Toward Understanding the Underpinnings of the Social Mind*, eds. Alexandre B. Todorov, Susan T. Fiske, and Deborah Prentice (Oxford: Oxford University Press, 2011), 188–207.

12. Take for example the research of Losada and Heaphy, who found that teams that favor inquiry over advocacy perform better (Marcial Losada and Emily Heaphy, "The role of positivity and connectivity in the performance of business teams: A nonlinear dynamics model," *American Behavioral Scientist* 47 (2004): 740–765). This favoring of listening and asking questions could also be likened to Greenleaf's servant leadership (Robert K. Greenleaf, *Servant Leadership: A Journey into the Nature of Legitimate Power and Greatness*, New York: Boston: Paulist Press, 2002), Goleman, Boyatzis and McKee's coaching leadership styles (Daniel Goleman, Annie McKee and Richard E. Boyatzis,

Primal Leadership: Realizing the Power of Emotional Intelligence, Boston: Harvard Business Review Press, 2002), and Srivastra and Cooperrider's Appreciative Leadership (Suresh Srivastva and David L. Cooperrider, *Appreciative Leadership and Management*, San Francisco: Jossey-Bass, 1999).

13. Other resources are: Ingrid Bens, *Facilitating with Ease!: Core Skills for Facilitators, Team Leaders and Members, Managers, Consultants, and Trainers*, with CD, New and Revised Edition (San Francisco: Jossey-Bass, 2005), Mark Goulston, *Just Listen: Discover the Secret to Getting Through to Absolutely Anyone* (New York: American Management Organization, 2010), and Madelyn Burley-Allen, *Listening: The Forgotten Skill: A Self-Teaching Guide* (Chichester: Wiley, 1995).

Chapter Five

1. Randy Pausch and Jeffrey Zaslow, *The Last Lecture* (New York: Hyperion, 2008). See also: http://www.thelastlecture.com, accessed January 12, 2012.

2. Tigger, a stuffed tiger, and Eeyore, a stuffed donkey, are characters in A. A. Milne's *Winnie the Pooh* children's book series. Tigger is bouncy, hyperactive, talkative and rarely gets sad or down. Eeyore moves slowly, exudes tiredness, says very little and always sees the negative in life.

3. Elizabeth J. Carter and Kevin A. Pelphrey, "Friend or Foe? Brain Systems Involved in the Perception of Dynamic Signals of Menacing and Friendly Social Approaches," *Journal Social Neuroscience* 3 (2008): 151–163.

4. Carol S. Dweck, *Self-Theories: Their Roots in Motivation, Personality and Development. Essays in Sociol Psychology* (Philadelphia, PA: Taylor & Francis, 2000).

5. Roy Baumeister, *Willpower: Rediscovering the Greatest Human Strength* (New York: Penguin Press, 2011).

6. Yuichi Shoda, Walter Mischel, and Philip K. Peake, "Predicting Adolescent Cognitive and Self-Regulatory Competencies from Preschool Delay of Gratification," *Developmental Psychology* 26 (6) (1990): 978–986.

7. Kerry Patterson, Joseph Grenny, David Maxfield, Ron McMillan, and Al Switzler. *Influencer: The Power To Change Anything* (New York: McGraw-Hill, 2008), 116.

8. Peter Meyers and Shann Nix, *As We Speak: How to Make Your point and Have It Stick* (New York: Atria Books, 2011), 155.

9. Craig Hassed, "Meditation as a Tool for Happiness," Presentation at "Happiness and its Causes" conference 2006, http://www. themeditationroom.com.au/Documents/Meditation_as_a_tool_for_happiness.pdf, accessed January 12, 2012.

10. Jean-François Manzoni and Jean-Louis Barsoux, *The Set-Up-To-Fail Syndrome: Overcoming the Undertow of Expectations* (Boston: Harvard Business School Press, 2002).

11. Tali Sharot, *The Optimism Bias: A Tour of the Irrationally Positive Brain* (New York: Pantheon Books, 2011), 56–58.

12. Art Gardner, *Why Winners Win* (Gretna, LA: Pelican Publishing Company, 1981).

13. The technique of passing a silver nitrate bar over a wound was a healing procedure from the 1970s.

14. Andrew Grove, *Only the Paranoid Survive: How to Exploit the Crisis Points That Challenge Every Company* (New York: Crown Business, 1999).

15. Micha Popper and Ofra Mayseless, "The Building Blocks of Leader Development: A Psychological Conceptual Framework," *Leadership & Organization Development Journal* 28/7 (2007): 664–684.

16. Bill George, *Authentic Leadership: Rediscovering the Secrets to Creating Lasting Value* (San Francisco: Jossey-Bass, 2003).

17. Lawrence A. Bossidy, Noel M. Tichy, and Ram Charan, "CEO as Coach: An Interview with AlliedSignal's Lawrence A. Bossidy," *Harvard Business Review*, June 2000.

18. Jacqueline Byrd and Paul Lockwood Brown, *The Innovation Equation: Building Creativity and Risk-Taking in Your Organization* (San Francisco: Jossey-Bass/Pfeiffer, 2003).

Chapter Six

1. CBS, "Kennedy Jr. On His Dad" (Funeral Mass), http://www. youtube.com/watch?v=a_bbl5DkUQY, accessed January 12, 2012.

2. Mihaly Csikszentmihalyi, *Flow: The Psychology of Optimal Experience* (New York: Harper & Row, 1990).

3. Daniel Goleman, "Leadership That Gets Results," *Harvard Business Review*, March 2000.

4. Richard Ryan and Edward Deci, "Intrinsic and Extrinsic Motivations: Classic Definitions and New Directions," *Contemporary Educational Psychology* 25 (2000): 54–67.

5. Daniel Pink, *Drive: The Surprising Truth About What Motivates Us* (New York: Riverhead Books, 2009), 23.

6. Martin Dewhurst, Matthew Guthridge, and Elizabeth Mohr, "Motivating People: Getting Beyond Money," *McKinsey Quarterly* November 2009, http://www.mckinseyquarterly.com/Motivating_people_Getting_beyond_money_2460, accessed January 12, 2012.

7. Roderick Gilkey and Clint Kilts, "Cognitive Fitness," *Harvard Business Review*, November 2007.

8. Richard M. Ryan and Jerome Stiller, "The Social Contexts of Internalization: Parent and Teacher Influences on Autonomy, Motivation and Learning," in *Advances in motivation and achievement*, Vol. 7, eds. Paul R. Pintrich and Martin L. Maehr (Greenwich, CT: JAI Press, 1991), 115–149.

9. Mary Ainsworth, Mary C. Blehar, Everett Waters, and Sally Wall, *Patterns of Attachment: A Psychological Study of the Strange Situation* (Hillsdale, NJ: Erlbaum, 1978).

Chapter Seven

1. Paul Rusesabagina with Tom Zoellner, *An Ordinary Man: An Autobiography* (New York: Penguin, 2007), xvii.

2. Jack Wood and Gianpiero Petriglieri, "Getting the Most Out of Your Leadership Program," *Perspectives For Managers/IMD* 113 (2004).

3. Your children should not be your secure base. It is destructive when a parent uses a child as a secure base because children need to feel the freedom to explore and be protected rather than being put into a caretaker role. Putting them in that position simply places too much stress and responsibility on him or her. The child should only be a secure base for the parent when the parent

becomes old and the roles change. Then, in the spirit of love, the grown child may become a secure base for the parent. That said, the family unit and the extended family can certainly be secure bases.

4. Daniel Pink, *Drive: The Surprising Truth About What Motivates Us* (New York: Riverhead Books, 2009).

5. John Kador, *Great Engagements: The Once and Future Johnson & Johnson* (New Brunswick, NJ: Johnson & Johnson, 2004), 146.

6. Charles S. Jacobs, *Management Rewired: Why Feedback doesn't Work and Other Surprising Lessons from the latest Brain Science* (New York: Penguin, 2009).

7. "Surgery Under Hypnosis a Pain-Free Event," Medical Procedure News, April 20, 2008, http://www.news-medical.net/news/2008/04/20/37534.aspx, accessed January 12, 2012.

Chapter Eight

1. The Characteristics Wheel provides a quick self-assessment about your strengths as a Secure Base Leader. A tested 360° feedback instrument is available to gather a more complete picture based on the perceptions of your reports, your colleagues and your boss(es). For more information, contact: duncancoombe@careto-dare.com

2. Over the years, the idea of attachment styles has been refined and developed by numerous researchers, but the original ideas of Bowlby and Ainsworth have continued to be supported. See Mario Mikulincer and Phillip Shaver, *Attachment in Adulthood: Structure, Dynamics and Change* (New York: The Guilford Press, 2007), 25–28.

3. Kim Bartholomew and Leonard M. Horowitz, "Attachment Styles Among Young Adults: A Test of a Four-Category Model," *Journal of Personality and Social Psychology* 61 (1991): 226–244.

4. Karen Horney, *Neurosis and Human Growth* (New York: W.W. Norton & Co., 1950).

5. Daniel Goleman, *Social Intelligence: The New Science of Human Relationships* (Hutchinson: London, 2006), 40–43.

6. The full impact and importance of these four types of energetic signals (body, emotions, mind and spirit) is explored in more detail in George's previous book, *Hostage at the Table*. He explains that when a person combines all four aspects, he communicates with his "whole being" (p. 126) and really enters into "a fully engaged dialogue with another person for shared learning through shared meaning" (p. 127). In such a dialogue, "no one person has 'the truth.' There is a perception, an interpretation, a subjective part." Powerful negotiation can occur in this space of mutual searching; successful negotiation is an extension of effective sensing/interpretation of signals and of effective dialogue. In fact, picking up on the four types of signals and interpreting them is intrinsic to six of the ten steps of negotiation outlined in *Hostage at the Table* (p. 152); these six steps are bolded in the list below:

1. **Forming a bond**
2. Separating the person from the problem
3. Identifying needs, wants and interests of self
4. **Identifying needs, wants and interests of the other person(s)**
5. **Using focused dialogue**
6. **Creating a goal and finding common goals**
7. **Finding options, generating proposals and making concessions**
8. **Bargaining for a mutual benefit**
9. Coming to an agreement
10. Ending or continuing the relationship on a positive note

For more detail, see Chapters Six and Seven of George Kohlrieser, *Hostage at the Table: How Leaders Can Overcome Conflict, Influence Others, and Raise Performance* (San Francisco, CA: Jossey-Bass, 2006).

7. Paul Ekman, "Basic Emotions," in *Handbook of Cognition and Emotion*, eds. Tim Dalgleish and Mick Power (Sussex, UK: Wiley, 1999), 45–60.

8. Albert Mehrabian, *Silent Messages: Implicit Communication of Emotions and Attitudes*, First Edition. (Belmont, CA: Wadsworth: 1971).
9. Marco Iacoboni, *Mirroring People: The New Science of How We Connect with Others* (New York: Farrar, Straus & Giroux, 2008).

Chapter Nine

1. Although "results and relationships" is not the language of secure bases as we have used it thus far, it served as a relevant proxy and language for Investec. "Results" represented challenge and "relationships" represented bonding and safety.
2. Both awards were granted by *Funds Europe*, a business strategy magazine targeting Europe's asset management professionals. The "European Asset Management Personality" award in particular honors individuals who have made outstanding contributions in terms of leadership abilities, results and performance, innovation and implementation of corporate and social responsibility initiatives.
3. The Hay Group, "Dangerous Liaisons, Mergers and Acquisitions: The Integration Game," 2007, http://www.instituteforgovernment.org.uk/pdfs/white_paper_haygroup_dangerous_liaisons.pdf, accessed January 12, 2012.
4. Peter Killing, Tom Malnight, and Tracey Keys, *Must-Win Battles: How to Win Them, Again and Again* (Upper Saddle River, NJ: Wharton School Publishing, 2006).
5. Peter Senge, *The Fifth Discipline: The Art & Practice of the Learning Organization* (London: Random House, 1990), 48.
6. Peter Senge, *The Fifth Discipline*, 3.
7. Organizations may also become secure bases for stakeholders other than employees; consider the SwissAir story shared in Chapter 4. For the purposes of this chapter, we concentrate on the employee point of view.
8. Note that there is no period at the end of the vision. Tetra Pak left it out purposefully in order to show that the vision had no end.

Chapter Ten

1. Institute of Leadership & Management and Ashridge Business School, "Great expectations: Managing Generation Y Institute of Leadership & Management and Ashridge Business School," 2011, http://www.ashridge.org.uk/website/content.nsf/FileLibrary/5B 2533B47A6D6F3B802578D30050CDA8/$file/G458_ILM_GEN_ REP_FINAL.pdf, accessed January 12, 2012.
2. Hans Toch, *Violent Men: An Inquiry into the Psychology of Violence* (Chicago: Aldine, 1969), 180.
3. Diane Coyle, *The Economics of Enough: How to Run the Economy as If the Future Matters* (Princeton, NJ: Princeton University Press, 2011).

INDEX

CPSIA information can be obtained
at www.ICGtesting.com
Printed in the USA
BVHW082316060122
624164BV00007B/193/J

9 781119 961574